Annie
Adams
Fields

Annie Adams Fields

The Spirit of Charles Street

Judith A. Roman

INDIANA UNIVERSITY PRESS
Bloomington & Indianapolis

The paper used in this publication meets the minimum requirements of American
National Standard for Information Sciences—Permanence of Paper for Printed
Library Materials, ANSI Z39.48–1984.

Manufactured in the United States of America

Library of Congress Cataloging-in-Publication Data

Roman, Judith.
Annie Adams Fields : the spirit of Charles Street / Judith A. Roman.
p.   cm.
Revision of author's thesis (Ph. D.)—Indiana University, 1984,
under title: The spirit of Charles Street
Includes bibliographical references.
ISBN 0–253–35022–0 (alk. paper)
1. Fields, Annie, 1834–1915—Biography. 2. Authors,
American—19th century—Biography. 3. Women and literature—
Massachusetts—Boston—History—19th century. 4. Authors and
publishers—Massachusetts—Boston—History—19th century.
5. Literature publishing—Massachusetts—Boston—History—19th
century. 6. Boston (Mass.)—Intellectual life. 7. Ticknor and
Fields—History. I. Roman, Judith. Spirit of Charles Street. II. Title.
PS1669.F5Z87   1990

818'.409—dc20   89–46328
[B]   CIP
1 2 3 4 5 94 93 92 91 90

For the members of all my families, especially my parents;
my "children," Andrew, Patrick, Emily, Molly, and Bridget;
and friends Bonnie, Carole, Mary, Susie, Susan, Tam, and Virginia

Contents

Preface

I first heard of Annie Fields in the late 1970s when Don Cook, the teacher of a seminar on Realism and Naturalism (James, Howells, and Norris) suggested I add her to a group of women writers I was reading about that included Sarah Orne Jewett and Rebecca Harding Davis. Professor Cook told me that Annie Fields was an interesting figure who had, incidentally, never been the subject of a book.

As I discovered in the seminar how much fun doing research could be, Annie Fields stayed with me. Women's Studies was a relatively new field, and Susan Gubar's first feminist criticism seminar at Indiana University in Bloomington inspired me to rediscover women writers who had been forgotten.

As I progressed and decided to write my dissertation on Fields, I was plagued with the difficulty of explaining to people who Annie Fields was and why she was interesting. Among those few who did know who she was, responses ranged from "Didn't she write something called *Memories of a Happy Hostess?*" to "They'll be writing dissertations about Mickey Mouse next." I tired of explaining that Fields was "the wife of James T. Fields" or "the companion of Sarah Orne Jewett." Scholars of American publishing or of Jewett, Stowe, or Dickens at least knew who Annie Fields was, and I was grateful to them. Yet Fields was not an easy figure to focus on directly—she seemed to dwell in some region of peripheral vision.

What Annie Fields became to me finally was, perhaps, a woman who lived an extraordinarily rich and self-reflective life, despite the fact that she never had children, never wrote a "great" book, never distinguished herself as an abolitionist, suffragette, or muckraker. When evaluated by some criteria, Annie Fields didn't do anything right. According to others, she did the most important things right: she strived, she thought, she wrote, she nurtured, she loved, she worked. As a human being, Annie Fields wore very well.

I began working on this project in about 1980 and had completed the original manuscript for my doctorate from Indiana University in 1984. Little new appeared on Annie Fields while I was revising the manuscript, with the exception of a chapter on Fields in Josephine Donovan's *New England Local Color Literature*. However, in late 1987 and 1988, while my final draft was being read by the Indiana University Press, three significant articles appeared: Rita K. Gollin's profile of Annie Fields in *Legacy,* a relatively recent journal of nineteenth-century American women's studies (Spring 1987: 27-36); the same author's essay "Subordinated Power: Mrs. and Mr. James T. Fields" in *Patrons and Protégées: Gender, Friendship, and Writing in Nineteenth-Century America,* edited by Shirley Marchalonis (New Brunswick: Rutgers University Press, 1988); and George Curry's "Charles Dickens and Annie Fields," which appeared in the *Huntington Library Quarterly* (Winter 1988). These items do not appear in the Bibliography since my work preceded their publication.

Many people helped me complete this book. Don L. Cook provided an invaluable combination of moral support and expertise. Other faculty members at Indiana University who helped me in a variety of ways include Cynthia Kinnard, Philip Appleman, Wallace Williams, James Justus, and Robert Gross. In addition, Gwen L. Nagel, Josephine Donovan, Maren Stange, Karla DeFord, Mrs. Benjamin Bole, and Mrs. Thomas Neal all helped me with my work on Annie Fields.

I would like to thank the Lilly Library, especially Elizabeth Johnson, and the Organization of American Historians, especially Joan Hoff-Wilson, for providing me with employment that made it possible to feel part of a community of scholars while I worked on my book.

The Indiana University Department of English and Graduate School provided me with employment and grants-in-aid during the writing of this book. The American Association of University Women gave me a crucial dissertation fellowship, and Indiana University East awarded me a summer faculty fellowship to work on revisions.

The Huntington Library, especially its former Curator of Books, Carey Bliss; the Masschusetts Historical Society; and the Houghton Library all welcomed me and assisted me with my research.

My parents, Kenneth and Mary Roman; my colleagues at Indiana University East, especially Ronnie D. Carter, Mary Fell, and George Blakey; Roger Mitchell; and many other relatives, friends, and neighbors all deserve my thanks for their support.

Abbreviations of Works
Cited in the Text

AF/*JTF*	Annie Adams Fields's biography of her husband, James T. Fields
AFL	Annie Adams Fields, *Letters of Sarah Orne Jewett*
BPL	in the collection of the Boston Public Library
CL	Cary, *Letters of Sarah Orne Jewett* (1967)
HBS	Annie Adams Fields's biography of Harriet Beecher Stowe
HH	in the collection of the Houghton Library, Harvard University
HL	in the collection of the Huntington Library
Howe *Mem.*	M. A. DeWolfe Howe, *Memories of a Hostess*
JTF/AF	in the Huntington collection of letters from James T. Fields to his wife, Annie Adams Fields
LCM	Whiting, *Louise Chandler Moulton*
LWJ	in the Huntington collection of letters from Annie Adams Fields to Laura Winthrop Johnson
MHS	in Annie Adams Fields's diaries at the Massachusetts Historical Society
RHD	Rebecca Harding Davis Collection, Alderman Library, Univ. of Virginia, Charlottesville, Va.
WL	Pickard, *Letters of John Greenleaf Whittier*

Annie Adams Fields

1.
Early Life and Marriage
1834–1859

Annie Adams Fields, wife of James T. Fields, companion of Sarah Orne Jewett, author of eleven books and founder of Boston's Associated Charities, belonged to an elite circle by virtue of her family heritage. A member of the eighth generation descended from Henry Adams of Braintree, Massachusetts, Annie was a true Boston Brahmin. Her marriage to a distinguished publisher was also part of the tradition of alliances between old families and commercial success, as were her vitality, her reticence, and her long life. According to Cleveland Amory's book about Boston families,

> In an Adams face . . . one can always see three things: intellectual power, iron will and calm determination. . . . If one is an Adams he can almost take for granted the fact that he will live a long time. . . . No Adams has ever been considered retired until he is in his grave. (147)

Like her friend and neighbor Oliver Wendell Holmes, Annie was devoted to Boston and would have concurred in its being the hub of the solar system. Like her husband, Annie admired English and European culture but preferred American life.

In her first book, the novel *Asphodel*, Annie declared her primary allegiance to her homeland and echoed her friend Hawthorne about the decay of the Old World:

> It is a fortunate lot to be born in New England; to find one's self stepping from the cradle out into the fore world of thought stirred by breezes fresh with the freedom of humanity. . . . The child of New England looks toward the East, saying, Now is the high noon of the world; we will bid farewell to the mists of earlier hours, and lands overladen by the history of ages, gathering from these what we need, but leaving the rest to decay upon the parent soil. (1)

Annie was peculiarly well placed to observe, enjoy, and participate in the American Renaissance.

Born in Boston in 1834, marrying there in 1854, and dying there in 1915, Annie Fields witnessed both the era when people were still asking "Who reads an American book?" and the dawn of the modern age. Oliver Wendell Holmes described the literary scene of the early 1830s in his introduction to *A Mortal Antipathy* (1885):

[N. P.] Willis was by far the most prominent young American author. Cooper, Bryant, Dana, Halleck, Drake had all done their best work. Longfellow was not yet conspicuous, Lowell was a schoolboy. Emerson was unheard of, Whittier was beginning to make his way against the writers with better educational advantages whom he was destined to outdo and to outlive. Not one of the great histories, which have done honor to our literature, had appeared. (5)

Within a few years of Annie's birth, Longfellow, Emerson, and Hawthorne had published *Outre-Mer, Nature,* and *Twice Told Tales,* and three great literary magazines were founded shortly thereafter—*The Dial* in 1840, *Harper's* in 1850, and the *Atlantic* in 1857. Of this later period, Holmes wrote:

In the mean time the nebula of the first quarter century had condensed into the constellation of the middle of the same period. When, a little while after the establishment of the new magazine [the *Atlantic*], the "Saturday Club" gathered about the long table at "Parker's," such a representation of all that was best in American literature had never been collected within so small a compass. Most of the Americans whom educated foreigners cared to see—leaving out of consideration official dignitaries, whose temporary importance makes them objects of curiosity—were seated at that board. (*Mortal* 9–10)

At the center of these men was James T. Fields, who was on his way to becoming the most influential publisher and editor in America.

The contrast between the Boston political scenes of 1834 and 1854 was equally great. In 1833 Massachusetts had recently broken all official ties between government and religion, although society, including Harvard College, was strongly Unitarian. In the year of Annie's birth an anti-Catholic mob burned down the Ursuline convent in Charlestown. Public sentiment against abolitionists was strong, and a mob attempted to seize William Lloyd Garrison. Despite Boston's prosperity, it lacked a public library, public high school for girls, and paid fire department.[1] By 1854, however, an increasing number of Bostonians opposed slavery, and the women of Boston had begun their efforts to gain political rights.

During Annie's youth the city grew from 46,226 to 136,881 people and its hills were levelled to fill the South, Mill, and West Coves, the land for the Fields house at 148 Charles Street coming from the last.

The face of the city changed in other ways as well. By 1854 the Pearl and Milk Street section where Annie was born had become almost entirely industrial, although a few beautiful buildings from the former time remained. Reminiscing about her childhood on Pearl Street in the 1830s and 1840s, Mrs. Fields described her birthplace as "a region of fine old houses with a succession of beautiful gardens, for which, indeed, it was famous" (Rossiter 40).[2] The street overlooked both town and harbor and received "the cooling breezes of the bay."

Annie was born into this beautiful, pre-industrial Boston as Ann West Adams on 6 June 1854, the sixth of seven children (two of whom died in infancy) and the fifth girl (Adams 460). Her father, Dr. Zabdiel Boylston Adams, was descended from a line parallel to that of the presidential Adamses: two Adams brothers had married two Boylston sisters; one of these lines produced Presidents John Adams and John Quincy Adams, while the other produced Annie's father. He was named for an ancestor on the Boylston side, Dr. Zabdiel Boylston, a pioneer of smallpox inoculation in America (Howard 157, 278). Annie's father and at least three of his namesakes also became noted doctors (Bole).

Annie's grandfather had been born in Quincy, Massachusetts before moving to Roxbury; the Quincy Adamses were his cousins, aunts, and uncles; Mrs. Fields remembered Sunday afternoons in Quincy spent visiting her great-aunts. Dr. Adams's sister, Eliza, married a man named Simeon or Simon Willard, related to the famous Boston clockmaker. Annie met her future husband through this family, for James T. Fields was closely associated with them when Annie was still a child (Tryon 106, 136–37).

Annie's mother, Sarah May (Holland) Adams, was a distant cousin of Louisa May Alcott's mother, Abba. Unlike her husband and four of her five surviving children, Mrs. Adams did not live any of her life in the public eye. The indomitable qualities of the May blood provided Sarah Orne Jewett, Annie's companion in her later years, with one of her favorite teases, that Annie "must be doing something on account of [her] grandmother's having been a May" (AFL 165).

Although little is known about Annie's childhood, her writing contains a few thinly disguised anecdotes about girlhood which are almost certainly autobiographical. One such account opens her essay "Tennyson" in *Authors and Friends* (1896), the most popular of her books. In the essay, Mrs. Fields recalls a little girl who memorized and recited in class all 152 lines of the "The Lady of Shallott," only to have the teacher, an admirer of the eighteenth-century moralists, sternly demand an interpretation as well (*A & F* 337–38). In another anecdote, Annie wrote about a girl who quoted Longfellow on making "our lives sublime" to her older sisters, chatting busily about "clothes and proposed pleasures" (87).[3] Like Annie, the girl in this story loves history, biography, and poetry; Washington and Mrs. Adams are among her favorite subjects, and Bryant, Whittier, and Lydia Maria Child her favorite writers.

Although Annie was close to her mother and dedicated a long poem, *The Return of Persephone*, to her, Dr. Adams may have been the more influential parent. An 1816 graduate of the Harvard University Medical School, he is described by W. S. Tryon, James T. Fields's biographer, as "widely respected, obviously well-to-do, much interested in public education, and one of the best and most renowned physicians in Boston" (210). When he died, numerous obituaries spoke of his remarkable record; in more than thirty years as a physician and councillor of the Massachusetts Medical Society, he never missed more than a day's work from illness. According to his obituaries, he was responsible for many unacknowledged charities.

A member of Boston's School Committee for many years, Dr. Adams became an advocate of education for girls ("Good" 26 Jan. 1855). As a child, Annie had attended a "plain little schoolhouse" near her home, but by the time she was ready for high school, Boston's short-lived school for girls had closed its doors because of *over*-enrollment (Rossiter 41). When it came to public education for women, Boston's record was dismal; until 1828, girls had been allowed to attend grammar school for only six months of the year (Gilman 439; Koren 103). Except for 1826 to 1828, no public secondary school accepted girls until the late 1850s (Woody 520).

Even before 1823, however, a group of concerned fathers formed a committee to arrange for their daughters' secondary education and persuaded George Barrell Emerson, one of the country's leading educators and the first principal of Boston's Classical School for boys, to leave that job to open a school for girls (Emerson, G. *Rem.* 65–66). Emerson was at first reluctant, but the fathers argued persuasively that well-educated women were the cornerstone of an educated citizenry. Their efforts to form a school succeeded, probably because they offered Emerson a salary which permitted him to marry. The George B. Emerson School for Young Ladies educated girls from old Bostonian families from 1823 until 1855. Its students reputedly earned "the equivalent of a B. A. degree" (Hale vii). Many of Annie's ideas and principles reflect those of her famous teacher: her love of English literature, her lifelong commitment to Christianity and Christian charity, and even her good health may have resulted from Emerson's influence.

Although Emerson's school superficially resembled female seminaries such as those at Troy, Mt. Holyoke, and Hartford, it differed in essence. Like the leaders of female seminaries, Emerson promoted reverence and moral principles, but unlike them he refused to dilute his curriculum with etiquette and domestic arts. His students studied Latin daily for two or three years, added French and Italian, and eventually read both Virgil and Dante in the original. Emerson taught Colburn's *Mental Arithmetic,* a book he had field tested before its publication, and assigned six or eight pages of history from an original text each night. His students studied maps, attended lectures on Newton, La Place, Galileo, and Lavoisier and memorized excerpts from the work of "the best English poets" (*Rem.* 67–69).

Had it not been for his more famous cousin, George Barrell Emerson would be better known today. One of the major educational theorists of the early nineteenth century, this Harvard graduate began teaching in 1817 and was appointed principal of the new Classical School in 1821. In the intervening years he thought a great deal about education and rejected the widespread use of harsh discipline, replacing it with a system based upon honor (Barnard 336–37). Emerson documented his contributions to education in two books, one a manual of instruction for prospective teachers and the other his autobiography, *Reminiscences of an Old Teacher.*

In *The Schoolmaster,* Emerson describes his innovations in class discipline and outlines a model curriculum for the benefit of the beginning teacher. Some of his recommendations are surprising; he included "good health" among the mental and moral attributes a teacher should possess and advised both male and female teachers to exercise vigorously for one to two hours each day. An amateur botanist, Emerson considered gardening an excellent way to combine recreation and exercise. Annie must have taken his advice, for she was an avid gardener and designed large gardens at both her Boston and her Manchester homes.

Emerson's academic recommendations were less unusual but equally rigorous; he believed, for example, that potential teachers should study the Laws of Creation, the Natural Laws, and the sciences in general. His list of indispensable classroom subjects included reading, spelling, grammar, writing, drawing, arithmetic, accounts, geography, history, physiology, and composition. Even when Emerson described his curriculum, however, his true mission emerged: he wanted teachers to be cultured, to form their students' moral character, and to govern with love.

Reminiscences of an Old Teacher concludes with Emerson's commencement address to his last class of female students. Emerson urged his students to cultivate to the fullest any talent they possessed. He advised his pupils to study languages and literature, especially Shakespeare, Milton, Wordsworth, Cowper, Scott, Bryant, Gray, Goldsmith, Coleridge, and Pope, and stressed the importance of reading biography. Students should keep a diary of "good thoughts or beautiful images" which were suggested to them "by [their] observation, by [their] reading, or by conversation," calling conversation itself "the most delightful of all arts" (145).

But it was "the duty of educating yourselves for a life of charity, of devoting to charitable uses the talents you will have improved" to which Emerson devoted most of his address (147). He articulated the crusading principle of Annie Fields's Associated Charities when he said that "what has been done to relieve the wants of the poor has often been unavailing, because it has been done in ignorance . . . of their character, wants, and circumstances" (151). He asked his students to search for the true needs of the poor instead of engaging in traditional feminine occupations like reading novels, embroidering, and socializing.

Emerson's curriculum helps to dispel an assumption, frequently encountered in writing about Annie and James Fields, that she was a malleable piece of clay molded in Pygmalion fashion by her older and more experienced husband (Tryon 211; Rotundo 39). On the contrary, some evidence suggests that it was Fields, rather than Annie, who changed in the early years of their marriage. Annie was better educated than her husband, whose formal schooling ended at age thirteen. The image of Annie as a clean slate, waiting to be written upon, is a myth which can be discarded.

Although Annie's mother remains in the background, Annie's two older sisters, Sarah Holland and Elizabeth Adams, led lives of creativity and accomplishment. Neither married. Sarah Holland Adams, named for her mother and maternal grandmother, was the eldest of the five surviving children. Eleven years older than Annie and crippled throughout her life, she outlived her younger sister by a year and a half, dying at age ninety-three. Her nephew, Dr. Zabdiel Boylston Adams, an orthopedic surgeon, guessed that she had been a victim of polio (Bole). A scholar of German, Sarah Adams lived for many years in Weimar, Germany and gained a reputation as the first English translator of Hermann Grimm. Louise Chandler Moulton, a Boston poet, described Sarah Adams as an essayist as well, although I have not located any published essays (Whiting, *LCM* 261).

Elizabeth Adams, called Lissie or Lizzie, was nine years older than Annie and seems to have been her closest sibling; their relationship, however, was not always calm. An artist, Lissie was eulogized as "among the first of those brave spirits who, casting away the old prejudices, dared to believe that a woman might dedicate her life to a profession." According to a family story, Lissie studied art at the Boston Museum school but became angry when she was forbidden to draw a nude model (Bole). Annie and her husband invited Lissie to join them on their delayed European honeymoon in

1859 so that she could see the great paintings of Europe (Tryon 243). Later, Annie helped Lissie obtain Mrs. Adams's permission to remain in Florence to paint.

Lissie probably spent some of her time as a copyist, as did Sophia Peabody Hawthorne and other women artists of the time. She sketched, worked in crayon, and painted with watercolor and oil (Burton 10). Portraits were considered her best work, and Annie supported her here, too, by modelling and arranging for models. Lissie eventually destroyed an oil portrait of her sister that Annie mentioned frequently in her diary, but a crayon portrait survives in the collection of the Boston Atheneum.[4] Elizabeth's portrait of Grace King, a close friend, was the writer's favorite (King 91). According to Lissie's memorialist, Robert Burton, her work was shown in the French Salon, a rare achievement for an American woman at the time (11). But for a lifetime of effort, Lissie's accomplishments were pitifully few; Annie grew exasperated with what she perceived as her sister's lack of drive and confided her disappointment to her diaries.

After living in Europe for a number of years, Lissie moved to Baltimore with her friend Miss Burnap, whose father, a Baltimore minister named George Burnap, wrote a book called *The Sphere and Duties of Woman* (1854). The two women built a home in Baltimore, where Lissie taught art to young women, performed charity work, and helped found the Decorative Art Society, the Women's Literary Club, and the Arundel Club.

Annie and her older sisters shared interests in art, foreign travel and culture, intellectual conversation, and social and educational clubs. Although neither Sarah nor Elizabeth ever married, both they and Annie maintained close ties with women friends that included lifelong commitments to one woman. Both Lissie and her older sister Sarah were active, intellectually and artistically committed women. Their lives say much about the cultural and intellectual climate in which Annie Fields grew up.

As a child, Annie attended the Federal Street Church of the Rev. Dr. Gannett and was married by him in King's Chapel. After her marriage, she belonged to the West Church of Cyrus Bartol, Fields's friend and minister, but she and her husband attended a number of different churches in order to hear the sermons of their friends and acquaintances among the notable ministers of the day (Tryon 615). After Annie's mother moved into a residential hotel in Roxbury, they often walked to this suburb to hear Dr. Putnam before paying their Sunday call on Mrs. Adams.

Religion played an important part in Annie Fields's life, but she became increasingly disillusioned with the spiritual leadership of ministers, the average quality of sermons, and churchgoing in general. Annie shared her culture's curiosity about various Eastern religions, Spiritualism, Swedenborgianism, and the Shakers. She enjoyed reading the popular books about Jesus written by Eastern philosophers. Hers was an eclectic religious philosophy that eventually embraced all liberal religions sharing an essentially Christian view.

The excellence of Annie's early education is illustrated by contrasting it with that of Alice James, the only daughter of the notable literary family. Because Alice was fourteen years younger than Annie, their lives crossed infrequently although Henry

James, Sr., was often a guest of the Fieldses, and Henry James, Jr., a friend of Annie's until her death in 1915.

The families of Dr. Zabdiel Boylston Adams and Henry James, Sr., differed markedly in character although both belonged, roughly speaking, to the same segment of society. Dr. Adams's family was more stable in both heritage and environment than that of Henry James: Annie grew up rooted to one section of Boston near many relatives and family friends, attending first a neighborhood school, then the best secondary school for girls in the area. Alice James, on the other hand, spent the years between seven and twelve in Europe, travelling according to the whims of a father determined to find the ideal education for his gifted sons.[5] Educated solely by governesses, and then only intermittently, Alice lacked the relationships with peers developed in the school environment.

Annie was the third daughter in a family that raised four daughters and one son; Alice was the sole girl in a family that focused its energy on four sons. Annie's father contributed time to the cause of public education, for girls as well as boys; Mr. James sacrificed Alice's education to his quest for the best of all possible educations for his sons. He himself admitted, on the family's return to the United States in 1860, that his "chief disappointment also on this side of the water has been in regard to Alice, who intellectually, socially, and physically has been at a great disadvantage compared with home" (Strouse 59).

Their fathers, siblings, and education made a crucial difference to Alice's and Annie's development and chance for success. A contemporary scholar might debate which of the two is the more important or interesting to literary history, but in their own lifetimes, such a question would have been ridiculous. Annie Fields married an intelligent and influential man and contributed greatly to his success. Her own influence on the literature of the time, though indirect, was significant. She helped to create an environment that fostered the production of literature and recorded for later biographers the details of the lives and events she saw. Her diaries are quoted or cited in most books about the famous people of her time; without them, the record would be considerably less complete. She founded an organization that helped make the field of social work what it is today and wrote books and articles that were highly regarded in her lifetime. She enjoyed an unusual nineteenth-century marriage and a long companionship with another woman that was the equivalent of a satisfying second marriage. By any standard, her life was a success.

Alice James, however, suffered the effects of a childhood lived only in the home. She brightened the lives of a few close family members and friends but never reached the potential of her intelligence and talent. Her life was circumscribed by her limited education and her role within her family, where she was diminished by the pedestal on which she was placed. Her upbringing resulted in debilitating psychosomatic illnesses. Although her life and her diaries are fascinating, the life of Alice James was in many ways a tragic failure.

It is tempting to consider what Annie Fields would have done or become if she had not married Fields at age twenty or not married at all. With two unmarried elder sisters,

Annie may not have seen marriage as inevitable. Whatever course she chose would be based on a desire to be useful or fulfill her talents, not on a need for money. She might have been influenced by George Emerson to become a teacher in the grammar schools, but Annie evidently had little interest in and a limited tolerance for children.

She was not artistic, like her sister Elizabeth, but did share an interest in languages and translating poetry with her sister Sarah. Her love of Tennyson and other poets may have led her eventually to writing poetry, although in 1854 she had not yet written, according to Fields. She probably would have dedicated her life to social work, an appropriate career for a woman who did not need to work and possessed enough money to give some away. Both Annie's father and her teacher George Emerson believed in working for the betterment of society. If Annie had not lived in such close proximity to authors, her literary ambitions might never have materialized. Because of her marriage to Fields, however, she pursued not one but several careers which led to her becoming, if not the greatest, certainly one of the most versatile women of her time.

James T. Fields exaggerated when he wrote Mary Mitford in 1854 that he had known Annie Adams "from childhood and [had] held her on my knee many and many a time." It is unlikely that Fields met Annie before his 1844 engagement to her cousin, Mary Willard, when Annie was ten, and he may have met her later during his marriage to Annie's cousin Eliza when both girls were in their teens.

James T. Fields was born in Portsmouth, New Hampshire, probably on 31 December 1817 although some sources, including Annie, give the year as 1816 (Austin 7). His original surname was probably "Field," and he is listed that way in the Adams genealogy, but the Boston Transcript gives the name as "Fields" in its announcement of James's marriage to Annie (Adams 460). According to one story, Fields changed his surname when he was a boy because he enjoyed writing the "s" at the end, but the variant probably arose as a result of inconsistent use of the apostrophe (Austin 7; Tryon 3). As late as the 1870s, lecture posters announced "James T. Field's lectures" (AF mss.)[6]

Fields's father, a ship's captain, died when James was two. James had a close relationship with his mother, who brought him up in "the straitest sect of the Unitarians" and took him to church several times a day on Sundays (JTF 2–3). An avid reader, he was delighted when a family friend obtained a place for him in a Boston bookshop, Carter & Hendee's, after his graduation from high school at thirteen. When the bookstore became Allen & Ticknor, James went to live with William D. Ticknor, his future partner. Eventually he moved into the rooming house at 2 Suffolk Place, where he lived for nearly twenty years (Tryon 28).

Fields was handsome, moderately tall, well proportioned, and slender. He dressed so meticulously that friends teased him about being a dandy (Tryon 34–35). According to E. P. Whipple, Fields was confident enough to be himself—a witty, high-spirited charmer—only with close friends. Among less intimate acquaintances, he was "eminently polite, irreproachably dressed, irreproachably decorous, and guarded in his conversation" (Tryon 31; Whipple 254). Although he was never taken seriously as a poet, Fields wrote well enough to participate in literary circles as both writer and publisher. He was popular with both men and women and avoided alienating people by being essentially apolitical, which later gave rise to the criticism that he waited to see which side would win before he took one. In 1852 Fields was a Whig, William Ticknor's affiliation. At the time of his marriage to Annie, Fields was undecided about the abolitionists, while Annie supported them ardently (Tryon 179, 250). According to his biographer, "Once [Fields] said he was opposed to capital punishment" (250).

Fields's views about food and health were more vehement. He disliked smoking, believed in moderate drinking, took long walks, and did deep breathing exercises. Annie noted in her diary his disapproval of the huge quantities of food some well-known men consumed. Fields became stout himself, however, and may have hastened his death by working too hard. He suffered from severe headaches and was sometimes disabled by illnesses with psychological components (Tryon 99). Around 1870, a breakdown led to his complete withdrawal from publishing and editing.

By 1844 Fields could afford to think about marriage. He had become acquainted with the Simon Willard family that lived nearby at 15 Kingston Street. The Willards had four children, Mary, Zabdiel, Eliza, and Helen (Nelly); Mrs. Willard, whose maiden name was Eliza Adams, was Annie's aunt. Fields became engaged to Mary when he was twenty-seven and she was twenty-one, but she died of tuberculosis less than a year later. Fields's relationship with the Willards continued, however, and on 13 March 1850 he married the second daughter, Eliza. This time he was thirty-two and his bride eighteen.

Although they were married only a year and a half before Eliza's death from tuberculosis, two descriptions of Eliza survive. The writer Grace Greenwood (the pseudonym of Sara J. Clarke) described her as "winning one's regard by her soft and unassuming ways" and as possessing a "half-timid, half dignified manner" and an expressive face (Austin 14). Eliza became ill almost immediately after her marriage. She recuperated long enough to make a trip to the Berkshires in August of 1850, where the Fieldses went on a picnic with Oliver Wendell Holmes, Nathaniel Hawthorne, Herman Melville, and Evert Duyckinck. However, Eliza's new blue silk dress and Fields's patent leather shoes made them reluctant participants on a short hike up a mountain path (Tryon 137–38; Tilton 220).[7] The next spring both Eliza and James fell ill, Eliza with tuberculosis and Fields with a mysterious disease, perhaps sympathetic, perhaps a mild case of tuberculosis. She died in July of 1851.

Utterly depressed by his second loss, Fields could not work or write and became ill again. This time, a trip to Europe was proposed by his associates, and he travelled part of the time with Eliza's brother, Zabdiel Willard, and his wife. After staying away eleven months, he returned reluctantly at the insistence of his partners. On this European trip (his second), Fields solidified his relationships with such English writers as Thomas DeQuincey, the Brownings, Mary Mitford, Thomas Carlyle, Walter Savage Landor, Barry Cornwall, Samuel Rogers, William Thackeray, and Charles Dickens.

Two years after his return from this trip and three years after the death of Eliza, James T. Fields was once again wooing a young woman. He remained within the same family, choosing a cousin of his previous fiancée and wife. Fields had sailed for Europe for the third time in June of 1854 but became so ill—with a fever in addition to his usual seasickness—that his ship put him ashore just north of Boston. By October of

1854 James and Annie were engaged, celebrating their engagement in Bostonian fashion by attending a theater performance with Annie's mother (Tryon 210).

The earliest written description of Annie is a letter Fields wrote to Miss Mitford announcing his engagement. Superficially, Annie was another quiet figure in the background like the first Mrs. Fields:

> After an engagement of a few weeks I am, on the 7th or 10th of next month to go to church with one of the best Yankee girls of my acquaintance. Indeed she is the best in anybody's acquaintance. Just the girl you wd. choose for me. She has never written books altho' she is capable of doing that some; never held an argument on Woman's Rights or Wrongs in her whole life, and so full of goodness of heart and beauty that you would say at once "that is the maid of all other for my friend Fields." . . . Her father (and this must recommend her to your favor) is one of our leading Physicians & a great admirer of Miss Mitford, as well as his daughter. In short Annie is a girl after your own heart and she told me to give her love to you and to ask you to love her. (Austin 14)

James T. Fields and Annie Adams were married at King's Chapel by the Rev. Dr. Gannett (the same minister who officiated at Fields's first marriage) on 15 November 1854 (*Transcript*).

Unlike Eliza, Annie stepped gracefully and assertively into her new position as Fields's wife and literary hostess. Her immediate popularity among Fields's literary friends signalled the start of a long career. Perhaps Fields consciously chose Annie for the combination of charm and power that would make her, as Austin said, "almost as prominent as her husband," but after such a short courtship and engagement, he probably had little notion of the effect she would have on him (15). According to Tryon, "It was she who made [the Fields home] the most famous gathering place in all America" (215). From the outset, Annie entertained her husband's friends and clients with "tact and dignity" and a poise that never failed. She is said to have "entranced everyone" by her beauty and charm, exhibiting just the right amount of "adulation" for the male writers and a heartwarming friendliness for the women (Tryon 215–16; Austin 3, 15).

Numerous authors describe Annie's effect without being able to pinpoint its cause. According to Tryon, "She dazzled no one by her wit, her conversation, or her brilliance. Always she stood in the background." Yet, "to all these varied individuals she was perfection itself"; "she made her guests comfortable" and "her house provided the perfect setting for the army of egos that marched into it." Willa Cather, who knew Annie in her later years, applied her novelist's insight to her analysis of Annie's success:

> No woman could have been so great a hostess, could have made so many highly developed personalities happy under her roof, could have blended so many strongly specialized and keenly sensitive people in her drawing room, without having a great power to control and organize. It was a power so sufficient that one seldom felt it as one lived in the harmonious atmosphere it created. . . . Nobody can cherish the flower of social intercourse . . . without also being able very completely to dispose of anything that threatens it. (Cather 58)

Cather alone perceived that behind Annie's success lay not only beauty and graciousness but also the intelligence and power to use them. Mark DeWolfe Howe, Annie's protégée and literary executor, admitted in a memoir that a friend of his, Charles Townsend Copeland, used to call Annie Fields "Clytie" (Howe, *Venture* 153–54). Copeland may have meant the beautiful maiden who was transformed into a sunflower, but more likely the powerful Clytemnestra.

Annie's reputation as one of the most beautiful women of her day has undoubtedly contributed to her characterization as docile and "Madonna-like." Harriet Prescott Spofford's description of Annie in about 1860 is typically extravagant:

> She was a vision of youth and beauty,—with the peach bloom on her lovely cheek, the gleam in her brown eyes, with a luxuriance of jacinth-colored [auburn] hair whose innumerable dark waves broke full of glancing golden lights,—of exceeding feminine grace withal, a tall, regnant young being. (1)

The surviving portraits and daguerreotypes of Annie confirm that she possessed a classic beauty. A recent description calls her best-known picture "one of the loveliest daguerreotype portraits ever made." In the portrait,

> Her head is turned to emphasize a graceful neck, and to present slightly more of her unusual face than a profile. . . . She sits quietly wrapped in an atmosphere of her own, as if absorbed in private thought but capable at any moment of noticing another's presence and rising with a polite welcome. (Pfister 160–61)

Both Henry James, Sr., and Henry James, Jr., left records of their impression of her beauty, the father calling her "that angelic woman, whom I shall remember in my last visions" (Howe *Mem.* 82) and the son "the singularly graceful young wife, her beautiful head and hair and smile and voice" ("Mr. and Mrs." 24).

Her friends also described Annie's sense of humor and her occasional sentimentality, sometimes referred to as "preciousness." Like unobtrusiveness and social control, humor and sentiment seem a paradoxical combination, unlikely to occur in the same person, unless they are considered as different manifestations of the same trait—in this case, a relaxed responsiveness, an ability to be easily moved and a willingness to show emotion. Both Mark Howe and Henry James, Jr., commented on these traits in Mrs. Fields. Howe wrote that "In Mrs. Fields the capacity for incapacitating laughter" was great, while he never recalled "in a single instance, in the excellent telling of innumerable anecdotes . . . unkindness, in word or suggestion, toward the persons involved in them." He added, "Mirth and mercy do not always, like righteousness and peace, kiss each other" (*Mem.* 7). Henry James, commenting on the same duality, wrote that "All her implications were gay, since no one so finely sentimental could be noted as so humorous . . . and no state of amusement, amid quantities or reminiscence, perhaps ever so merciful" ("Mr. and Mrs." 29).

The less appealing quality of "preciousness" was commented upon by enough of the Fieldses' acquaintances, both friendly and hostile, that its existence cannot be disputed. However, the two anecdotes most often cited as proof of preciousness illustrate the occasional pretentiousness of the Fieldses' circle as much as they reveal

Annie's personality. In a comment written to Louise Imogen Guiney in response to some poems, Annie noted "preciosity" as a quality she herself disliked.[8]

One story used to illustrate Mrs. Fields's preciousness appears in Van Wyck Brooks's *New England Indian Summer* as a typical instance of New England writers' airs (74). As told by Tryon, Mrs. Fields sometimes lost herself in the middle of one of her own dinner parties, sitting with her chin in her hand and gazing off into space. One evening, when she realized she had been daydreaming, she said, "Forgive me, dear friends, I thought I was in Rome" (217). The other ubiquitous anecdote, told by Harvard undergraduates who enjoyed poking gentle fun at the stately and aged Mrs. Fields, describes Annie saying "There's a gazelle in the garden" when she noticed food in her husband's beard at the dinner table. In one version of this story, the gazelle represents the piece of food, making the garden Mr. Fields's beard and the statement a kind of code directed at him. In the other version, Annie used this phrase and a gesture toward the dining room window to distract the company while Fields tidied himself (Tryon 217; Austin 3; Howe, *Venture* 156). Howe cites this story as evidence that "the feminine segment" of the nineteenth-century Bostonian literary circle "may have been a little excessive." He concludes, however, that the anecdote is apocryphal because Mrs. Fields had too good a sense of humor to say such a thing, at least seriously. In any case, these stories illustrate the kind of evidence upon which Annie's "preciousness" is based.

After their marriage, Annie and James lived with her parents at 37 Boylston Street, where they remained for a year and a half largely because of the unexpected death of Annie's father on 26 January 1855 only two months after her marriage ("Good"). In the spring of 1856 they found a house they liked on the western slope of Beacon Hill. The house, built on land created by filling in the West Cove, stood at the very end of Charles Street and the lot behind it looked over the Charles River. A four-story red-brick structure, the house was attached to a block of similar new houses. The assistance of Ticknor & Fields was required to buy the land and dwelling, which cost $14,000. The firm bought the property, maintained the house, and paid the taxes and interest charges, while Fields paid a rent of $1100 annually (Tryon 213). Fields's income was then only about $1500 per year; Annie may have contributed from the $2000 and annual income of $500 she received in her father's will (Tryon 209). The firm later purchased the lot behind the house for a garden, and a much smaller garden remains, now covered only with sparse grass and straggling bushes; the house was torn down after Annie's death and was replaced by commercial buildings. The original address of the house was 37, changing later to 148 Charles Street.

According to Tryon, the house was a "late Greek Revival style," as befitted the Fieldses's classic taste (213). The door opened onto a hallway and a flight of stairs; on the left was a reception room furnished in dark blue velvet. The dining room, containing a large oval table, was behind the reception room, and the dining room windows overlooking the garden became partially covered by ivy. On the second floor the most famous room, the library, ran the whole length of the house. It was furnished in matching green carpet, curtains, and sofa. The room opened on one side to two small studies used by James and Annie in the early years of the house and by Annie and Sarah Orne Jewett later on. Annie's study contained a tall, broad desk with a green felt writing surface and many pigeonholes. The long wall of bookshelves was broken only by two white marble fireplaces. Both James and Annie wrote articles about their collection, which included two hundred volumes from Leigh Hunt's library, purchased by Fields after Hunt's death. Many of Fields's books were either first editions or autographed copies; some were both.

The remaining library walls were gradually covered with pictures and sketches by William Morris Hunt, Eduardo Zamacois, Sir Joshua Reynolds, and others. Some of the artwork was by friends, some of it portrayed friends. The Fieldses purchased old furniture for both this house and their summer home at Manchester, an idiosyncrasy at the time. The room contained, in addition to the pictures and furniture, numerous busts and statues, some of them replicas of Greek and Roman masterpieces, and a grand piano. The library windows overlooked the street at one end and the garden and the Charles River at the other; the beauty of the sunset over the river, as viewed through the rear windows, was remarked upon by many visitors. There are extant photographs of the library and the dining room and sketches of the front and rear of the exterior.

The third floor contained three bedrooms, two large and one small; the reticence of the time prevented anyone from describing these rooms. One was used by Mr. and Mrs. Fields, leaving two available for guests. Both were often full. The fourth or attic floor is said to have contained two rooms, either occupied by servants or used as guest rooms, according to different accounts (Tryon 215; Cather 60). The house did not contain bathrooms for most of its existence; instead, each room had crockery bowls and pitchers supplied with hot water for washing and chamber pots under the beds. The kitchen was in the basement.

The smooth running of such a house depended a great deal upon servants; the Fieldses employed one male servant and usually between two and four female servants. Patrick Lynch, who was with Mrs. Fields for many years, is described in a sketch about Sarah Orne Jewett's Irish setter, Roger, as the dog's "best friend" who took him for walks in Boston (Wickham 545). Annie Fields often mentioned her women cooks and maids in her diaries and in letters to friends. She was a well-meaning but demanding employer. Despite the simple facilities of the Charles Street house, the small number of guest rooms, and the fact that it was eventually one of the few residences on a noisy street, Annie Fields lived there for just short of sixty years. Modern plumbing, a telephone, and even an elevator were eventually installed.[9]

In the first sixteen years of marriage, before Fields's retirement and his frequent lecture trips altered their lives, Annie and James were together constantly. Annie wrote to her friend Laura Winthrop Johnson in January of 1873 that "Jamie is lecturing in New York tonight. He goes almost for the first time in our married life so far away without me." She added, "You may be sure we shall rejoice to meet tomorrow night."[10] Throughout their marriage Fields frequently sent Annie flowers and gifts to supplement their dinners, especially when he brought home an unexpected guest. When Annie departed for the seaside in the summer, James wrote her anxiously every day, telling her the news and who had called—her sister Louisa, or Charlotte Cushman, the actress. In one such note, he told her poignantly, and apparently truthfully: "I think of you every hour."[11]

2.

"The Sleeping Partner"
1859–1870

In June of 1859, the Fieldses set out together on James's long-delayed trip to Europe. At the time of their departure, Annie was twenty-five and James forty-one. Annie thought that James took enough books for three voyages, but his invariable seasickness confined him to his cabin for most of the trip (AF/*JTF* 83). Their first stop was England, where Fields renewed old friendships and introduced Annie. Miss Mitford had died in 1855, but they visited Tennyson, Dinah Mulock Craik, Mr. and Mrs. Macmillan, Charles Reade, Bryan Waller Proctor (who wrote under the name Barry Cornwall) and his daughter Adelaide Proctor, Gerald Massey, George Bennett, and others. Annie's first taste of English manners was supplied by Tennyson, who was accustomed to read at breakfast and disturbed to find Annie up early enough to sit at the table with him. After politely asking Annie if she had something to read, he pursued his *Times* in silence for the rest of the meal.

Although Annie, like her husband, almost revered the English writers, she was not too much in awe to criticize them occasionally; for example, she liked Miss Proctor but said Cornwall's daughter was "not graceful in manners nor in the every day expression of the mind." Her response to English landscape was more cordial than it was to Anglican Catholicism. She often complained about the difficulty of finding Unitarian churches, "the hastily muttered high church prayers," and the formality of Anglican and Roman Catholic churches (Tryon 240). She was dissatisfied with the English sermons as well, calling them "the same 'vain repetitions' of Catholicism."

Annie showed a surprising willingness to disagree with noted men far older than she. One heated discussion about Dickens with a Mr. Russell forecasts the intimate relationship she would have with the novelist later on:

> Is it not religious to discover that, within and around the meanest of God's children[,] which can elevate them and give them a purpose and aim in life? He said there was no reference to a higher power. But do not the lessons of charity and cheerfulness which he [Dickens] teaches spring from a sure faith in God and a future life and desire to inculcate the knowledge of how to begin our immortal career?

She exchanged views on art with Tennyson, responding to his question, "Is not the highest painter . . . the exactest copyist?" with her opinion that it was "he who can inform the picture with the largest expression of Deity." And she noted privately her disagreement with Gerald Massey, who had said that Shakespeare and Burns were truer poets than Tennyson because they were more objective and therefore of more use to humanity. Annie thought that some people, including both Tennyson and Shakespeare, "live nearer heaven than others and interpret what they see to those who touch the hem of their garments."

Fields continued his practice of bringing Annie flowers while they were abroad: "I did not rise early . . . but my darling did and came bringing me flowers before I arose, lilies and roses in melodious confusion and while I lay still looking and loving him and then I heard Mr. Bennett's [knock]. Soon my locks and the posies were in order." This passage provides an unusual glimpse of Annie and James in the privacy of their own room; Annie did not often describe scenes as intimate as this.

Before leaving England Annie met Charles Reade, who struck her as "most interesting[;] a man of true genius and as much power of self-excitement as any I ever saw indeed I sometimes fear it is too strong in him[.] It is a most rare failing." Annie made some extracts (probably from American papers or magazines) for Reade, and he responded in a letter to Fields: "Mrs. Fields is a duck—for making the extracts, and you another for sending me them. The ladies for ever. She has just cut the things out I should have taken myself" (Austin 387).

The Fieldses crossed to France in August. They moved slowly toward Paris, stopping in Calais, where they landed, then proceeding though Belgium, Germany, and Switzerland before finally reaching Paris in early October. Most description of their travels reads like a guide book; without the now ubiquitous camera, Annie sought to capture every detail of the scenery and architecture in words. Although she succeeded admirably, these pages of her journals offer little insight into either Annie or the people the Fieldses encountered along the way. In Antwerp, Annie and James found the paintings in the cathedral draped for a festival day. Annie wrote: "The pictures which we wished so much to see were shrouded in their veils. . . . Our hearts were oppressed with the sad idea that the Christ who had lived and died for [Catholics] was not yet received or known by them." After seeing the great unfinished cathedral in Cologne, Annie wrote:

> I think they will never finish it. Catholicism must die as civilization continues and the tide seems slowly turning that way. . . . Went to the church of St. Ursula and saw the monument to her and the bones of the 11,000 virgins. A painful mummery.

The relics of martyrs and saints, which she saw as shams, particularly affronted her.

The news of Leigh Hunt's death awaited them in Zurich, where they arrived in a chill rain. James was depressed by the loss of his friend while Annie, herself suffering from an unnamed illness, worried about her husband's morale: "Poor Jamie's spirits now horribly low. Poor fellow! I can hardly move and what then can I do to cheer him." A little later she wrote that "Jamie is sick of the people, the smokers and gamblers one is so apt to meet in hotels," and upon reaching Berne, she noted, "Poor J. was overtaken with the old enemy, the headache, directly after our arrival." Annie was often called upon to apologize for interrupted plans and answer her husband's letters until his indisposition had passed. Annie mentioned illnesses of her own, usually a cold or a nameless indisposition, less frequently.

Immediately after their arrival in Paris, James departed for London on business, leaving Annie alone in the hotel. On the Fieldses' next trip to Europe, in 1869, Annie provided for her husband's absences by bringing Mabel Lowell, the daughter of James Russell Lowell, as her companion. When James returned from London they visited the great Parisian sights and heard the famous singer Pauline Viardot in Gluck's *Orpheus,* an event Annie remembered vividly for years and recounted to Willa Cather (Cather 62).

James brought Annie both flowers and a poem when they celebrated their fifth wedding anniversary on 15 November 1859 in Paris, where they waited for a letter from Annie's sister Lissie, who had been invited to travel with them in an effort to improve her health (Tryon 243). Providing a chance for Lissie to see the art and beauty of Europe was also a motive, as was Annie's need for companionship when James was engaged with business. By early December, Lissie had arrived in England but not yet crossed the channel to Paris, where she would meet the Fieldses and depart for Italy. Annie took French lessons and read Carlyle and Rousseau. After meeting some minor French women writers with major egos, she noted sarcastically:

> Sometimes I think author-ship spoils women. This is all nonsense but *small* authors men or women are apt to belong to a lower grade than the average remainder of *un*writing humans. Chiefly because their vanity overpowers in the end their fraction of common sense.

On Saturday, 18 December 1859, the Fieldses received word of John Brown's execution, which sparked harsh criticism from Annie:

> We hear that Brown was executed the 2d of December. I wept strong hot tears, not for him but for our country. The wound it makes in my heart is as deep as the love I bear her. . . . I believed and hoped it could not, would not be—May we wipe out this national sin.

Lissie reached Paris in late December and on 2 January 1860 the party left for Italy. Their final destination was Florence, but they stopped at several Italian cities along the way. In Florence, Annie met Harriet Beecher Stowe for the first time and rebuked herself for not finding the words to tell her how much she admired her. But the sight of Mrs. Stowe was soon part of everyday life in Florence (*HBS* 254–55). The Fieldses made their first call on the eighty-five-year-old Walter Savage Landor, who admired Annie immensely. They also met Isa Blagden, a close friend of the Brownings, and she showed them Casa Guidi in the Brownings' absence. Thomas Adolphus Trollope, the novelist's brother, was in Florence, as was Kate Field, an American journalist. Landor invited the Fieldses to dinner and sent Annie a flirtatious letter that asked her to call but advised: "Be sure to bring your husband with you for I would not an on any account make him jealous. I wish I could persuade myself that I shall not be so. I *have* been, heretofore, and my ears have been pulled for it" (Austin 15). Landor even walked to the Fieldses' lodgings to pay a call on them, a rare event since he lived in an upstairs apartment with steep narrow stairs and seldom went out.

On 10 February Annie and James returned to Rome, leaving Lissie, who was unwell, in Florence. They visited the Vatican and St. Peter's, where Annie said they "lingered about an hour longer than we intended in order to hear the Vespers. The music was certainly very beautiful but the sight of men singing with the voices of women was something so revolting we could not stay."

Although they had missed the Brownings (whom Fields had met before) in Florence, Annie met them at last in Rome. Mrs. Browning's political fervor and the couple's familiarity in public impressed Annie:

> Browning talked about "Sordello" and his desire to finish it at which his wife looked at him with a curious doubting expression which at last came out in words. "Oh Robert I'm afraid you'll never make *that* clear!" He was arranging the fire when she spoke so that his face was hidden but when he turned to look at us and answer there was not the least shadow of annoyance about him only a radiant expression of confidence in himself and belief in her.

Although Annie was clearly in awe of the Brownings at this meeting, she later criticized Elizabeth Barrett Browning's political support of Napoleon III and her attack on America.

While in Italy the Fieldses frequently saw Charlotte Cushman, a noted American dramatic actress who played both male and female roles, and her friend Emma Stebbins, a sculptor. Harriet Hosmer, another sculptor, often accompanied Cushman and Stebbins, and these three women formed part of the semi-permanent colony of American artists living in Rome and Florence who greeted American visitors as they came.[1] James and Annie visited the studios of both American and English artists but were most impressed by the English:

> We feel continuously here that the largest interest and highest truth is to be found by Pre-Raphaelistic study—the whole tendency of the age is now in that direction in literature as in art. . . . The world was indeed "delaying long" to find this truth.

The months of tramping around Europe finally took their toll on Annie, as would the endless entertaining at home in the next decade. In early March Annie wrote that "We have seen palaces upon palaces and churches upon churches. I hope this frail tenement of memory will stand up bravely and retain what is best retaining for me."

On 21 March, Annie and James woke up at night both dreaming about Charles Dickens. Annie had not yet met the novelist, but James, who knew Dickens from his earlier trips, liked him immensely. In James's dream, he and Dickens were visiting a school and "Dickens continually made the boys laugh, till at last the teachers were obliged to dismiss them with a prayer wh[ich] Dickens interrupted with the apparently convulsing words, Fortuna [Porcara] [luck of a swineherd]." In Annie's dream, she

> had been forced to pass the evening with Uriah Heep. I turned supplicatingly to ask Jamie how such creatures were allowed to exist in the world? He answered me, *They are abortions of Nature,* and like the hen, are the result of long imprisoned misery.

These were only the first of many dreams about Dickens that Annie and James would share with each other over the years.

At the end of March the Fieldses visited Perugia, where Annie, like many other visitors, remarked upon the many beggars who assaulted the tourists. On the way back to Florence on 2 April the driver of a postillion tried to cheat them on the fare and Annie argued with the man in what she called her "extraordinary Italian" and eventually won. On the fifth of April she received Mrs. Browning's new book, *Poems before Congress* (1860), including "A Curse for a Nation," an attack on American slavery. Annie found the book

> full of fine enthusiasm but for the largest part Poetry seems forgotten in fire and ire—for Napoleon and against the world. "A Curse for a nation" is for poor America.

Annie referred to Napoleon III, whom Mrs. Browning admired, as the greatest murderer of them all.

They returned to London, where there was "plenty of work for Jamie," on 23 April. They visited Anthony Trollope, Charles Reade, and George Bennett, among others. Annie talked to Reade about Spiritualism, and said of Oxford, Reade's home: "Ah! it seems a lonely place, that college, in spite of its beauties. I believe he must write that he may people a world after his own heart to live in." They later visited Dinah Mulock Craik, the Macmillans, and others, before going to Edinburgh where they visited Dr. John Brown, the Scottish essayist, and the DeQuinceys. On 8 May Annie at last met Dickens, sitting next to him when she and James dined with him and Willkie Collins. Annie "tried to be as little awe-struck as possible at my position that I might enjoy it to the full." She thought Mary Dickens the more interesting and better looking of the two sisters; Georgina Hogarth, who would become a lifelong friend of Annie's, was not there. Annie noted the "shadow over Dickens' household" which kept him from being a happy man.

They departed for home from Liverpool on 16 June 1860, almost exactly a year from the date they had left America, travelling on the same ship as the Hawthorne family and Harriet Beecher Stowe. During the voyage Fields was seasick as usual and stayed in his room, eating little; the generally unsociable Hawthorne, returning from his consulship in Liverpool, also kept to himself, partly because he disliked Mrs. Stowe. However, the three women, Sophia, Hattie Stowe, and Annie, struck up a friendship. Sophia, Una, Julian, and Rose Hawthorne frequently visited the Fieldses in Boston and both Hawthorne and Sophia came to admire Annie enormously.

Annie and James arrived home on 28 June 1860, having spent about $8000—enough to have made the trip a "royal progress" indeed (Tryon 236–37). Fields returned to his publishing business with the additional responsibility of running the *Atlantic Monthly,* which Ticknor had purchased in his absence (Austin 29). Annie returned to being a literary hostess, a role she found was at least as much work as play.

Annie's public life came into being in response to what one might normally consider the private side of her life—her marriage. In the nineteenth century a middle-class husband and wife often lived in two completely different spheres—the sphere of business and work with its emphasis on material success and the sphere of home and domesticity with its emphasis on esthetic refinement and spiritual elevation.[2] Men spent most of their time with men, and women with women. A wife and mother would have supervised her children's nurse and various other servants and attended to the early education of her children. She might not know much about her husband's work and have little interest in it; he might have little knowledge of how she spent her day and even less interest. Their conversation might have been limited to discussion of the children, matters of political interest such as the Civil War, other family members, vacations, and perhaps, if they were problematic, household expenses.

To the extent that this model was typical, Annie and James had an atypical marriage. There were three reasons for this, all perhaps equally important—James's great love for Annie and his desire to be with her as much as possible; their childlessness; and the nature of the literary business, which made involving Annie in James's work possible. Eliminate one of these conditions and the Fields partnership might never have existed.

Despite James and Annie's separate activities—James was at the office all day and regularly attended the Saturday Club, Longfellow's Dante Club, and other exclusively male dinners and events, while Annie supervised the home, made calls, and visited with other ladies—they managed to see a great deal more of each other than most husbands and wives. The pattern of their affection can be clearly seen in James's notes to Annie, written from the office to her at home or from Boston to Pigeon Cove, Rye Beach, or Manchester if Annie preceded him on a summer vacation.

Fields's notes contain numerous small signs of affection. The following note, echoing Wordsworth's poem "She Dwelt Among the Untrodden Ways," was written "At the store":

> I don't get a moment free from people or things. How I do want to be with you this evening! But oh! the difference to me! . . . What a life I lead to be sure. But we, you and I, get glimpses of something better.[3]

When Annie had gone to the North Shore one summer before him James wrote, "Eat and sleep generously and don't forget your absent lad in town who loves you."

James lectured infrequently in the 1860s, but when he did, Annie received notes like this one from Springfield, Massachusetts: "Just arrived. Well and Hungry but no Annie! O how lonely. Well, well, we shall meet in a few hours I hope." The notes that survive—fifty-eight in all—represent only a fraction of the notes Fields must have written to his wife at a rate of one or two a day when he was in town and one a day when apart.

Although none of Annie's letters to James survive (probably destroyed by Annie herself), her diary reflects her love and devotion. A walk along the Singing Beach of Manchester, Massachusetts reminded Annie of their spiritual union:

> As I walked I discerned the foot-prints of feet which lay parallel to mine—I looked again—they were my husband's! Surely this incident was no accident nor was it without signification—So we walk side by side in spirit. (19 July 1866)

In 1867 she wrote from Manchester: "Jamie goes to town & will not return tonight. I feel as if life were ebbing somehow when he does this." After reading Mrs. Augustus Cravens's *Récit d'une Soeur,* a sentimental memoir describing her brother's romantic marriage and his death, she wrote:

> I see so strong a likeness between any true story of married happiness and our own life, that it comes to me with peculiar force, as if written for, if not from, myself, when I reflect that within this tale death separated these lovers in two years and we have already enjoyed nearly fourteen. (7 March 1868)[4]

Because of her characteristic reticence, references to physical contact are rare. Annie wrote of James, who had both a cold and a headache, that "The dear boy has snatches of sleep when he is more comfortable and dreams I am in his arms!!! He is made up of tenderness." A reference to reading Milton's *Comus* shows that Annie did keep some secrets from her diary:

> Very very warm. The morning was dewy clear and of seraphic beauty. We redde (see Byron and common sense) Milton before breakfast, that passage where virtue is called upon as light in herself to guide the sweet lost maiden. The thrushes sang plenteously and life is sweet and silent and apart. How far apart it seemed indeed after such a close contact as we have had—. (3 July 1868)[5]

Not all the shared intimacies that crept into the diary were serious; after returning to town from Manchester, Annie wrote that she and "Jamie" enjoyed "one bohemian evening of wandering and came home singing Shakspear's song 'Fear no more the heat of the sun' all the way down Beacon St." until she thought they might be arrested for a mysterious Victorian mania called "mania a potu"—which probably meant intoxication.[6]

James and Annie's observance of the anniversary of both their engagement and their marriage was perhaps exceptional. In October of 1868 she wrote:

> This is the month we were engaged 14 years ago!! It seems but yesterday from one point (tho' there are always the two points, as Dickens' [sic] said)—Dear J. has given me an exquisite Aqua Marina stone to mark the loving time—.

James wrote poems for Annie on the sixth of June, her birthday, and on their wedding anniversaries. Annie did not feel confident enough of her own poetry to reciprocate until 1865, when she presented James with the first series of her poems, "Canticles of Married Love," the collective name for three series of poems, never published, written for James in 1865, 1866, and 1868. The ten poems written for their eleventh anniversary, on various aspects of love, are written in a formal style full of classical figures of speech and allusions and resembling the poetry of Donne's era more than that of the nineteenth century.

The poems achieve more personal warmth and intimacy than many of Annie's published poems. For the most part, they convey thanks for blessings sprinkled with descriptions of nature and avowals of love. Several begin with apostrophes to a Platonic ideal or embodiment of a specific kind of love:

> O earthly love! O human married love!
> Time holds no grace transcending thy estate;
> Clear as the starry spheres that circling move
> Circles thy joy, unknowing death or fate. (HL)

Some of the more successful poems suggest the wit contained in the work of such American metaphysical poets as Anne Bradstreet and Michael Wigglesworth:

> Once but a seed, and now a tree full grown,
> Once crescent moon, and now a perfect sphere,
> Then, maiden blushes, all too quickly flown,
> Now, sunlight to illume the rounding year.
> . . . .
> The widening river widens to the main,
> The trees' broad shadow broadens with the May,
> We watch their growing strength, the seasons gain,
> And know Love's morning ripens into day.

The "Canticles" reveal more of Annie's inner life than do most of her published poems and may be her best poetry. It is unlikely, however, that the poems would be read today for any but biographical reasons.

The poems do provide information on a subject about which Annie was otherwise silent—the Fieldses' childlessness. In the second series of "Canticles," Annie mourns the void in their household:

> No young bright curls nor sound of little feet,
> No baby voices ringing up the stair,
> Nor budding grace to follow the hours fleet,
> And laugh to see them make youths' gold more fair!

Using the conventional imagery of her time, Annie struggled to express the emptiness she felt. As the poem progresses, Annie describes what she believed to be the duty of the childless to devote the energy and money they would have given their own family to the poor and to orphans:

> But ever up and down the weary way,
> Forever, pass the infant multitude,
> All motherless and friendless, and astray,
> And ignorant of holy gratitude.

Annie saw heaven as the reward for doing one's humanitarian duty and tried to console herself and James with this vision:

> They who have loved these wandering children best
> Shall hear their voices falling on the ear,
>
> And singing "Glory" through the lofty skies,
> And "Welcome" to the sad, and then "Well done,"

> While leaning on bright harps, their loving eyes
> Guide like fixed stars and lead us to the Sun.

This theme, that the childless have a moral obligation to the homeless, recurs throughout Annie's diaries and letters.

Although Annie considered adopting a child—or, to put it in more nineteenth-century terms, considered taking in a homeless child on a permanent basis—she never did. Perhaps she and James did not adopt because of the widespread belief that heredity was the predominant, if not the only, shaper of personality. Most of the children available for adoption would have been members of the poorest classes and possibly the children of criminals or alcoholics. According to the thinking of the day, a child so displaced would be a misfit, doomed to unhappiness among an alien people.

There may have been other reasons why the Fieldses did not choose to adopt. The few references to children in Annie's diaries suggest that she had little tolerance for children and high expectations. In 1869, when Annie cared for one of her sister Louisa's sons during an outbreak of fever, she expressed ambivalence about her sacrifices:

> Day after day slips away but as I give five hours of each to our baby I absolutely cannot write here but my German comes on swimmingly and I know it is better to be writing on this infants' [sic] mind than any where else. . . . [3 Feb.] Baby still here and I do not write at all.

After the birth of Louisa's second son, Annie tried to entertain one of Louisa's older stepchildren: "I caught Ida in my arms and tried to stimu-late [sic] her to try to paint the scene; but the poor children have not much divine fire in them." In a letter to her friend Laura Winthrop Johnson about a recent family vacation, she wrote:

> I have a great dread of change of climate and of living for young children—one of the little boys was ill at N. Conway, so I was all the more in haste to go elsewhere. (HL 15 July 1874)

In these and other comments, Annie shows little patience with children and a reluctance to give up her time for them. Annie was plainly terrified by a street urchin whom she and Harriet Beecher Stowe brought home to Charles Street one night. Harriet washed him and put him to bed, remarking that "The household was far better constituted to look after young cherubim than young humans." Perhaps it was just as well that the Fieldses never had any children of their own.

The literary business differed from other businesses because it required, or at least benefitted from, sociability. Fields's capacity for friendship accounted for part of his success. He functioned well with men, who welcomed him as a member of the male literary clubs of the time, and he functioned well with women, who found his manner charming and free of condescension. Fields had been popular as a single man, but the addition of an efficient and charming wife expanded his social potential. Women had presided over literary salons in France for years; they had succeeded as writers in

England since the eighteenth century at least, and by the middle of the nineteenth century were prominent as both editors and writers in the United States. The involvement of an editor's wife in his work was natural and even helpful.

The compelling reason for the Fieldses' entertainment was James's business as publisher and editor, and this motivation underlay all Annie's activities as a hostess. She did not entertain the great writers, artists, musicians, and actors of her time for the reflected glamour or as a way to fill empty days. Hospitality was her profession. Had James been the minor poet he was but earned his money differently, by banking or medicine, his friends may have been the same but his entertainment would not have reached the same dimensions.

Annie's job was to make their home a pleasant haven for authors so they would continue to place their work with Fields. Because of his love for the theater and other arts, Fields also invited nonliterary people, such as actors, singers, and other musicians. These people were good company and enhanced the Fields salon with their conversation and with impromptu performances. In the nineteenth century, the arts were closely allied; it was possible for a cultivated person to be familiar with the best in theater, art, and music as well as in literature. Everything was arranged to create an environment that was simultaneously hospitable to creativity and advantageous for Ticknor & Fields.

Annie was, in fact, an early example of an executive wife, a rarity in the nineteenth century because of the separate spheres in which middle-class husbands and wives generally lived. She shared several duties with executive wives of today: she created an environment congenial to the entertainment of clients, she gave excellent parties, and she was herself a good guest.[7] In addition, she participated in civic affairs and charitable work not unlike the Junior League activities in which the wives of young executives are encouraged to participate today. Unlike contemporary couples, the division of labor between home and office was by no means complete. James often solicited Annie's opinion about books and articles, and he sometimes guided her selection of a menu when an important guest came to dine, especially in the early years of their marriage (JTF/AF).

While James's desire to be with Annie admitted the possibility of partnership, Annie made it happen. Few of the wives of Fields's friends shared Annie's combination of good health, cultivation, personality, critical instincts, and organizational ability. Mildred Howells, Lilian Aldrich, Amelia Holmes, Sophia Hawthorne, Lidian Emerson, Frances Lowell, and, later, Olivia Clemens are all cases in point. Annie's energy and drive, typical of a certain kind of Boston grande dame, were essential to the Fields partnership; if Annie had not possessed these traits, Fields might have been just another successful publisher instead of a Boston landmark.

Annie's salon personality was consonant with the business nature of her position. Her pre-eminent quality was tact, and she was seldom exclusive except in ways that can be explained by the business nature of the undertaking. In the numerous comments about her personality as a hostess, there are few denigrations, and these are clearly related to jealousy of her position.[8]

In addition to tact, Annie's virtues as a hostess included her ability to blend into the background, her refusal to dominate the conversation, and her studied avoidance of disagreements among the guests. She was what a later generation would call a good facilitator. At the same time, her parties were not shapeless; she exerted her intelligence to put the right people together and to control the atmosphere. She made rare comments in her diary about the undesirable qualities of certain guests; Forceyth Willson, for example, smelled, and she thought both Lowell and Norton a little conceited. She did not, however, express these opinions to others, as Ellen Ballou suggests in her history of Houghton Mifflin. It was only natural that Annie, Sarah Orne Jewett, and T. B. Aldrich, all of whom quarrelled with Horace Scudder in the 1890s, should share an occasional joke at Scudder's expense; this is hardly evidence, as Ballou bluntly states, that Annie was a "demolisher of reputations." Similarly, when Louise Tharp, in her biography of Sophia Hawthorne and her sisters, portrays Annie as a "queen bee" and an insincere friend, she is defending Mrs. Hawthorne's attack on the integrity of James T. Fields.

Most descriptions of Annie as a hostess praise her combination of graciousness and effectiveness; as James C. Austin says in his biography of her husband: "Fields would have been far less successful in business without the aid of his wife, who could be counted upon to charm into compliance anyone whom her husband wished to impress" (120). James Parton closed a letter to Fields with a pun which captured the essence of Annie's dual role: "With my love to the Firm, and my respects to the sleeping partner" (Austin 346). In her biography of Oliver Wendell Holmes, Eleanor Tilton explains why he and many other male authors felt comfortable with Mrs. Fields: "Although he admired some of his feminine fellow-authors, Holmes could not help thinking that women who were not aggressively literary satisfied his tastes and furthermore provided the means for indulging his sociability" (Tilton 276). The key word here is "aggressively"; paradoxically, because she retained a feminine grace and manner, Annie succeeded in penetrating the male sanctum better than other, more talented women writers. Although Annie gave her youth to this secondary role, she benefitted later; her quiet observations provided her with a unique womanly perspective upon which to base her memoirs. Whether Annie's career as a writer would have been more impressive had she not participated so enthusiastically in her husband's work is a moot point.

Although Annie was much younger than most of her guests, she played a maternal role in protecting them. Like James, she wanted to keep adverse criticism away from "their" authors; she seldom invited the disrespectful, and criticized anyone who derided either her beloved authors or her beloved Boston. This is the atmosphere which Samuel Clemens disrupted at the 1877 Whittier dinner with his indecorous story of Emerson, Longfellow, and Holmes as three tramps (Rusk 500–01). Although James and Annie were reverent, Annie showed that she was aware of the danger of too much adulation when she wrote about William Dean Howells in her journal: "Howells worships [Lowell and Norton] too much for manliness, but he is young and his eyes will open by & by." James and Annie undoubtedly shared with Howells an excess of admiration for their authors, at times, but this admiration is at least partly explained as the normal solicitude of a businessman for his client.

If either Annie or James had been a more serious writer, they could have been viewed as competitors and their value as publishers might have diminished. As dabblers in occasional verse, Annie and James posed no threat to either male or female authors. This, and fear of a charge of nepotism, may account for the fact that until the early 1880s all of Annie's published writing appeared anonymously and most of it was privately printed.

In addition to entertaining her husband's clients, Annie often read manuscripts, recommending the publication of Elizabeth Stuart Phelps's bestselling novel *The Gates Ajar* when James was uncertain about it (Phelps 147). John Townsend Trowbridge wrote to Fields about his article "The Wilderness," "I must confess also to the keen gratification it gives me to know that the story is commended by so practiced & competent a critic as your wife" (Austin 135). Whittier often asked both Fieldses their opinions of a new poem, which was as likely to arrive in a letter to Annie as to James.

Annie's participation in the editorial process was not limited to expressing opinions on manuscripts; she was called upon by Harriet Beecher Stowe—more than once—to correct proof and even to make major revisions and additions. Stowe wrote to James regarding an article for the *Atlantic*:

> Please let Annie look it over & if she & you think I have said too much of Waltham watches make it right. . . . If Annie thinks of any other thing that ought to be mentioned & will put it in for me she will serve both the cause & me. (Austin 273)

In fact, Annie's editorial work included a good bit of unacknowledged writing. According to her diary, she and James co-authored an article on Dickens that appeared in the *Atlantic* shortly after Dickens's death which was published over James's name only. He inserted excerpts from her diaries without acknowledgment into *Yesterdays with Authors* and probably other works as well. Since Annie may have thought of her journals as records she was keeping for her husband, they were, in a sense, part of her service to the firm (Rotundo 39).[9] She opened her diaries to other readers over the years: Henry Alden and Edward Emerson relied upon them for information about DeQuincey and the Saturday Club, respectively. It would be difficult to determine how much both the reminiscences of the period and later biographies owe to Annie's diaries, but the debt could be surprisingly large.

The vast majority of the Fieldses' business-related friendships were amiable and more. Annie realized that their friendships with the major writers of their time were in part an accident, a gift of Fields's business. The range of their friendships was enormous; their intimate circle consisted chiefly of individuals who had made their mark in some way. Annie became a frequent associate of Emerson, Longfellow, Holmes, Lowell, Whittier, and, during his last few years, of Hawthorne. Of these men, the only one with whom she shared a truly personal friendship was Whittier; among the others, she seems to have been fondest of Longfellow and Holmes. She was a little in awe of Hawthorne and Emerson and ambivalent about Lowell. Other frequent guests in these years were Louis Agassiz; Otto Dresel, a close neighbor; Charles Eliot Norton; Henry James, Sr.; Cyrus Bartol, the minister of Fields's church and a neighbor at Manchester; various members of the Dana family, who also summered in Manchester; Thomas Bailey Aldrich; and William Dean Howells.

Annie played a special role among the women writers who did business with Fields, a role described by Tillie Olsen in her work on Rebecca Harding Davis and by Josephine Donovan in her book *New England Local Color Literature*. Fields is generally acknowledged to have been at the center of a loosely knit circle of women writers that not only included New England writers but also extended well into what is now the Midwest. Although many of these writers never met, and even those who lived relatively close to each other seldom had the time or the means to visit each other, they supported each other with letters full of encouragement. They exchanged photographs, manuscripts, and published books. They congratulated each other on marriages and children and consoled each other on the deaths of family members. They understood, as most of the male writers did not, the difficulties that women faced when they tried to achieve distinction in the arts. In addition to writers, the support network included women painters, sculptors, stained-glass artists, educators, reformers, actresses, and others. The network was international as well, including English and a few French women.

The list of notable women with whom Annie corresponded included many of the women writers who have started to be noticed in the recent flowering of women's studies and others who have not. Some of the women Annie wrote to were probably aspiring writers or artists like her whose names and aspirations have been forgotten. The Huntington Library collection of Annie's correspondence contains, in addition to major figures discussed elsewhere, the names of Alice French, Jane Addams, Elizabeth Agassiz, Ethel Margaret Arnold, Anna Hempstead Branch, Alice Brown, Frances Hodgson Burnett, Alice Cary, Rose Terry Cooke, Dinah Mulock Craik, Catherine Crowe, female couples Charlotte Cushman and Emma Stebbins and Olive Dargan and Anne Whitney, Margaret Deland, Anna Eichberg (Mrs. John Lane), Mary Halleck Foote, Agnes Irwin, Helen Hunt Jackson, Grace King, Lucy Larcom, Anna Leonowens (Anna and the King of Siam), Mary Livermore, Louisa Powell Mac-Donald, Alice Meynell, Helen Modjeska, Violet Paget, Alice Freeman Palmer, Harriet Waters Preston, Anne Proctor, Lizette Woodworth Reese, Agnes Repplier, Laura Richards, Anne Thackeray Ritchie, Christina Rossetti, Catherine Maria Sedgewick, May Sinclair, Ellen Terry, Elizabeth Stuart Phelps Ward, Frances Willard, and Sarah Chauncey Woolsey. Some of these letters illustrate the extravagant affection characteristic of nineteenth-century women—Celia Thaxter, Louisa MacDonald (Mrs. George MacDonald), Sophia Hawthorne, and Rebecca Harding Davis are only a few of the women who seem almost worshipful of Annie or of Annie and Sarah Orne Jewett as a couple. Not all of these women knew Annie well—some of the letters are mere thank-you notes or responses to invitations—but the list of names provides some idea of the extent of the contacts among the women of the time.

One of the most interesting of these friendships, which illustrates the earlier phase of Annie's patronage of her husband's clients rather than the later phase when she and Jewett reigned over the Charles Street salon, is that of Annie and Rebecca Harding Davis. Annie's correspondence with Rebecca Harding began in the early 1860s after Rebecca's "Life in the Iron Mills" marked her impressive entrance into the pages of the *Atlantic*. Rebecca was a a woman of limited experience in her early thirties who felt herself to be a literary outsider. Her home state of Virginia made her sympathetic to the South although she opposed slavery. Like Harriet Beecher Stowe, Rebecca assumed Annie had more time for her anxieties and qualms than did James, and so looked to her for support. She requested and received pictures of both Annie and James, saying that Annie "ought to thank God for such a face—it must be so natural to love her" (RHD). She asked Annie for criticism of her work and evidently received the suggestion that she try to be more cheerful—remarks similar to those Sophia Hawthorne passed along to Annie about Davis's work.

Rebecca carried on a passionate correspondence with Annie for many years, meeting her at last in 1862 on her first momentous visit to Boston, when Annie calmed her anxiety about the literary lions she feared would devour her. Rebecca's romance the next year touched Annie greatly, and she wrote a poem marking the wedding day for Rebecca. The friendship continued with ups and downs—Rebecca wrote angrily to Fields when his successors at the *Atlantic* cut her name from their contributors' list. Annie and Rebecca did not meet again until early in 1873, ten years after Rebecca's marriage to Clarke Davis, and the friendship seems to have declined thereafter. But Rebecca's adoring letters to and about Annie leave little doubt of the impression Mrs. Fields made on many women writers who felt largely excluded from the male-dominated Boston literary circles. According to Donovan, the local-color school "could not have existed without the Boston publishing network that surrounded and issued from" James and Annie (38).

Despite the generally amicable nature of the Fieldses' business relationships and James's reputation as a jovial, kind, and generous publisher, his career was not free of feuds and unpleasantness. Annie noted in her journal for September 1865 a conflict that was typical of the minor disagreements that occurred. Dr. Frederic Hedge, a Unitarian minister then serving in Brookline and an old friend of Emerson's, wrote a book called *Reason in Religion* which John Weiss, another minister and a close friend of Celia Thaxter's, was to review. Fields had offered to let Hedge approve the review—not an uncommon practice in those days—and when the review proved too long for the available space, he instructed John Nichols, his proofreader, to cut it. Hedge later mentioned to Weiss that he had been allowed to approve the review; Weiss became angry and called Fields a coward. Annie noted indignantly that Hedge should not have told Weiss he had approved the review, evidently without considering the ethics of Fields's action.

Before the year was over, Annie helped her husband weather one more crisis. In late October Fields decided to eject Howard Ticknor, William Ticknor's son and Fields's junior partner in the firm, for immorality. Fields had never much liked Ticknor, who had been caught "kissing one of the new women employees . . . behind a counter after hours" (330). Annie's version of the story utilizes its dramatic possibilities:

> Yesterday Jamie had a terrible day—for five mortal hours confronting a man found in adultery—the cause of ruin to two women besides the wreck of his wife's happiness & that of his mother. The vanity and shallowness of this man's character came out startlingly & after the long solemn session—his last remark was "Mr. Fields, if you had taken me

by the hand and introduced me to your social circle perhaps this would not have happened, for I was always counted a clever young man in society!!!"

Annie's picture is more vivid than anything in her fiction or her poetry:

> The calmness of the young girl who called God to witness her innocence when she was most guilty, and heard my love's kind voice questioning her & telling her that because she was an orphan he would over-look her sin and she should retain her position, to think of her denying everything unmoved and without even a tremulous movement of her pen's point. . . . He left her saying . . . "if I know anything of human nature this girl is perfectly pure" and went immediately to her seducer who confessed the girl had been his victim for two years!!

Annie concluded the tale with a characteristic bit of literary allusion: "I came today upon Burns's Song, 'The Ruined Maids' [sic] Lament' which appeared to me to have unspeakable sweetness & force."[10]

These minor squabbles anticipated the serious feuds with Mary Abigail Dodge and Sophia Hawthorne which would make Annie bitter about her hard work for her husband's firm and prompt both James and Annie to plunge themselves into Dickens mania, perhaps the best nineteenth-century equivalent of Beatlemania.

3.
Literary Ambitions
1860–1870

The image of Annie as a literary hostess, full of beauty and grace, entertaining Holmes at breakfast, Emerson at lunch, and a party of eleven famous men from Agassiz to Whipple at dinner, is accurate as far as it goes, but no one, not even her husband, knew how intensely Annie wanted to be one of the great writers herself. The time she devoted to entertaining brought her many rich friendships, but it represented time lost for her own talents. Annie felt ambivalent about her role: proud to be Mrs. James T. Fields, yet capable of expressing her resentment about the ways her life limited her. In 1868, five years after her debut as a poet, Annie wrote in her diary:

> J. says I shall never do a better thing than the Ode on the Organ—It will certainly depend upon circumstances what I may do but I feel I can do something far more sustained and as truly lyrical—but not under the ordinary condition of my city life—Burns was always a poet—surely we ought always to be ourselves, and yet I am too much a woman to be always a poet, I cannot live for that—I cannot have a woodland walk when I feel like it because somebody will lose their dinner—Annie Thackeray was right—our American life is a strange mixture of magnificence and scrub just now, and that goes to the wall. Yet I know there is a heart of a singer hidden in me and I long sometimes to break loose—but on the whole I sincerely prefer to make others comfortable and happy as I can now do and say fie! to my genius if he does not sing to me from the sauce-pans all the same.

This is a side of Annie Fields which may come as a surprise to scholars who have thought of her as a "happy hostess."

Contrary to her image, Annie loved to be alone, longed to study languages and write, and frequently complained (to her diary) about the extensive socializing Fields's work involved. During a business trip to New York in 1866, she wrote, "What a strange full life this is of ours—So many pleasant friends! Will the solitary days be rich for us when this is over—I love them best and yet I love my friends too" (2 Jan.). The Fieldses' social schedule was always full; Annie commented in her diary that "The Ladies Club, the Thursday Club, the Dante Club are all in full swing, also Mrs [Julia] Dorr's dinners.[1] It is easier to go out every evening than to get the chance of staying in" (Dec. 1865). Annie came to resent the demands her husband's profession made upon her. In herr own mind, she was not merely an adjunct to Ticknor & Fields: after reading Carlyle's *On Heroes, Hero Worship, and the Heroic in History,* she noted:[2]

> There are a few thoughts which give me perpetual rest whatever fatigue or weariness I
> may suffer—first[,] thoughts of those I love and revere[;] second[,] of the heroic
> possibilities of all life—even my own. (Feb. 1867)

In the 1860s Annie tried to find a place as a linguist and translator, like her sister Sarah;
as a poet; and as a fiction writer. But her gift was analytical and intrepretive rather
than imaginative or lyric. Although she never excelled as a creative writer, her
intelligence and keen understanding of human nature contributed to her success in
nurturing writers, serving the poor, and writing diaries, memoirs, and biographies.

Although being the wife of an important publisher seems like an advantage for an
aspiring writer, the reverse was true for Annie. Fields encouraged his wife to be a
dilettante but not a serious writer; he may have felt that his business would benefit
from nominal participation in the writing community but suffer from genuine competition. He was too astute to fill coveted *Atlantic* space with his wife's work. His
sensitivity had unfortunate consequences for Annie; he cancelled a long review of
Blake's work that he had asked her to write because one of his "name" writers
exceeded her space (MHS). Fields published a number of Annie's poems in the
Atlantic, but always as "filler" at the end of an essay or story. Everything that Annie
published through *Under the Olive* in 1881 appeared anonymously, under a pseudonym, or was privately printed. Annie's discretion had to be impeccable, and she
censored her creative impulses from fear of a misstep.

Fear of offending sensitive contributors may not have been the only reason Fields
seems to have published as little as possible of his wife's writing. She occasionally
confided to her diary her husband's lukewarm praise of poems she had struggled over
for months. Fields could not and did not mislead Annie about the value of her writing,
and this may have been her one hidden grievance. Sarah Orne Jewett proved to be
much better at cheerleading Annie's efforts.

Living in close proximity to the greatest writers of the age meant that Annie must
have constantly compared her own work with the best of her time. Dissatisfaction was
inevitable. The frustration and sense of failure she felt are illustrated in this passage
from her diary, written at the peak of her success as a literary hostess:

> How fine it is to work up to the top of one's bent all the time[,] to the top of one's power.
> What happiness to have the gift to do so—I look upon Longfellow with his two tragedies
> this busy month as a man on whom Providence has smiled—I feel bitterly sometimes,
> how little [illegible]—. (2 March 1868)

Such comparisons made Annie's amateur standing more pronounced.

Initially Annie may have seen herself as a scholar and writer along the lines of
Emerson, Longfellow, or Lowell. She wanted to know French, German, Italian, Latin,
and Greek; to achieve this end, she set herself a difficult schedule of reading books in
foreign languages, taking lessons, and translating poems into English. She published
only one translation but completed many more, usually from German or French. She
knew enough Greek to render the translations for epigraphs and provide copious notes
on Greek mythology in her books of poetry. During the 1870s she belonged to a group

of women who read their translations to each other in the manner of Longfellow's Dante Club. Translation proved a dead end for Annie, however, probably because she lacked the time for concentrated study and the fluency for translation.

The genre Annie pursued most persistently over the years was poetry. She confided to Sarah Orne Jewett her belief that her "genius" lay in poetry. Her literary reading was primarily poetry; it included both genuine and spurious Chaucer *(The Court of Love* and *Romaunt of the Rose),* Browning, Dryden, Swinburne *(Poems and Ballads),* Byron, Landor, Morris, Eliot, Holmes, and Burns. Although competent, her poems lack originality and work a familiar vein of classicism. Her earliest poetry notebooks are dated 1857, just three years after her marriage to Fields (HL). Annie's lyrics fall into familiar categories: she wrote poems to celebrate birthdays, anniversaries, and weddings; poems which reflect her love of nature; poems about the Civil War; poems on religious subjects; and a few narrative poems in the manner of Longfellow or Whittier. Of the hundreds of poems Annie wrote in the 1860s, only a small number were printed and those anonymously. Aside from a few short personal lyrics, her most interesting poems may be *The Children of Lebanon* (1872), a sentimental treatment of the Shakers, and *The Return of Persephone* (1877), an interpretation of the myth that focuses on the mother-daughter relationship.

The Children of Lebanon is a blank verse poem of over 400 lines about the romance of Phoebe and Nathan who were adopted by the Shakers as children and chose to leave the Lebanon community so they could earn independent incomes and eventually marry. Phoebe, an orphan, was cared for by Sister Dorothy, who struggled against loving Phoebe as a daughter and thereby placing too much emphasis on worldly love. Nathan came to the community with his mother, who had been forced to bring her "little brood" to the Shaker community after her husband had abandoned them. After discovering their love for each other, Nathan and Phoebe asked the Church conclave for its blessing (and presumably a share of its savings for a start in life) but were forced to work for five years to earn enough to marry. Eventually Dorothy, who had let Phoebe leave without a word, left the community to search for her adoptive daughter.

The poem is interesting primarily for its choice of subject matter. Annie had evidently heard such a story of true love among the Shakers and considered the Shakers' rejection of "worldly love" a misinterpretation of Christianity. Although she does maintain iambic pentameter for the length of the poem, neither the rhythm nor the language achieve distinction.

The Return of Persephone, published shortly after the death of Annie's mother and dedicated to her memory, is also written in iambic meter. Annie works from Walter Pater's story of the myth of Demeter and Persephone. In Annie's version of the story, Demeter is a possessive mother who seems to feel that her daughter should remain hers indefinitely. Persephone, still a child when kidnapped by Aidoneus, the ruler of Dis, seems to fear admonishment from her mother more than the darkness of the underworld, for she protests twice, "'Mother! mother dear! / I did not disobey thee!'" Demeter eventually softens her grudge against the world enough to nurse a male infant, Demophoon, but continues to seek Persephone. By the time Helios (the sun) intercedes and asks Aidoneus to let Persephone visit her mother, Persephone has evidently come to love her husband, for she tells him, "'I would away, since thou, my love, dost bid.'"

She says she will tell her mother "'what calm abides with thee.'" Annie seems to be reading the natural cycle of the earth's seasons as a metaphor for the natural departure of the daughter from the mother, the natural transference of allegiance from parents to spouse, although the daughter still returns periodically to visit her original home. Whether the poem is a comment on Annie's relationship with her mother is unknown, since she said so little about it in her diaries and letters.

As luck would have it, Annie's first published poem received a hostile reception and caused a furor that must have dimmed her enthusiasm and her eagerness to become part of the writing community. In 1863 Boston installed a large organ in the newly remodelled Music Hall, and Charlotte Cushman, a noted actress and an old friend of the Fieldses, was chosen to recite a dedicatory poem. Perhaps because of this friendship, Annie, then less than thirty years old and an inexperienced poet, was invited to write the piece. Her excitement about her commission is evident in her diary:

> There has been an ode written to be spoken at the organ opening—No one is to know who wrote it. Miss Cushman will speak it if they are speedy enough in their finishing. This is of interest to many. I trust they will be ready for Miss Cushman. (25 Sept. 1863)

On 6 October she noted, "Today they have begun to tune the great organ. If no accident occurs Miss Cushman will read *the* ode."

The Ode is a poem composed of six sections and nearly 200 lines of rhymed verse. The first section will give the reader a good idea of the general quality of the work:

> Listen to the invocation!
> Now awaking, praiseful breaking,
> It shall bear the heart of a nation,
> Swelling in vast convocation,
> Full of honor, full of song,
> Upward to the Source of Praise where harmonies belong.

The poem proceeds to discuss the settling of America, the decision to build an organ, the selection of the builder, the design, the onset of war, the completion of the organ, and the hope that "Through all the tones the voice of Freedom rings/ One choral chant, one song of praise,—A NATION'S VICTORY!" Although it is probably no worse than a good deal of other poetry of its type and time, the effort has little to recommend it.

After the dedication on the evening of 2 November, she dropped the third person in describing the event: "Miss Cushman read my ode in a most perfect manner. . . . It was a night never to be forgotten."

Nothing more appears in the diary about the ode itself, although one passage refers obliquely to an incident it caused. The item appears over a year later: "Mr. Bartol came to bring a message from Julia Ward Howe asking us to forget an article she wrote in the 'Commonwealth' which was an unpleasant piece of business on her part" (4 Dec. 1864). The "unpleasant piece of business" was a review which resulted from Julia Ward Howe's anger that she had been ignored and Annie asked to write the ode. (She might also have been irked by the amount of time Fields let elapse between publication of a series of poems he had accepted for the *Atlantic* in 1862.)[3] Mrs. Howe sharply criticized Annie's poem in print, and the Fieldses and Mrs. Howe ceased to be friendly until Mrs. Howe's note of apology.

A look at Howe's review explains the length and the bitterness of the hostilities. Both the ode and the review were ostensibly anonymous, but Harriet Beecher Stowe's brother Henry was the editor of the *Commonwealth* and her identity became known. Mrs. Howe discussed her previously high expectations for the evening and attacked the remodelling of the building before vilifying the ode itself:

> The Ode which was now presented to the public, judged from a literary point of view, deserves neither praise nor criticism. It had no characteristic of a poem other than phrase and rhyme, and presented the mere wardrobe of poetry, without a body or soul. A poem in the true sense of the word is a conception, claiming birth. . . . A mere statement, couched in the usual phraseology, and interrupted by irrelevant rhyme can in no wise be called a poem. Such, alas! the present Ode proved to be, with no stamp of originality, and with no line that will remain. Considered as an expression of feeling, simply, and as the work of an unpracticed hand, we ourselves might find something to say in its favor. But the occasion was one calling for poetry, and the false ambition of this attempt merely blocked the way from something better. Surely, among the literary men and women of Boston, among those who really *could,* might have been found some one who *would* have spoken the word for the hour which, whether in prose or in verse, was what the public wanted to hear. ([Howe, J.] "How")

Mrs. Howe completed her review with an attack on the music and the inadequacy of the organ itself.

The effect on Annie must have been devastating: her first venture into poetry greeted not only by harsh criticism, but also by ill will. Today, most readers would probably agree with Mrs. Howe's evaluation of the poem, but that is not the point. Fields was Mrs. Howe's publisher; they were in the same social circle. In the context of reviewing practice of the time, her review was an outrage, especially when aimed at a friend. Even if a friend's book was terrible, a critic generally wrote a kindly, balanced review; in this case, the other papers called the ode "a fine poem," and Oliver Wendell Holmes rose to its defense ("One").

Mrs. Howe's apology helped to assuage the break and soon Annie sent a poem to Howe's paper, "The Boatswain's Whistle," which was sold at the Seaman's Fair to raise money for a National Soldier's Home (Tharp, *Three Saints* 266). The poem Annie sent was probably "An Appeal to the People for an American Seaman's Home," which is found in her poetry notebook for October and November of 1864 (HL).

While an outward sociability was restored, over the years a number of critical remarks about Mrs. Howe crept into Annie's journal. In November of 1865, Annie noted: "[Ladies] Club at Mrs. Andrews. Mrs. Howe read a clever vulgar salutatory at which everybody laughed outwardly and were ashamed inwardly." A few years later, when the Fieldses visited Venice during their second European trip, Annie referred to a private joke about Mrs. Howe:

> We have had Bleak House with us & have remembered our picture of Mrs Howe in Mrs Jellyby. Jamie laughed heartily over a description Tom [Appleton] gave him from a

college friend who had been visiting at her house in Newport[.] He said the order of the house seemed to be "the Devil take the hindmost." (Aug. 1868)

Another negative description of Mrs. Howe appears in January of 1868 after their return home. Annie wrote:

> Col. W. B. Green & his family took tea with us—He has organized a Society of Working Women—Mrs Julia Ward Howe came upon them like a whirlwind the other night declaring she had been spoken of disrespectfully there, bringing her little narrow personality into a meeting occupied with business and heated with high enthusiasms.

Annie's resentment eventually dissipated—a good thing, because the women saw one another often. Near the end of Mrs. Howe's life, she visited Annie while Mrs. Humphry Ward, a prominent British antisuffragist, and her daughter Dorothy were in town. Annie remarked:

> Mrs Ward talked with her [Mrs. Howe] somewhat of early New York but [Mrs. Howe] avoided the subject of suffrage about wh. Mrs. Ward really knows nothing but it was dangerous ground [Mrs. Howe] felt. I was sorry—it would have been very interesting to hear the dear old woman [Mrs. Howe] telling of her faith and its causes.

After nearly fifty years of sharing the Boston literary scene, old quarrels were forgotten.

Annie continued to write and publish poetry but she was alone in her belief that it was her best work. She had less confidence in her ability to write fiction, and in this case her self-evaluation was correct. *Asphodel* was virtually the only fiction Annie wrote, although she occasionally recorded ideas for a story in her diary. Annie never thought very highly of her own prose writing, and Sarah accused her of being a "poor supporter of story writers." In the 1860s the only novels Annie mentioned reading were by George Eliot, Victor Hugo, Dumas, Dickens, Oliver Wendell Holmes, and Henry James, a selection which suggests that she read only writers of international reputation and friends.

Annie's first and only novel, *Asphodel,* was her second publication. The book was published anonymously by Ticknor & Fields, and this time its authorship was more carefully concealed, although by the end of the 1870s both Lowell and Howells knew the book was Annie's (MHS). The destructive criticism of *Asphodel* was delivered privately, and the person who delivered it, Sophia Hawthorne, probably never knew what she had done. Annie brought this grief upon herself by sending a copy of her novel to Sophia and soliciting her opinion of the book without acknowledging its authorship.

Neither Sophia nor Nathaniel was in the habit of mincing words about contemporary writing. In 1859, Hawthorne had bluntly expressed his views on women writers in a note acknowledging some books Fields had sent him ("Mrs. F." is not Annie):

> As a less awkward mode of doing the business, I have preferred to acknowledge Mrs. F's books in a note to yourself, than to her. You will find it enclosed; and if it meet your

approbation, please to forward it. I really do not know that I have said any more than the truth, in a good-humored mood, will warrant; but nevertheless, I can very well conceive of a person's tossing the books aside as tedious twaddle. My favorable opinion of the book has evaporated, in the process of writing it down. *All* women, as authors, are feeble and tiresome. I wish they were forbidden to write, on pain of having their faces scarified with an oyster shell. (Oldham 144)

That Sophia shared her husband's ideas about women writers is evident from this letter to Fields in 1859, declining to publish her own travel letters in the *Atlantic:*

You forget that Mr. Hawthorne is the Belles lettres portion of my being, and besides that I have a repugnance to female authoresses in general, I have far more distaste to myself as a female authoress in particular. (Oldham 144)

Annie certainly knew the Hawthornes' prejudice about women writers and their frankness as well, for Sophia had bluntly criticized Rebecca Harding Davis, a Ticknor & Fields author and a friend of Annie's, a few months earlier. According to Mrs. Hawthorne, her husband couldn't read Mrs. Davis's work because of its "bad style and slimy gloom." She also criticized Davis for using the words "pulse" and "pulsate" as verbs, and finally declared:

But I do wish that Miss Harding, who is now Mrs Davis would cease to write about disgustful flabby men and "dried up old women," and present truth in a rather more graceful style—She makes me sea sick—Why will she be so "mouldy" as my husband told her she was—Why does she love squalor—oh why? There is mire enough in the streets without smearing the pages of books with it. (BPL 25 April 1866)

Given the well-known antipathy of both Sophia and her husband to women writers, it seems foolhardy of Annie to have sent the book to Mrs. Hawthorne in this manner. Sophia's candid reply must have crushed Annie:

I began but *could not* read Asphodel on account of its lack of nature, truth, simplicity, *vraisemblance*—Perhaps I was not in the mood, and perhaps it is better in the end. But I think I could not ever read it, and I hope you do not like it yourself well enough to care whether I like it or not. Is it some new young authoress, whom you are trying to befriend and bring forward? She is no artist certainly—I would rather have your Florence Mosaic (as I call it) than a library of such books as this. But you ought not to be mentioned on the same page as this one. A Persian lily! (BPL 1 Oct. 1866)

Annie smothered her feelings and continued to be a good friend to the Hawthornes until 1869 when Sophia joined Mary Abigail Dodge in an attack upon Fields and his methods of payment. Then Annie's irritation about Sophia found a voice in her diary:

I know she has felt discontent for a year or two because we no longer asked the children & herself to stay in our house for long periods, but they were most fatiguing and ungrateful guests, the only redeeming pleasure being Mrs. Hawthorne's real talent and apparent happiness in our friendship. I could never do anything; but was obliged to relinquish every moment while either of them was in the house to finding congenial occupation and change of occupation for them.

But Annie's responsibilities as a hostess always took precedence, forcing her to give up her time, her fair chance at publication, and even her wounded feelings.

A closer look at *Asphodel* is helpful in understanding some of the impediments to Annie's success as a writer. Although untactful, Sophia Hawthorne's comments about the literary quality of *Asphodel* are essentially correct. But the book shows Annie's determination to write literature, not popular fiction, and her interest in mild polemic. The opening hymn of praise for New England and New Englanders conveys Annie's commitment to her birthplace and to native American literature. The book illustrates her agreement with Transcendental philosophy, love of classical literature, and sympathy with nature.

In *Asphodel,* Annie attempted to write a novel in the form of a classic tragedy, casting its central character as the "great and good man" with a tragic flaw who commits *hamartia*. Although the action of the story takes place in several locations and over a span of months, Annie creates the illusion of unity of time by making the story begin at sunrise and end at sunset, with the sun playing a conspicuous part in the action throughout.

The book has a melodramatic plot. Russell, an egotistical writer who is mourning the recent death of his wife, takes his daughter Fanny to visit his friends Herbert and Alice Gregory, who live in a seaside town. Alice's school friend, Erminia, arrives to help take care of the Gregory children, Ernest and Allegra, because Herbert has been advised to travel for his health. Russell and Fanny decide to prolong their stay with the Gregory family; the stage is set for Russell and Erminia to fall in love.

As *Asphodel* develops, Russell continues to be obsessed with the perfection of his late wife and does not notice that Erminia loves him. When he finally falls in love with her, he remains silent, mistaking her maidenly reticence for indifference. He is called to the West Coast on business and leaves his daughter in Erminia's care.

On the ship to California Russell meets a family, the Van Ranses, who have a teen-age daughter named Amy. Lonely, unable to resist Amy's coy advances, Russell finds himself trapped into a gentleman's proposal when he discovers that Amy loves him. In the meantime, however, he has declared himself to Erminia by sending her his signet ring. She correctly assumes that the ring is a declaration and responds with a letter announcing her departure for the West Coast. Russell's note rescinding his proposal is delivered too late, and Erminia and Fanny arrive at the Van Ranse home just as the minister completes the wedding ceremony. As a result of this series of events Erminia loses her mind and Amy catches a cold which develops into tuberculosis. Russell, without domestic happiness once again, finds consolation in the prospect of Fanny's marriage to Ernest, the son of his old friends.

The plot resembles so many other plots and bits of plots in nineteenth-century novels that any prolonged attempt to trace literary influence would be pointless. While Annie was of course aware of the conventions of plot, character, and sentiment in the fiction of her time, the parallel between her novel and the social circle she knew is more striking and may further explain the anonymous publication. The book makes transparent use of names and character traits that can be identified as originating in the Fields circle. Of nine main characters, five have the same names as members of the Longfellow family.[4] Even more significant, however, is the name of the main character, Russell, and his resemblance in both character and history to James Russell Lowell.

To the extent that the book makes a point, it expresses sympathy for a pure, honest woman, Erminia, and condemns a selfish, egotistical man, Russell. The one man Annie repeatedly refers to in her diaries as egotistical is James Russell Lowell. She notes on more than one occasion that she does not think people in general, and Lowell in particular, sufficiently appreciated his second wife, Frances Dunlap. Lowell's first wife, Maria White, had been widely respected as an abolitionist and a woman of character; Lowell was devastated when she died in 1853. Frances Dunlap, his second wife, had been his children's tutor and was generally considered his social and intellectual inferior at the time of their marriage in 1857. Like Russell in Annie's novel, Lowell had one cherished daughter, Mabel, from his first marriage.

Perhaps the plot was suggested to Annie by Lowell, her dislike of him, and her feeling of advocacy for his wife, without her intentionally using him for a model. Her own unconscious insecurity at being a second wife may have resulted in an identification with Frances Lowell and played a part in the story as well. But the most surprising coincidence is that, in some respects, Lowell's future followed the course of the novel. When Lowell was ambassador to Spain in 1877, Frances contracted a disease which affected her sanity; she never recovered from it. Lowell and some of his friends held him responsible for Frances's disease and death because he had taken her to the foreign place where her health had been destroyed (Duberman 134, 284–94, 336).

A second noteworthy feature of the book is the relationship between Erminia and Alice, which began at school and ended in an intimacy so strong that Alice's marriage nearly caused a rift. Erminia later wrote to her friend:

> Seven years ago, upon your marriage day, I grieved and wept. In my girlish weakness, I feared I had lost something, being ignorant of the divine mystery of married love to enlarge the possibilities of life. (26)

On the morning of Herbert's departure, Alice calls Erminia to help her arrange a mass of flowers. We are told that Alice

> looked chiefly at her friend, who never appeared more lovely. The slender group of lilies and roses, relieved against the deep blue of her dress; the sunshine streaming through her rich "Venetian" hair, causing the gold gleams hidden there to shine; and . . . a sweet simplicity of manner . . . made her inexpressibly lovely to Alice. (20–21)

Annie may have merely observed this pattern in women's friendships or she may have drawn upon her relationship with Laura Winthrop Johnson, a schoolmate and Annie's closest female friend until the 1880s.

The relationship between Erminia and her father illustrates additional differences between the nineteenth-century point of view and our own. Erminia's mother had died when she was twelve, and until her father's recent death, the father and daughter, we are told, "had been an unspeakably happy pair" who succeeded in driving out of the house two "maiden aunts" who came to help raise their niece. After they left,

> the child who appeared so wilful and wayward under uncongenial control became with her father, what he believed her to be, the most docile of pupils, and humble as a lover. (25)

Evidently Annie felt no compunction about describing a father-daughter relationship in terms which the current century would consider suggestive. Even in 1911 Annie wrote a description of the love between a father and daughter that makes a post-Freudian blush. When writing in her diary about her Manchester friend and neighbor Georgiana Godland Eaton, who had just died, Annie recalled how Georgiana had been her father's "daughter, friend, wife, sister and . . . son" for many years. Her language echoed that of *Asphodel* when she wrote:

> Georgie became the joy and support of her father and after some years they were like lovers wishing for nothing else while they had each other. (MHS 8 Sept. 1911)

Like Annie's relationship with Jewett, the relationships Annie portrayed in *Asphodel* were commonplace in the nineteenth century but unfashionable in the twentieth.

Mrs. Fields's poetry and fiction are forgotten, but her diaries, memoirs, and even her biographies continue to be read by at least a small audience of scholars. Annie enjoyed reading nonfiction more than anything else, and it is appropriate that she did her best work in nonfiction genres. The bulk of her reading was journals and diaries, letters, biography and autobiography, essays, history and philosophy. Between 1862 and 1870 she read lives of Michelangelo, Samuel Butler, Hans Christian Andersen, Margaret Fuller, Voltaire, Lessing, Garrick, and Madame de Lafayette; the autobiographies of Gibbon, Horace Greeley, and Harriet Martineau; and the letters of Mendelssohn, Charlotte Brontë, and Madame Roland. Her philosophical and histori-cal reading included Plato, Virgil, Horace, Plotinus, and Plutarch and the more modern work of Swedenborg, Milton, and Rousseau. She mentioned Carlyle's *Shooting Niagara: and After?, The French Revolution,* and "The American Iliad"; Sainte-Beauve's *Portraits des Femmes*; Coleridge's *Biographia Literaria*; Hawthorne's notebooks; and Mrs. Henshaw's *Northwest Branch of the Sanitary Commission.* The notion of keeping literary diaries may have evolved from her interest in journals, letters, and autobiographies. Annie's earliest diaries were scrapbooks into which she inserted autograph letters, daguerreotypes, early photographs, engravings cut from magazines, and stories about writers, friends, books, lecture series, and anything else that she considered interesting. In one such album, the immediate forerunner of her literary diaries, she wrote about memorable current events such as the triumphant greeting that Boston gave to Colonel Robert Gould Shaw, the brave leader of the North's first black regiment:

The first colored regiment was welcomed into the city upon the common and after a magnificent demonstration said its farewells and departed for the seat of war. . . . Men blessed God that they had lived to see this prejudice wiped away. (May 1863)

The germ of Annie's writing is the literary diaries of the 1860s and 1870s, fifty-three blue books that represent her contribution to American letters. She began them with the intention of creating a publishable journal which would (tactfully) enlighten an interested public about the daily lives of its favorite authors. The first of this series indicates Annie's intention of creating a "Journal of literary events and glimpses of interesting people."

The diaries soon became Annie's most important writing project. But she was never satisfied with the amount of time she could spend on the diary and felt her notes were inadequate; in fact, the diary became an unpleasant reminder of her inability to carry out a major literary project. During Dickens's visit in November of 1867, Annie wrote:

He drew Mr and Mrs Lewes also, both exceedingly homely but he thinks the latter very interesting with her shy manner of saying brilliant things.—I grieve at the imperfection of these things—but time—. (29 Nov. 1867)

A review of Anne Bradstreet's poetry in January of 1868 gave Annie a chance to express what she hoped her diaries could be:

In looking over an account of the poems of Anne Bradstreet lately reprinted, I am struck by the truth of the remark that if she had given a simple womanly or witty account of things going on around her how delightful the book might yet be,—whereas it is dry as dust and must presently be blown utterly away in spite of these new leaves—
    Even on account of this simple diary I felt rather conscience-stricken when I read those words for it is often a mere record of doings & sayings uninteresting and valueless except perhaps for reference for my own use now & then—
    Yet a great deal does go on *around* if not *within* which might have permanent value if I could bring myself to setting down my words a little more painfully perhaps, or at least less [illegible]—.

Annie knew she was doing too little composing and too much mere recording, injecting too little wit and personality, for her diary to be considered literature. She wanted her diary to be a record of permanent value, but she did not have the time or the energy, and perhaps not the skill, to carry out her goal. In April of 1868, after several attempts to express her grief at Dickens's recent departure, she wrote in despair:

It is the most difficult task of all in writing a diary to tell the straight thing in a straight way which you have seen with your own eyes or heard with your own ears—In the first place the matter which fills us most deeply is the most difficult to speak of—

A few months later Annie indulged in self-mockery: "Not one word in this vastly important volume for more than a week." By 1870 Annie had stopped keeping her journal altogether and directed her energy into social work. But despite her disappointment with her work, the diaries are full of the writing she did best, literary history that drew upon her analytic ability and her intuition about people.

Annie failed to create a uniformly objective, outward-looking description of the literary life of her time, but what she did create is almost more interesting: a daily record of the anxieties surrounding housekeeping, servants, ungrateful writers, and similar burdens. Soon after their commencement, the diaries became a mixture of disparate elements. And in the many digressions from Annie's literary record we find a new source, virtually untouched, that provides information of a new kind about Annie's private life and the private lives of other women like her. The diaries vividly portray Annie's struggle against the decree that a woman's most important work was domestic rather than intellectual or creative.

Annie's ambivalence about the priority of woman's domestic role and her failure to produce a great work of literature are a constant theme throughout the seven years Annie continued these diaries. Her belief that every living being had a responsibility to develop his or her talent conflicted with the social imperative that a woman's first duty was to work for the comfort of others. Annie longed for the freedom she thought genius conferred: If she could produce one great novel, one great poem, she would have felt justified in neglecting her domestic responsibilities and consecrating herself to art. But how could she produce anything really worthwhile while she was supervising the home, entertaining daily, and assisting James with *his* work?

Annie's diary reflects her day-to-day struggle to define her duty and perform it with a little time left over for literary work. She wavered between a recognition of "the slight value of the world's praise compared with the true well-doing" and a wistful longing for "the old studious thoughtful days" before she had made her husband's ambitions her own. But even a publisher's wife needed some time off:

> LeBrun's motto for women is ever nearer my heart "Inspirez et n'ecrivez pas" but "to inspire" one must take seasons of meditation and repose from the world and must live listening to the eternal harmoniums while the tempests of earth howl and sweep round our heads. (19 Jan. 1866)[5]

"Inspire and do not write" was a bitter motto for Annie. She exchanged her dream of literary success for the reality of providing her husband's clients with good food, lively conversation, and a welcoming smile, and no one can blame her for grumbling a bit:

> I have had hardly an hour for study or reading except when too tired to give my best devotion to my work and I feel as Gibbon did during the first 7 or 8 months of his service in the Hampshire militia, only alas! This is not the first time in my life as it is with him. Society absorbs too much of my ~~time~~ best thought and time yet I cannot see well how to help this because [illegible] will. The [causes] are many and evident but I sometimes wonder at and blame myself for not seizing more time, only it is not my own to seize. The slight cares of housekeeping and entertaining beside of visiting cannot be neglected in the smallest of particulars, else others who depend upon me will be made uncomfortable.
>
> Gibbons' [sic] Autobiography is very absorbing and interesting[.] Now that the Spring

months are here I would devote many hours every day to Greek and Latin if I could find an instructor. I will look.

Eventually, Annie's inability to meet the high standards she set for herself resulted in an overwhelming sense of failure. Her time for books diminished in proportion to James's success and her family's growing inclination to leave their problems in her capable hands. She gave in to the inevitable by sublimating her ambition in a half-hearted commitment to the doctrine of "true womanhood."

4.

Family and Friends, Housekeeping and "True Womanhood"

Although she resisted the loss of her time for study, Annie felt morally bound to fulfill her womanly duties, as she might have called them. Annie believed that traditional roles for men and women helped to create a well-ordered world and that making those around her comfortable was a woman's responsibility. She felt that her childlessness gave her an additional responsibility to serve the needy and homeless, as well as those in her own family circle. Annie realized that the responsibilities allotted to women were time-consuming and not very satisfying, but she attributed this to God's plan, the natural affinities and talents of men and women, biological imperative, or the greater efficiency of divison of labor, not to social injustice. As she wrote in her diary when her mother and sisters Lissie and Sarah came to visit:

A kind of light has come to show me how it is happier better (yes perhaps happier) by far to live and make use of poetry such as some people can concentrate into poems than to live only for such concentration. It is well the light has come, for I have a little family of 5 now and 4 below stairs for a few days.

Her apparent acceptance of the traditional female role did not prevent her from drawing some surprisingly modern conclusions about the obstacles which stood in the way of women who hoped to make a lasting contribution to art or literature.

After her father's death in 1855, Annie seems to have become the head of the remaining Adams clan. In 1862 Annie's youngest sister, Louisa, married James H. Beal, a widowed banker with five children. Annie's only brother, Boylston, was wounded and imprisoned during the Civil War; he later attended Harvard Medical School. In 1870 he married Frances Kidder in the Fieldses' Charles Street home. Mrs. Adams and her eldest daughter, Sarah, moved to a residential hotel in Roxbury, the town where Mrs. Adams had lived before her marriage.

Annie's relations with her mother and siblings then fell into a pattern which they followed for many years. Boylston and the Fieldses were seldom in touch; hints of disapproval appear in Annie's infrequent references to him. Annie and James often visited the various members of Annie's family on Sundays, walking to Roxbury to have dinner with Mrs. Adams and Sarah and spending the evening with Annie's youngest sister, Louisa, and her family. Louisa's two sons, for whom Annie sometimes babysat, and Boylston's son and daughter were the only children in the succeeding generation and became James and Annie's heirs.

The relationship between Annie and her sister Lissie was a close one, so close that Lissie appears to have been one of Annie's alter egos, a woman who had made different choices, choices that Annie sometimes wished she had made. Lissie was single and there were no impediments to her pursuing an artistic career. In her role as elder stateswoman of the Fields clan, Annie made it possible for Lissie to go to Europe and remain there to study and paint despite the objections of their sister Louisa and the uncertainty of their mother. Although she became Lissie's advocate and identified with her, Annie found their relationship a source of strain and frustration. Whenever Lissie failed to come through for Annie—as frequently happened—all of Annie's own unfulfilled longings and regrets came to the fore.

The first major strain in their relationship occurred in 1865 when Lissie, living in Florence, proved unequal to Bostonian hospitality and liberality. Edmonia Lewis, a young woman with black and Chippewa blood who was a protégée of Lydia Maria Child, called upon Annie in Boston shortly before leaving for Florence to study art. Annie gave Miss Lewis a letter of introduction to Lissie and urged Edmonia to call upon her sister right away. Lissie responded to her sister's letter by keeping it "long enough to read it," then sending it back to Edmonia (who had not yet been admitted) "without one word." Lydia Maria Child indignantly wrote to Fields, "Is this Miss Adams your sister-in-law? If so, you must tell her she is lagging behind the age" (HL 13 Oct. 1865).

A week later, the *Commonwealth,* an abolitionist paper in Boston, included a small story about Edmonia Lewis's successful transition to Florence, aided by Mr. Marsh, the American minister, and two American artists, Mr. Thomas Ball, a sculptor, and Mr. Hiram Powers. The article ended, "In contrast with this generosity should be mentioned the conduct of a Boston lady there residing, who, when Edmonia sent in a letter of introduction given by her own sister in this city, *returned it to her,* and declined to receive her,—because she was 'colored!'" ("Artistic"). Annie defended her sister, although she was undoubtedly displeased. Child backed down, writing to Annie that "There has been an unpleasant misunderstanding, and Edmonia is evidently much excited; but that is not to be wondered at, considering the trying position in which she is placed by her complexion." It is impossible to know exactly what happened, but evidently Lissie was exonerated of turning away Miss Lewis because of her color. Annie was very sensitive about her husband's clients, however, and this incident probably created some resentment against her sister.

In the fall of 1866, Lissie returned to Boston after an absence of eight years, taking up residence at the Fieldses'. Lissie made many demands on Annie, who felt obliged—as hostess or sister—to plan trips into the country so that Lissie could sketch, to take walks with her, to spend hours looking for children to pose for Lissie's paintings, all of which she recorded irritably in her diary. She herself posed at length for Lissie, although she managed to faint once right after they started (the only record of Annie's fainting). Annie was continually frustrated by her sister's lack of ambition, her refusal to complete paintings and sell them. Her feeling that Lissie lacked professionalism came through loud and clear:

I have felt saddened lately by Lissie's remark, that we continually said she had never yet done anything, and she continued ["]I never shall do anything which will please you.["] I see I have overstepped the mark somewhere ! should not have allowed myself to be frank with her I should have preserved a better silence if I wish to please her—but I do not I can say frankly—"Do [unto] others" et—and I prefer others for instance to tell me when a poem is a failure than to praise it untruely [sic]—How much healthier is this than praise (provided a recognition of labor given is granted).

Annie evidently meant that she was not being hypocritical in criticizing Lissie, unaware of the extent to which she was making Lissie carry the burden of her own failures and disappointed expectations.

Annie's journal is a record of her own daily defeat, in this case, after returning to Boston from a summer in Manchester:

Written nothing here lately—am trying to begin housekeeping just right. It absorbs everything at first—that and the few visits which must be paid. But I shall keep a few hours out of each morning sacredly as soon as we are established, except when I have friends staying in the house—Then I see no help for it I suppose those hours must be given up—I will struggle through.(Sept. 1868)

But Lissie had no household responsiblities—indeed, no responsibilities at all, except to her art. How frustrating to Annie:

We are bound to be disappointed in poor Lissie's work[.] She does not finish anything and indeed does so little anyway that six months work would never pay her even for the rent of a small studio. . . . I tell her of the necessity for more vigorous action but the poor girl works steadily every morning and what more can she achieve. . . . At present she is stumbling and falling (as are we all more or less)[.] She has not been able to [send] anything to the Wheelock fund although her name is advertised.

A few months after an illness, during which Lissie accused Annie of not caring for her and saying unkind things about her work, the conflict between the sisters reached a crisis. Annie wrote that

Lissie gives up my portrait [blacks] over the face which she had made very sweet & leaves it. . . . She is inert (like most of us only it amounts to disease with her) and she is apt to fail before reaching [her] goal.

Three months later Annie recorded that her sister had sailed once again for Europe. After a healthy two-year separation, Annie wrote philosophically to her mother and Sarah that Lissie should be allowed to remain in Europe but that

As for any money-making on her part that should not be considered as possible. . . . It is worse than foolish to look upon any efforts she may make as results to depend upon. This is usually the case with artists but especially it is the case with her.

Annie and Lissie corresponded frequently and visited after Lissie moved to Baltimore; despite their problems, Lissie was undoubtedly Annie's favorite sister.

Annie's criticisms of her youngest sister, Louisa Beal, seem mundane by comparison. The two women having little in common, their conflicts were less charged and more familiar. For example, Annie noted with disdain that after a trip to Europe, her sister and brother-in-law "have bought so many dry goods that their journey seems to have been chiefly a shopping excursion except for Switzerland and the tower of London—But they have done, according to their own lights, well." Annie observed that "few people could count their intimate friends among their own relations and that family parties always were and always must be, trying things."

Annie's sense of family responsibility extended, at least once, to her distant cousin, Louisa May Alcott, for whom the Fieldses made room in their home in 1861 when Louisa was teaching in Boston. The arrangement apparently worked well enough, but Annie and Louisa, only two years apart in age, were never friends. Nor was there much affection between James and Louisa—he is said to have advised Louisa early in her career that she had no talent for writing. Later, after the success of *Hospital Sketches,* Fields expressed interest in publishing a possible sequel called *Plantation Sketches,* but the project was abandoned. Although Fields read and rejected *Moods,* he did finally accept a book of her fairy stories, but managed to lose the manuscript.

The contrast between these cousins must have irked Louisa, who was brought up in a home always on the verge of poverty that made success a necessity. Annie, with her responsible father, "feminine" mother, and wealthy husband, could have been the model for the princess-like girls Alcott's less fortunate characters often envy. It is no wonder that Louisa resented and perhaps even disliked James and Annie.[1]

Annie's problems with her servants are a good example of the reasons she had little time to write and felt she "wasted her substance" in housekeeping. The average middle-class person has trouble imagining what housekeeping a woman with three or four servants had to do. Annie's diary entries about her servants tell us.

In her attempts to get along with her servants, Annie met with a puzzling mixture of success and failure that later carried over into her efforts to aid working people. One troublesome sequence of household events began in October of 1866, when the lure of westward expansion reached Charles Street. Annie wrote:

> My good faithful Ann talks of going to California lured thither by her sister who has found a good husband and good wages in San Francisco. It will be a trial to lose her, for what good can equal that of a faithful servant.

After hiring a replacement for Ann two weeks in advance, Annie recorded "A sudden household convulsion. Katy the cook thinks she must go with Ann and so both will depart tomorrow. I 'flew around' yesterday and have a new cook coming." A month later, however, Annie had dismissed the new cook, who had complained about cooking for six people (three family members, including Lissie, and three servants) on a salary of five dollars per week.

Annie's efforts to create an orderly household continued through the winter and spring. In July of 1867 she found a new maid, "our Irish Marcella," who pleased her. Marcella had been hired as a laundress and housekeeper, but she also waited on table and spread the supper and "as much by her interested way of winking at us & whispering to know one thing and another, put us through well." When a former servant returned unexpectedly from Canada, though, the household suddenly had

> four servants with only room for 3—However Marcella did not go to bed till 2 at any rate so I fancy there was not much sleeping done. Catherine the chamber maid too has a dreadful cold. . . . Wednesday morning found my maids had slept not at all because they were 3 in a bed and busied until two clearing up after supper.

The very next weekend, the Fieldses awoke on Sunday morning to find the house had not been cleaned up after their company had left at ten the night before. They set out immediately to look for new downstairs servants; a few days later, the two upstairs servants informed Annie that they also wished to leave. As October of 1867 came round, Annie had replaced two of the servants but been "obliged to turn off my waitress who proved dull-witted and incompetent, though clean & a girl of excellent intentions which made it a rather sad thing to be obliged to do." She replaced her with an English servant, and Annie was finally able to report: "I have three able servants, my only hope is I may keep them & that they may learn to love & respect us" (19 Oct. 1867).

Annie eventually modified her demands, after repeated instances of losing and rehiring staff. She noted in her diary after hiring another laundress that

> I think I found too much fault with ours though she was sometimes very careless nevertheless I would have kept her and said less if I had not thought she would take my reprimands kindly and improve under them; instead of which as is so frequently the case she has gone away and given me the trouble of finding another who may be worse.

A few weeks later when Annie's upstairs maid was ill, she noted that she was "still making my own bed Katy being *in* hers," but that

> We get on capitally having no company but I frequently reflect what a different thing it must be to have a large and troublesome family to engineer with all the varieties of mood & taste not to speak of the varieties of bad servants one *might* get.

One of Annie's principal objections to building a summer house in Manchester was the difficulty of hiring and retaining servants: "It is sufficient reason for not living a suburban life . . . the impossibility (speaking humanly) of getting servants for the *winter,* and no sane person should have two houses." How much more difficult were the lives of such writers as Harriet Beecher Stowe, Celia Thaxter, or Louisa May Alcott, who lacked Annie's financial security and comparative freedom from worry.

Although many of Annie's women friends were a part of the literary world, her closest friend throughout the 1860s and 1870s was an old school friend named Laura Winthrop Johnson. A native of Boston, after her marriage Laura moved to Staten Island, New York, where she lived most of her life. Despite numerous children, Laura published books of poetry and nonfiction and actively participated in social work. Although disagreements and tensions appeared in their correspondence from time to time, Annie and Laura wrote frequently and visited each other about once a year. Because Laura did not live in Boston, Annie's letters to Laura describe her activities and interests in more detail than does her diary. Laura remained the friend to whom Annie spoke most freely and with the least need of professional tact until her intimate friendship with Sarah Orne Jewett began shortly after James's death; only in Jewett did Annie have a dearer friend.

Annie's extant letters to Laura, which begin in 1864 and continue through 1883, illustrate Annie's circumspection and Victorian sense of privacy. Many letters point up the differences between nineteenth-century sensibility and our own; for example, Annie sometimes swore Laura to secrecy before telling her something so vague it is hard to understand its confidentiality. In a letter written to Laura at the time of William Ticknor's death in 1864, Annie quotes Hawthorne as having said, "I hate all undertakers. . . . There are some callings which no man ought to follow even if they are never followed—A hangman is better, he does as he is told and has some feeling in his soul" (April 1864). Annie commented to Laura:

> Dear Laura, these are things I never can repeat to anybody but I believe you will understand them, will take them as we should take everything from such a man, sacredly to be held with judgment and reverence, otherwise I should feel as if I were violating friendship to repeat them.

The passage contains a capsule summary of Annie's philosophy about greatness: she felt that it excused a lot. Years later she gave a talk about great men in which she exculpated Byron and Shelley of their personal weaknesses because of their great achievements, and she clearly applied this to Dickens as well.

The principle of privacy was an important one with Annie; she noted with interest the many abuses of friendship that plagued great writers. She herself wrote about writers she had known but published her thoughts only after their death, and even then her tacct was extreme. Annie savved any and all literary memorabilia which came her way, but she occasionally worriied that something she saved might be misused. Shortly before her death she affixed a note to letters written by the Scottish author John Brown asking her literary executor to destroy them because Brown's mental powers were failing when he wrote them.

Annie shared with Laura an intense interest in religion and she expressed her views about it forthrightly in their correspondence. Annie had begun adulthood with a firm commitment to regular churchgoing (Fields was rather indifferent to it), but her boredom with sermons led her to believe in the greater importance of private faith. Annie wrote to Laura:

> We have seldom spoken in our letters of the light which Christ brought to us but however neglectful we may seem of his life I find there the mightiest exposition of all truth. Is it not so with both of us? In him faith is made evident. And yet—yet—to what depths of unfaith it is possible for me to sink! Fred[erick] Robertson explained much to me when

he talked quietly (as if each of us knew such) of "unloving moments." That expression went deep down into my soul and I have felt better ever since. (March 1864)[2]

In the 1870s when Laura became an agnostic Annie tried to win her back to belief.

Another subject Annie could discuss with Laura was her increasing desire to be alone. Since Laura lived safely outside Boston, Annie could be sure that her disinclination for society would not be broadcast to James's clients:

> I, partly from indisposition of body and partly of spirit, remain at home.... What is called general society never did have a strong hold upon me and this year I have even withdrawn from the Ladies Club which was organized three years ago. It is not that I feel older or like people less but because I like them more and it hurts me to meet them too often on what seems to me like a false basis. (5 Jan. 1867)

Although Annie discussed the same subjects both in her letters to Laura and in her diaries, the letters contain more personal information about some of Annie's activities, such as her charity work; more about James; and more of Annie's opinions about the role of women. Since Annie occasionally offered her journals as a resource to her husband and other writers, the need for circumspection was greater there. As a result, the letters to Laura provide us with Annie's uncensored opinions as they could be told only to the most intimate of women friends.

Many of Annie's opinions about women and the justice or injustice of the claims which life made upon them illuminate her own choices and frustrations. The friction between Annie and her sister Lissie stemmed from Annie's own inability to produce the work of art that her association with Fields and his clients had made important to her. Annie's comments about women with talent show that she felt herself moving further away from the possibility of success as a writer. She suppressed her fierce drive and longing for freedom from household responsibilities but blamed others if they did the same, particularly her sister Lissie:

> Between the offer of marriage from England, her studio, and her desire of coming home, the poor child is perplexed. How hard it is for women to work in this world, they are made to love, to sympathize, to console, to labor for others, but only when their lives are cast on desert sands do they attain pre-eminence in art. With all her talent[,] with her hours of exile which have brought their fruit and given her a certain pre-eminence in Art, now comes this man who wishes her for himself—well, we shall see.

Since Annie knew many women who failed as artists, every success was a cause for rejoicing. When the work of sculptor Anne Whitney finally began to receive the recognition it deserved, Annie wrote:[3]

> How beautiful a woman can be after the world has forgot [sic] to call her beautiful—after she has forgotten to think of beauty for herself except as it may come in spite of herself through love or life. (Jan. 1867)

Anne Whitney was also the stimulus for this bittersweet passage that hinted at Annie's longing to accomplish more herself:

> Last night letters from Mrs. Stowe, Laura, Mother and news that Miss Whitney has done an exquisite work at last in sculpture. . . . Hard as it is for anybody to do anything well, the difficulty is heightened for women. They are hampered somehow by their very petticoats—by the very preciousness of their womanhood. (24 Aug. 1867)

Despite Annie's praise of "true womanhood," she possessed an understanding of the reasons for women's failures as artists that was both feminist and ahead of her time.

One of the women who most inspired, influenced, and, surely, frustrated Annie Fields was Harriet Beecher Stowe. According to one of Stowe's biographers, Forrest Wilson, Annie was Harriet's "most intimate friend during the remaining years of her life" (after 1860) (451). Stowe played an important role in Annie's life and their friendship was sometimes intense. Their correspondence and Annie's diaries provide ample evidence that the two women conversed with great enthusiasm when they met and wrote faithfully when they were apart. Perhaps because of Stowe's age and status, however, they may not have enjoyed the kind of reciprocal friendship Annie had with some of her younger friends.

Although Annie was full of awe for Stowe at their first meeting in Florence, this soon gave way to a mixture of friendship and eagerness to help. Annie would have been less than human if she had not sometimes bristled at Stowe's assumption that her friend would intercede with James and raise money for her pet causes, in addition to occasionally editing and rewriting her articles (Wilson 459, 464, 565). Annie usually produced as expected, but unfortunately, neither Annie nor James could provide Mrs. Stowe with the evidence she wanted of a marriage between George Eliot and George Henry Lewes, even a nominal one (608). Annie dutifully performed Stowe's errands and either raved about or apologized for Stowe's work by letter, in person, and in her tactful "authorized" biography. In return, Annie received gratitude and friendship but lukewarm praise of her literary efforts (607).

Fields's retirement from publishing inevitably led to a less active relationship. Annie and James never managed to visit the Stowes in Mandarin, Florida, despite heartfelt invitations. After Fields's death, Annie was too busy with Sarah Jewett to respond quickly to Harriet's letters. The two women made a trip to Hartford in 1884 so that Sarah could meet one of her literary heroes (608, 623).

Harriet Beecher Stowe espoused "true womanhood" to the end and was not above using her womanhood as an excuse for her failures—and apparently not because of social injustice. In a letter to Oliver Wendell Homes, Harriet wrote: "I make no mental effort of any sort; my brain is tired out. It was a woman's brain and not a man's, and finally from sheer fatigue and exhaustion in the march and strife of life it gave out before the end was reached" (636). When Annie came to write her life of Harriet Beecher Stowe, she insinuated her own perhaps unconscious belief that her subject had indeed been hampered as an artist by her commitment to her family responsibilities and her womanhood.

Although Annie made sacrifices for her husband's work and for her family, she was critical of women she felt sacrificed too much. She was equally critical, however, of women whose poor health or "selfishness" prevented them from adequately performing what Annie considered a woman's duties. Annie was not a radical feminist, even compared with the women of her own time, but she ardently held a number of feminist views and supported a woman's right to live an independent, fulfilling life unhampered by the prejudices and restrictions of a narrow-minded society. Most of the comments she made about women are spontaneous and offhand, but they derive from a consistent and well-considered philosophy about woman's role.

Annie often noted the important contributions women made to their husband's successes. She wrote of Mr. and Mrs. Louis Agassiz:

> What a wife that man has! The labor of his books falls chiefly upon her. Hers is the writing and the drudgery. Hers the almost judicial wisdom. Hers the patience with trifles without which no complete result could be given. (Aug. 1866)

A single line written in July of 1863, not long before Hawthorne's death, had expressed Annie's evaluation of that household: "Mrs. Hawthorne is the stay of the house." After Hawthorne's death, however, when Sophia was less able to cope with the children, Annie was often critical of her. Annie recognized, even when Mrs. Hawthorne was pressuring James for money, that Sophia was burdened by the unreasonable demands made by the men in her family. In August of 1866 Annie wrote:

> The poor woman is in a sad quandary. Her brother having come with his family to visit by invitation, now considers that she should support him and wishes to remain in her house. This is a sore trial—first because she wishes to support her brother and cannot[;] second because she cannot form any plan by which he shall support himself. The most unhappy feature of the case seems to be that *he* considers she ought to do what she really cannot and accuses her of not doing her utmost for him.

Sophia also suffered from hardships caused by her son Julian, who lived for a time at the Parker House and, according to Annie, "in spite of his mother's assertions to the contrary spends a good deal of money." Long after Sophia had ended their friendship, Annie expressed sorrow about the burdens Mrs. Hawthorne had suffered in the last years of her life.

Annie clearly took pleasure in any favorable comparison of a woman to her husband, such as this comment about Mrs. Carlyle: "'Cleverer than her husband,' says Miss Cushman. I put this into my German pipe and puff peacefully" (20 Sept. 1863). Annie intuited the frustration a talented woman who was married to a talented man might feel. She noted the following remark made by Harriet Beecher Stowe during a visit:

> Mrs. Stowe spoke of Mrs. Parkman as needing a larger space—a career in short! It came to me how fast the sphere is opening before any woman, especially if she had talent, to help to humanize and harmonize society to breathe "sweetness and light" into, & this

entirely apart from the vast labors of the benevolent (in this day & generation) in wh. we must all bear a part. (5 Feb. 1868)

Annie often noted that a wife of a famous man was also talented and needed an outlet; she apparently advised Frances Lowell to find some suitable work for herself before the trip to Spain which ruined Mrs. Lowell's health. In writing about a Boston woman named Mary Felton, however, Annie expressed a point of view more favorable to marriage: "I wish she might be well married—What a solution of life's difficulties this is for a woman! And how a wrong marriage makes all things look darker than before—" (Dec. 1868). Annie recognized that women faced many more obstacles in their search for fulfillment than did men—still referring to Mary Felton, she wrote:

> It shows weakness in a man to be oppressed by the opinions of society—in a woman like Mary Felton it shows simply a powerful contest with which she is sometimes wearied out.

Annie was particularly critical of Celia Thaxter's husband, Levi Thaxter. Though an intelligent man, Thaxter provided only limited financial support for his family. Annie was often indignant about her friend's situation:

> Mrs. Thaxter had a strange story to tell us yesterday of herself. She said she thought she should never write any more for she had no servant now-a-days and did all the work of her house, that she could not afford to do otherwise!! I could not help thinking what a mighty shame it was for this woman with a husband in the prime of health with three sons to be obliged to work for them in this manner. She washes and irons and scrubs and mends stockings and pantaloons and makes her own clothes while he does no business and pretends to be a philanthropist, a radical and all that is good—I don't believe in him, that's all! They are not very poor. I sometimes wish they were, then he would have to work. (Nov. 1865)

The decision to be poor was one over which the woman exerted no control; yet, as a result, a woman's talents were often wasted, as was the case with Celia Thaxter, Jane Carlyle, and others. The husband sat, thought, and wrote, but the wife must take care of the children, wash, and sew. Unlike the husbands, the wives were seldom able to abandon their household responsibilities in order to follow their literary inclinations.

Annie also quickly perceived situations where women were at a comparative disadvantage to men. Commenting upon the different effects of their hermit-like lives upon Hawthorne and his sister, she wrote: "Utter solitude lames the native power of a woman even more than that of a man, for her natural growth is through the sympathies" (Howe *Mem.* 69). In 1868, when Oliver Wendell Holmes decided to stay in town for the summer, despite the terrible heat, Annie was highly critical of his lack of consideration: "It hurts him less than his wife, partly because the intellectual vivacity and excitement keeps him up, partly because he is physically fitted to bear almost everything but cold" (37–38).

Annie's fund of sympathy for women did not preclude her from being highly critical of those she felt didn't do their part. Mrs. Dana received some harsh words in the diary one day:[4]

> Sallie Dana came in the afternoon. Those children seem in a degree sacrificed by the illness and inattention of their mother, who though a noble and interesting woman appears to have diseases of mind and body wh. prevent her from giving herself as mothers in America must to her family.

Mrs. Howells and Mrs. Aldrich often appear in Annie's diaries as examples of the sickly American woman. Annie's first description of Elinor Howells initiated what would be her constant theme:

> Mrs. H. is a pallid, wide-eyed little woman not without great sweetness and purity in her thin face which just escapes being what we call spiritual-looking, a kind of childishness which is a [charm] at the same time that it suggests this world and the enjoyment of it rather than another. (6 Aug. 1866)

In March of 1867, Annie used Mrs. Howells and Mrs. Aldrich as her illustrations in a general lament about the poor health of American women. She noted that "Mr. Howells came from Cambridge to pass an hour. His wife has lost her expected baby" and that "Lilian Aldrich is getting better and hopes soon to be in her tiny house." She continued:

> What wretched results of American education such women as Mrs Howells & Mrs Aldrich are.
>   How hateful a thing is ignorance! Lissie too [Annie's sister], whose health was injured years ago by over application and her nerves fatally disordered and diseased. It is very sad; for American women are full of power to be and to do. They have a friendliness of organisation which appears to me less common in other nations. But I [find] this also that where the fine organisation *does* exist in other nations the women are quite as apt to become nervously diseased. The great wonder is, the thing being so common in America, that we have not long ago studied to counteract the tendency to disease by greater care.

An appropriate conclusion to these remarks is Annie's note that Mr. Howells's wife "is ill too and he fears will not be able to receive or go into company all winter. She is a nervous little creature at best poorly fitted by nature it seems for the position in wh. she finds herself" (Oct. 1867). Annie herself, of course, was superbly "fitted by nature" for her position as a literary hostess and editor's wife. She tended to sympathize more with strong women who were overburdened but carried on than with women who were invalids. This is understandable in the context of her own excellent health and strength; she probably felt that if she were capable of exercising, eating well, and working hard all day, other women were too.

Annie noted a similar problem of ill health in the daughters of two friends. This passage has been crossed out in the journal, but it is still legible; perhaps she marked it as a note to herself or someone else that it was not to be published:

Kate Dewey[5] and Una Hawthorne have been to see me both young women of exquisite sensibility and pure sentiment for life and high aspiration—but the d—energy is wanting! They do nothing—can not even keep their spirits alive for lack of energy—poor children—I wonder if dear Una will never awake I trust so for I love the child and it makes me sad to see her so spiritless. (18 Sept. 1865)

This whole question of the "spiritlessness" of American women concerned both Annie and the age. Annie's interest is reflected in her partial endorsement of a book written by her own doctor on the causes of women's poor health.

In 1873, Dr. E. H. Clarke published a book called *Sex in Education,* which described the ill health of American women and provided a hypothesis for their causes. Annie described Mrs. Howells and Mrs. Aldrich as "wretched results of American education"; Dr. Clarke's book may explain what she meant. According to *Sex in Education,* the constitutional weakness of educated women resulted from forcing girls to attend school during their menstrual periods. Dr. Clarke believed this drew energy necessary for the development of the reproductive system to the brain. The insufficient energy directed to the developing reproductive system caused latent physical weakness which might not exhibit itself for years; thus, when a woman showed symptoms of nervousness or disease at any age, but most commonly in the twenties, it could be ascribed to the damage done while she was in school. What he advocated was not, however, removing girls from the educational system during these years, but arranging for them to stay home and rest during menstruation and any other time they felt weak. Annie did not accept Dr. Clarke's theory wholeheartedly. In a letter to Laura Johnson she discussed Dr. Clarke's book and its relevance to the death of a woman, Mrs. Badger, who had contested the doctor's theories. Annie wrote:

Still will I presume we all think that Dr. Clarke exaggerated and overstated his precise opinion of the reason why thinking women are not as strong as they should be, but we must believe poor Mrs. Badger['s] opinion sorely at fault when she was so overworking her own strength as to be living on the verge of madness.

One of the misfortunes Dr. Clarke attributed to the American system of educating girls was sterility, an idea that Annie, childless despite her excellent health, would undoubtedly have rejected.

Although Dr. Clarke's theory appears wrongheaded today and was rebutted by feminists, it was not so antifeminist as many other nineteenth-century theories of women's weakness. Clarke avowed that women's brain power equalled that of men and that women were perfectly capable of learning such subjects as Latin and higher mathematics, which many people believed injurious to women. His only stipulation was that girls not be educated in the same way as boys—that some allowance be made for their developing reproductive systems. Since Annie believed that sexuality influenced character and justified different roles for men and women, her willingness to accept a theory which advocated a slightly different philosophy of education for girls is not surprising.

Annie's ideas about woman's role identify her with what has been called "the cult of true womanhood," an ideal to which she occasionally referred in her writing.[6] Stimulated by a recent conversation with Dickens about dress, Annie recorded her conviction that "English ladies were more individual in their dress and therefore dressed more beautifully than the ladies of any other nation" and that "ideas exercised in dress . . . create true beauty." She realized, however, that this was the very reason why English women had "their reputation for bad taste, because there must be a fine reticence in the expression of the individual by externals, especially when before the world." Annie thought American women compared unfavorably with English women in other ways as well:

> We have not yet a *class* of women, grand in womanhood, noble in wife-hood, beautiful in saint-hood. Sometimes it seems to me no woman has ever yet said or shown *all* it may be to be a true wife. She has testified what it is forever and wears a crown therefore; but I would say that sometimes when I reflect how true love can cause a woman to blossom and bear perfect fruit not only of the body, but the spirit, how from a weak unfurnished twig, green and lithe and comely but still very weak, she can grow and gather light and heer lily shine perfected liike a star,—when I think of these things, I pray to God to bless all women, to make them more womanly, and to elevate only those things in their eyes which shall show them most truly their heavenly mission—. (May 1868)

Annie believed in woman suffrage, she believed in a woman's right to read, write, study, and be an artist; she regretted the limitations that creating a home and caring for children placed on women; but she also believed that woman had a God-given responsibility to be the creator of the home, the educator of children and the under-privileged, and the spiritual ideal of society. In short, Annie believed in *ladies,* and women of her class who were not ladies came in for their share of harsh words.

Two such women were Mrs. E. D. E. N. Southworth and a Mrs. Davis of New York.[7] According to Annie, Mrs. Davis

> wears her hair curled in a poor fashion and uses perfumery and powder, yet disgusting and vulgar as this is, by the side of southern and western women who have never had either culture or the opportunity to travel, she is refinement itself. (Sept. 1867)

Mrs. Davis told Annie what she evidently considered a humorous anecdote about Mrs. Southworth, but Annie drew her own conclusions:

> Poor Mrs. Southworth with all her excellence is so romantic in everyday life as to draw some ridicule down upon herself. It seems to me to show rather a lack than a [perception] of true ideality when it crops out in this offensive way in dress and manner. Her fancies[,] too[,] on practical affairs are crude and silly. She thinks it a great pity that an army of women had not been added to our army in the war. "But what department would you assign to them" somebody asked. "O the cavalry *of course,* they should have worn a uniform of orange and black bloomer dresses which would have produced a fine effect"—As some one said it would have been frightful enough to have driven the rebs into the Mexican gulf for very horror. (Sept. 1867)

Annie eventually modified her own ideas of appropriate dress to the extent that by the 1870s she had begun patronizing a dressmaker, Mrs. Flight, who had "invented the cleverest arrangement for women's underclothing I have ever seen . . . and I really think will do much to emancipate the race" (LWJ 6 June 1874). In the meantime, however, the movement for clothing reform elicited little sympathy from Annie.

Although Annie supported many of the feminist causes of her time, including woman suffrage, the suffragists themselves were targets of scorn because of their "unladylike" behavior. In November of 1868, Annie expressed her interest in the suffrage movement by attending a convention, but she was disappointed by what she found there, perhaps because James was put off by so many aggressive women:

> Grand Convention for advocating Suffrage of Woman came off yesterday & the day before. J. and I looked in, but there were so many hard faced unlovely women full of forthputting-ness about, we retreated hastily. My heart is wholly with the movement, but the movers alas! are often women who love to un-sex themselves and crave audience from the rostrum.[8]

Annie was far from alone in her ungenerous criticism of the Suffrage convention; Clover Adams and her cousin, Effie Shaw Lowell, attended the same convention and received the same impression as the Fieldses. Clover's sister-in-law, Fanny Hooper, wrote about it: "They [Clover and Effie] signed a paper petitioning for suffrage . . . but some of the strongest females made themselves so obnoxious that they must have injured the cause" (Friedrich 84).

Political organizations of women consistently elicited a negative response from Annie during the 1860s. In 1868, Kate Field, Annie's journalist friend, helped Jenny C. Croly, also a journalist, found a Woman's League or Club in New York which was initially called "Sorosis." Kate apparently wrote to Annie about her frustrations, and Annie replied with sympathy but little patience:

> What are those foolish women thinking of? Squandering time and opportunity over "Sorosis." . . . All the fools are not in the Woman's League,—but I am so unused to work with others that I learned and admired much at that first meeting and I think you will help to bring things out straight. (BPL 18 May 1868)

The members did not reach agreement, however, and Kate Field led a splinter group which formed its own club. Annie wrote reassuringly to Kate:

> I don't think it would ever have been possible for the Club to succeed with such components, so childish & ill-regulated as some members were who did much of the talking. Please erase my name also and transfer it, if it is wanted, to the one on the true foundation. . . . The Club must be made up of pure sterling material; at least, for a foundation. (BPL)[9]

Annie found much in these groups to criticize, but she never completely rejected either the cause or the women involved. Annie was able to make the crucial distinction between substance and style.

5.

The Dickens Years

1867–1870

The years from 1867 to 1870 broke the routine of the earlier part of the decade, when Annie had earnestly juggled entertaining, writing, and trying to "love and serve" her family and friends. Added to her other cares was worry about James, who was feeling the strain of carrying Boston's literary establishment on his shoulders. The next three years of Annie's life would be dominated by two events—the "second coming" of Dickens to America and the attack of two valued clients, Mary Abigail Dodge and Sophia Hawthorne, on her husband's integrity. These years marked the end of Annie's intense involvement with the publishing business. Her diaries show Annie alternating between the defensiveness of a mother lion protecting her cubs and the passion of a mature woman in midlife. Dickens had this effect on many women, but few had the opportunity for intimate friendship with him that his visit provided for Annie.

Fields had first met Dickens in 1852 on his second trip to Europe, a brief meeting that opened the way to their later friendship (Tryon 151). Annie met Dickens for the first time in 1859, shortly after he had separated from his wife.[1] By 1867 James had established a reputation for paying English authors fairly, and he and Dickens had joined forces in the fight for an international copyright agreement.

Fields had been urging Dickens to make a lecture tour to America since 1858 (Adrian 97). Dickens was attracted by both the financial potential of the trip, especially in the United States, and the opportunity to perform, which satisfied his restlessness and helped him forget the failure of his marriage. In making such a trip, however, his writing would suffer, his English readings would stop, and *All the Year Round* would be disrupted. His frequent ill health and his relationship with Ellen Ternan kept Dickens home for a number of years. When at last he decided that the trip was possible, Ellen Ternan proved the main deterrent.

The evidence of a serious relationship between Dickens and Ellen Ternan, "a meritorious young actress," was not made public until 1952.[2] Although eighty years had passed since Dickens's death, scholars protested when Ada Nisbet published the facts about Dickens's reluctance to leave Ellen, his desire to take her with him to America if possible, and his notes about her and to her in letters to W. H. Wills.

In 1865, Dickens had suffered a severe illness which resulted in a lame left foot; in 1867, the foot again became inflamed and swollen. He was strongly discouraged from making the trip by Georgina and other close friends, but Dickens refused to take his poor health seriously. The two biggest factors in his early death, according to many, were his trip to America and the reading he added to his repertoire in England after his return, "Sikes and Nancy," from *Oliver Twist,* with which he whipped his audience and himself to a frenzy.

Dickens was undoubtedly cheered by the knowledge that Annie and James Fields would be in America to help him feel at home, but their solicitousness exceeded the bounds of any expectation Dickens could have formed. In James, he found a companion as jolly as any he had known, someone who was always ready for a long walk or whatever else pleased Dickens. In Annie, Dickens found a beautiful and charming woman who possessed a sense of humor. She catered to his every whim, from food to company to flowers, and went a long way toward filling the gap created by the absence of Georgina, Ellen Ternan, and Dickens's daughters.

Dickens brought a new element into Annie's life. Although James Fields and Charles Dickens shared many traits—both were charming, astute, intelligent, attractive to women, and gentle—Dickens was a "genius." According to Beacon Street gossip, Annie was in love with Dickens; but Willa Cather thought it was more likely the other way around (Sergeant 64). There is sufficient evidence in the pages of Annie's journals and the history of Dickens's relations with women to support either theory. Dickens attracted people like a magnet, both men and women. Whatever the truth of her relationship with Dickens, he, Fields, and Sarah Orne Jewett seem to have been the three people Annie loved most passionately in her life.

Dickens arrived in Boston on 19 November 1867, four days after James and Annie's thirteenth wedding anniversary. Annie decorated Dickens's rooms at the Parker House with flowers, and Dickens noted his gratitude in a letter written to his sister-in-law and friend Georgina, to whom he described Annie as "a very nice woman, with a rare relish for humour and a most contagious laugh" (*Nonesuch* 3:572; 25 Nov. 1867). On the twenty-first, Annie was the only woman at a Parker House dinner for Dickens; the other guests, besides Fields, were Agassiz, Emerson, Judge Hoar, Holmes, Norton, Greene, and Longfellow. Dickens's friendship with the Fieldses quickly became intimate, and they became his American confidants. By 28 November, Dickens had complained to them of both his children and his wife. In her diary, Annie wrote:

> He appears often troubled by the lack of energy his children show and even allowed J. to see how deep his unhappiness is in having had so many children by a wife who was totally uncongenial. He appears to have the deepest sympathy for men who are unfitly married and has really taken an especial fancy I think to John Bigelow, our late minister at [Paris], who is here, because his wife is such an incubus. (28 Nov. 1867)[3]

The friendship between Bigelow and Dickens was of many years' standing, and Bigelow, who was among the first to publish his knowledge of the liaison, had written about Mrs. Dickens's jealousy of Ellen Ternan in his diary as early as March of 1860 (Nisbet 23).

Some of Dickens's confidences to Annie show how his lack of discretion led to the variety of rumors which flourished in both England and America about his private life. Annie misinterpreted one chance remark of Dickens's to mean that Catherine Dickens drank too much:

> Such charity! Poor man! He must have learned great need for that. (He told J. yesterday
> that nine out of ten of the cases of disagreement in marriage came from drink he believed.)
> He is a man who has suffered evidently. (4 Jan. 1868; Howe *Mem.* 155)

Accusations that Dickens himself drank too much were widespread, but Annie
defended him against them in her diary: "The idea of his ever passing the bounds of
temperance is an absurdity not to be thought of for a moment" (Howe *Mem.* 154).
Such rumors did not deter Annie from serving Dickens's potent punch after his
readings.

Annie's fascination with Dickens is evident in this passage from her diary where
she tried to analyze his charm:

> The perfect kindliness and sympathy which radiates from the man is, after all, the secret
> never to be told, but always to be studied and to thank God for. His rapid eyes, which
> nothing can escape, eyes which, when he first appears upon the stage, seem to interrogate
> the lamps and all things above and below, (like exclamation points Aldrich says), are
> unlike anything before in our experience. There are no living eyes like these, swift and
> kind, possessing none of the bliss of ignorance, but the different bliss of one who sees
> what the Lord has done and what, or some thing of what, he intends. (4 Jan. 1868; Howe
> *Mem.* 155)

The tone of hero worship in this passage, the description of the hypnotic power of
Dickens's eyes, the suggestion that the mind of God was open to him, all articulate
the strength of Dickens's charisma. As with most idols, however, the public impulse
to destroy him was equally strong: he was sharply criticized for separating from his
wife, opposing temperance, retaining custody of his children, and employing his
sister-in-law as his housekeeper. Regardless of the charge, however, Annie believed
in Dickens's innocence.

Dickens brought a new spirit of playfulness into Annie and James's lives. They
attended nearly all his readings, often accompanying Dickens throughout the whole
day despite the fact that Dickens lived at the Parker House until late in his tour. Annie
and James's post-reading visits became so routine that Annie found herself "smother-
ing a disappointment" when they were omitted.

Such disappointments were, however, the exception rather than the rule. Usually
Dickens, the Fieldses, and carefully selected friends got together to play parlor games
and drink Dickens's punch at the Parker House, Charles Street, or someone's hotel
room when they were on the road. Late in the tour, Dickens suspended his policy of
avoiding private homes and lived with the Fieldses for a time. Annie recorded their
daily schedule in her diary:

> We breakfast at half-past nine punctually, he on a rasher of bacon and an egg and a cup
> of tea, always preferring this same thing. Aferward we talk or play with the sewing-
> machine or anything new and odd to him. Then he sits down to write until one o'clock,
> when he likes a glass of wine and biscuit, and afterward goes to walk until nearly four,
> when we dine. After dinner, reading days, he will take a cup of strong coffee, a tiny glass
> of brandy, and a cigar, and likes to lie down for a short while to get his voice in order. . . .

Upon our return we always have supper and he brews a marvelous punch, which usually makes us all sleep like tops after the excitement. (Jan. 1868; Howe *Mem.* 154)

Annie took pleasure in minutely describing this routine; Dickens's presence gave her joy. Whenever Dickens was reading in town, she and Jamie participated in his life to the fullest possible extent. The usual social barriers between men and women were eventually dissolved, and Annie surrendered herself to Dickens's charm. In February, she wrote, "We played a game at cards which was most curious—indeed, something more—so much more that I have forgotten to be afraid of him" (22 Feb. 1868; Howe *Mem.* 157). In March Annie noted:

He helped me to win the game at cards. It was very pleasant to have him leaning over me to help me through. I have written to Syracuse to ask Mrs. White (wife of the President of Cornell University) to try to make him comfortable at the hotel—I feel somehow like one of his daughters and as if I could not take too good care of him—. (6 March 1868)

Such was the confused state of Annie's emotions.

A search for corollary passages in Dickens's letters or journals yields little because Dickens regularly destroyed them. An extant letter from this time reveals the degree of familiarity that existed between Dickens and the Fieldses:

As there is no question that our friendship began in some previous state of existence many years ago, I am now going to make bold to mention a discovery we have made concerning Springfield. . . . Ticknor reports the Springfield hotel excellent. Now will you and Fields come and pass Sunday with us there? It will be delightful, if you can. (*Nonesuch* 19 Mar. 1868)

The great Walking Match was the culmination of Dickens's visit.[4] Dickens and Fields were both tremendous walkers, often walking six or seven miles together in an afternoon. Dickens drew up papers announcing a six-mile walking match between James Osgood, Fields's colleague, and George Dolby, Dickens's companion and business manager, on 19 March. After driving to the Parker House to check on the arrangements for dinner, Annie caught up with the participants and, finding Osgood far in the lead, gave him bread soaked in brandy all the way back to town. Dickens wrote to his daughter, Mamie, on 2 March 1868:

We are not quite determined whether Mrs. Fields did not desert our colours, by coming on the ground in a carriage, and having *bread soaked in brandy* put into the winning man's mouth as he steamed along. She pleaded that she would have done as much for Dolby, if *he* had been ahead, so we are inclined to forgive her. (*Nonesuch* 2 March 1868)

At the dinner which followed the Match, Annie and Mrs. Charles Eliot Norton were the only ladies, and Annie wrote that Dickens "divided his attention loyally between us." Her journal entry after the match and dinner states that "Jamie and I are truly penetrated with grateful love to C. D."

In contrast to the gaiety of Dickens's visit was the anxiety occasioned by his poor health. He suffered from two different complaints, constant colds and a recurrence of his problem with his left foot, neither of which Dickens took seriously. In the summer before he had left England, Dickens could not wear a shoe on his left foot because of an enlargement that had become irritated and inflamed. Dickens had an "American" cold (which he considered more potent that an English cold) nearly the whole time he was in America. Insomnia was a third health problem. His trip to America exacerbated his problems, just as Georgina, John Forster, and William Henry Wills, Dickens's associate on *All the Year Round,* had predicted.

In early April Dickens wrote to Mamie that he was so ill he couldn't eat solid food and lived on a liquid diet which consisted of rum, sherry, and champagne, supplemented by cream, an egg (beaten into the sherry) and beef tea. Shortly before a large farewell dinner, Dickens's foot swelled so badly that he had to attend the event with his foot sewn in black silk. Although the Fieldses were both solicitous about Dickens's health, they do not seem to have understood the seriousness of his symptoms until much later, when they saw him again in England.

The fairy tale had to come to an end. On 10 April Annie and James accompanied Charles Dickens to New York for his last readings prior to sailing home. Annie's diary became a chronicle of her feelings about Dickens and his imminent departure. By now, Dickens's exhaustion was severe. When they visited him after a reading in mid-April, Annie and James found him

> a perfect picture of prostration, his head thrown back without support on the couch, the blood suffusing his throat and temples again where he had been very white before. This is a physical peculiarity with Dickens which I have never seen before in a man, though women are very subject to that thing. Excitement and exercise of reading will make the blood rush into his hands until they become black, and his face and head (especially since he has become so fatigued) will turn from red to white and back to red again without his being conscious of it. (20 April 1868; Howe *Mem.* 181)

Annie later wrote, "Mr. Dickens has now read 76 times. It seems like a dream." To Dickens, whose foot was so badly swollen he could not bear any weight on it and who slept very badly, it must have been more like a nightmare. The press gave Dickens a farewell dinner on 10 April. Women were excluded from the event so Annie was unable to attend; Dickens later repeated his speech for her word for word and minutely described the events.

On Tuesday 20 April Dickens stayed in bed all day resting his foot. Annie was heartbroken:

> I lay awake since early this morning (though we did not leave him until half-past twelve) feeling as if when I arose we must say good-bye. How relieved I felt to brush the tears away and know there was one more day, but even that gain was lessened when I found he could not rise and even this must be a day of separation too. (Howe, *Mem.* 187)

Mark DeWolfe Howe, a late Victorian himself, omitted such passages from his book based on Annie's diaries, saying that Annie continues "in terms which the diarist herself would have been the first to regard as more suitable for manuscript than for

print." He correctly adds that the further passages "throw more light upon Mrs. Fields
. . . than upon Dickens." On Wednesday Annie wrote:

> Rose at six this morning sleep being out of the question—I must confess to sitting down
> in my night-dress in a flood of tears—When I remember all Dickens has been, had become
> to us in these short months and that I can never see him again under the same conditions,
> even if we should ever meet at all in this world it seems more than I can bear—Jamie
> feels this too but he will go to the steamer and will always have perhaps a more repose-full
> connection than is possible on earth between men and women— . . . what to him [C. D.]
> can be the tenderness of one woman like myself.

Back in Boston two days later, Annie wrote:

> I find in the pain of parting I have written more than I knew at the time, above . . . Jamie
> felt it sorely and it was in one way harder for him, being obliged to go to the ship. When
> he came back we put our arms about each other and then for the first time his grief gave
> vent to itself in tears. My memory goes back again and again to the last scene, the last
> embrace the look of pain; the bitter bitter sobs after he had fairly gone—. (24 April 1868)

In another passage Annie imagined herself in Georgina Hogarth's position:

> It is not an easy service in this world to live near such a man, to love him, to desire to do
> for him. He is swift, restless, impatient, with moods of fire, but he is also and above all,
> tender, loving, strong, forthright, charitable and patient by moral force. Happy those who
> live, and hear, and do and suffer, and above all love him to the end—who love and labor
> with and for him[.] He *can* be, he *must* be, the whole world and the light of the future to
> them. . . . May his mistakes be expiated—. (24 April 1868)

These passages suggest that Annie's feelings for Dickens were far more complicated
than simple friendship. Either consciously or unconsciously, Annie loved Charles
Dickens, an interpretation which is supported by a dream she had about him shortly
after he left:

> By night as we lie down we pray for him, and in the morning I awoke dreaming that he
> has just come to say "goodbye"—I see that sharp painful look dart up his brow, like a
> lightning of grief. I feel his parting kiss on my cheek and see my arms stretched out to
> hold him—vanished. It was but one dreadful moment, yet now that it is over the pain of
> it lasts—lasts—we both of us tried to avoid it—but it was inevitable—. (26 April 1868)

The passage shifts abruptly. Did Annie mean that she and Dickens had tried to avoid
falling in love, "but it was inevitable"? Or that she and James had tried to avoid the
emotional intensity of their friendship with Dickens and the devastation caused by his
absence? One thing is certain: if Annie fell in love with Dickens, her love for him
involved no diminishment of her love for James, perhaps because he also "fell in love
with" Dickens. Dickens affected the emotional lives of both Annie and James and their
daily activities; his visit influenced the course their lives would take in the next decade.

   The immediate effect of Dickens's departure on Annie was to send her to bed exhausted. She read a poem by Crabbe, "The Lover's Journey," which Dickens had mentioned to her in the last days before his departure. She vowed to herself that "when the skies clear I shall try to work for others and forget not *him* but myself" (24 April 1868). She imagined Dickens's triumphant landing in England when his ship, the *Russia,* was reported to have arrived in Liverpool: "I can't help rehearsing in my mind the intense joy of his beloved" (2 May 1868). Annie and James loyally took Dickens's side in his separation from his wife and affair with Ellen Ternan. Like Georgina, Annie believed that genius and greatness excused much, and the existence of a beloved created more distance between her and Dickens.

News of Dickens's landing in Liverpool was followed by their first letter from Dickens on 14 May, which sent Annie into her Dickensian effusions. Her diary is uncharacteristically negative at this time; she wrote that she "hated" working on a fair to help the recently freed blacks, and she harshly criticized a visiting explorer and writer, Paul Du Chaillu,[5] who accompanied the Fieldses to a musical party. Annie wrote that Du Chaillu "looks too much like a gorilla to satisfy one's sense with regard to the superior creature who is supposed to have discovered the gorilla simply; he is horribly suggestive of the idea of being the gorilla's cousin or some not too distant relative" (15 May 1868). Annie said, however, that he "did well enough for the party," which she described as a "physical boil, a mental depression, a moral retrogradation."

One effect of Dickens's visit was to make it impossible for Annie to read and study, for, as she wrote, "This winter has scattered [illegible] all in such a ruthless way that I feel it will be more difficult than ever to make any steadfast plans and hold on—." A little later she wrote:

> I have not yet done any literary work. I feel a great need of reading and reading with a memory so I try to be satisfied with that. I know by and by the time will come but I long for absorption in something of the kind. (15 May 1868)

On Saturday 23 May, the Fieldses held a farewell dinner for Longfellow, about to leave for Europe. They invited, in addition to the guest of honor, Emerson, Agassiz, Holmes, Lowell, Greene, Norton, Whipple, and Dana. Annie envied Longfellow his chance to go abroad and see Dickens, and confided to her journal her distress that Dickens wrote so seldom.

Sincere though his regard for her was, Dickens must have seen Annie as simply a diversion, the most charming woman in America. For Annie, there was a huge hole in her life where Dickens had been. As the wife of his American publisher and sponsor of his tour, Annie could legitimately take care of his every need, send him flowers, and prepare special dinners for him; she had even moved Christmas so Dickens could celebrate it with them between readings. She may have been commenting upon Dickens's forgetfulness when she wrote on 6 June, her birthday:

> Jamie gave me a pair of beautiful flower-stands for a birthday gift. He alone remembered the day! I do not say this regretfully but gratefully for I frequently think how solely we stand being *all* to each other in this world.

For a few months, Dickens had made a third in their family, but if Annie had imagined he would try to retain his place there, by now she knew that she was wrong.

The Fieldses' friends were puzzled by their obsession with Dickens. Mrs. Hilliard, who seems to have understood Dickens better in some ways than did Annie, had pointed out to her "how strong his power to attract is and oftentimes what a burden really to him when he cannot give a satisfactory response to the feeling he has excited" (June 1868). Annie wrote in her diary that she and James "both dream of dear C. D. by night and by day our thoughts wander to Gad's Hill . . . and all other things gather new hues from this love of ours which nobody else here can understand" (June 1868). Knowing Dickens permanently altered Annie's perceptions; she wrote that "Other men, many others, seem so dull and inapprehensive to me after dear C. D. and the few!" (June 1868). On 11 June 1869, Annie finished a blue book, ready to "begin another era and shut away in a drawer much of all I may ever be able to record of Charles Dickens."

In February of 1868, in the midst of Dickens's lecture tour, the Fieldses had been shattered by an action which they could not, at first, understand. Annie's puzzlement is evident in her entry about the situation:

> We had a real sorrow last night. Mary Dodge whom we have known so well and sincerely loved has seen fit to withdraw her friendship—and without a word, only a little note refusing to explain. She has thought she could make more money from her books but instead of talking her affairs over in a gentle way with J. has thrown up the whole matter. It has hurt us both. Not that we care for money but to think she could (or anyone but a maid-servant could) be so forgetful of all she owes to another who had been a true and steadfast friend. . . . I have written her a farewell note of two pages but J. thinks we should do well to say nothing for a week that we may speak dispassionately when we do speak so I have laid my note aside—.

This entry was Annie's first mention of the business quarrel which disrupted the continuity of Annie and James's roles as literary hostess and congenial publisher. Later in the month, Annie revealed the extent to which she felt betrayed in these apparently offhand remarks:

> Dr. Hedge and Mrs Agassiz were speaking of the savages here on Sunday night both in Brazil and Greenland & giving some of their peculiarities, somebody said how ready the savage was to break out even through all the [layers] of civilization and I could not help reverting immediately to this behavior of Mary Dodge.

Annie's perception of Mary Dodge's "savagery" was undoubtedly conditioned by the passion and hero worship which Dodge had bestowed on both Annie and James.

Mary Abigail Dodge, better known by her pen name, Gail Hamilton, had become a close friend of the Fieldses' in the early 1860s. In 1859 James had published an article by Gail, as Annie referred to her, in the *Atlantic*. Between 1862 and 1868 he published nine of Dodge's books and appointed her to the editorial staff of *Our Young*

Folks, the firm's magazine for children (a position which apparently required little work). Fields introduced Dodge to Nathaniel Hawthorne and his wife, Sophia, and invited her to social events such as the dinner that followed the gala dedication of the renovated Music Hall in 1863. By 1865, Annie and Miss Dodge were such intimate friends that they discussed James together, Gail saying that she thought James and Whittier "alike in a certain womanliness." "Womanly," used as an adjective for a man, could have been a term of either approbation or criticism, depending on the context; here, however, it was a compliment, denoting sensitivity. Since Dodge is said to have proposed to John Greenleaf Whittier, comparing Fields to him was a high compliment.

Although Annie liked Dodge she did not neglect to record in her diary an unfavorable comment made about her by Henry James, Sr., with whom Dodge carried on a long and curious philosophical correspondence. Comparing her conversational abilities to those of Sara Palfrey, the daughter of the historian and an acquaintance of the Fieldses',[6] James remarked that "'Gail' is like a clump of daisies by her side!" (2 Nov. 1865). For the most part, though, Annie continued to be complimentary about Miss Dodge, referring to her as "that jewel woman and friend" in her diary (21 Nov. 1865). Dodge was equally complimentary about the Fieldses; in an 1864 letter to a friend, she wrote:

> Mr. Fields is not only a handsome man, but one of the nicest men in the world, straight-forward, genial, simple-hearted, though in the thick of the city. I like him very much, and he has the sweetest wife, and beautiful, too, and they are as happy as can be. (*Gail* 1:393)

Jamie and Annie sometimes visited Dodge in her hometown of Hamilton, Massachusetts, where she lived with her mother. Like the Hawthornes, Miss Dodge sometimes stayed at the Fields home for several days. She and Annie went shopping together, and Annie advised her about clothes.

The quarrel which Annie described as "a real sorrow" had started when Dodge read an article in the *Congregationalist,* a religious paper, which declared that all authors received at least ten per cent royalty on their books, a statement which was untrue and proved to be inflammatory. Many of the Ticknor & Fields authors, Dodge included, had received ten per cent at one time, but during the war most contracts had been renegotiated to a flat payment system. In Dodge's case, she received fifteen cents per copy. Consequently, when inflation pushed book prices past two dollars per copy, Dodge was receiving only seven to eight per cent.

Although the alteration in payment had been initiated because of the uncertainty of business during the war years, when the war ended and economic conditions improved, Fields took advantage of his friendships and loose contractual arrangements to boost the firm's profits. Mary Abigail Dodge could not afford to be cavalier about money; she earned her own living and supported her mother with her writing (Austin 312–14; Tryon 334–49). She sent her note "withdrawing friendship" after her attempts to negotiate with Fields by mail had been met by genial suggestions she come to Boston to talk it over. These had not appeased Mary, who was much angrier than the Fieldses guessed.

Annie was upset about the feud, although she found ways to salve her pride, writing, "I feel sadly about 'Gail' when I think of it, but always somehow more for her than for myself, though I also lose much (for a very little time.)" James wanted to give Dodge "time to repent—to see what she really intends . . . time to retrieve herself if she wishes it." Annie suspected that their silence would make Dodge angry, but went along.

Fields both underestimated Dodge's fury and deliberately misunderstood her complaint. By late February, according to Annie's diary,

> A gentleman called without previous warning and drew out the amount of [illegible] all the money due her in the hands of Ticknor & Fields precisely as if she had been or expected to be robbed.

Annie now imagined that Dodge's friendship had been insincere: "But I really thought she cared for me! And now to find it was a pretense or a stepping-stone merely is something to shudder over—." By May, Annie wrote, Mary Dodge was "writing confidential letters all about the country with regard to Ticknor & Fields, saying that under the guise of friendship they have cheated her & paid her insufficient copyright— This is very bad and I don't know where these things will end."

An excerpt from a letter Mary Dodge wrote to an unidentified correspondent about this time offers an interesting contrast to her earlier extravagant praise of her publisher:

> Mr. ——— has not merely vanished from my regard . . . he dug his way out with a rough and relentless spade. . . . And in his wild journey-work he upturned so many earth-worms and unearthed venomous creeping things and revealed nests of unclean and hateful birds till I turn away shuddering. . . . He squirmed out of my sight . . . and I saw some one . . . with a mean face and ophidian eyes and puny voice. . . . *That* is not the man I cared for at all. . . . I am not half so vexed with Mr. ——— as I am with myself. . . . I worshipped a golden calf. I did not think he was a lion, but I did think he was a sprightly, agreeable, amusing, and friendly and virtuous beast. When he began to bleat, I found he was a jackal. (*Gail* 2:630–31; 11 May 1868)

Her passion suggests that Dodge may have been a little in love with Fields; it is difficult to understand this scathing condemnation in any other way.

All of this was going on just prior to, during, and after Dickens's visit, which provided Annie with an explanation for Dodge's attack:

> Having a woman's instinct in me I think she was mortally wounded because we did not invite her to meet Dickens and this is the root of the trouble—a trouble not clearly defined even to herself.

There is more than a little evidence that Annie was right. Dickens's second lecture tour in the United States had begun in late 1867, only a few months before Dodge's attack on Fields. Mary Dodge had offered Dickens three hundred dollars to come speak in her home town, Hamilton, Massachusetts, and had been chagrined when she discovered he was asking twice that for a night's engagement. Her omission from the guest lists of the exclusive Dickens dinners given by the Fieldses exacerbated her irritation. By November of 1868, a lawsuit had been filed which neither party really won.

Although losing Mary Dodge's friendship was painful, losing that of the Hawthorne family was even more so. Ever since Annie had met Sophia in 1860 on the steamer *Europe,* she had held an important place in Sophia's life. Sophia's notes and letters to Annie are gushing, worshipful, and extravagant in their praise. She called Annie "my Peri,"[7] "my Persian lily," and "Mrs. Meadows," and Fields "Heart's ease," because of his comforting manner and gentle assurances. Even before Hawthorne's death, the Fieldses introduced an element of normalcy into the children's reclusive and somewhat isolated lives. Julian, Una, and Rose attained the status of honorary godchildren, and Sophia and one or more children often came to the Fieldses' for visits which were often too long for Annie, who found it necessary to guard her husband's energy and her own time.

In later years, Annie acknowledged that Julian, Rose, and Una had lacked motivation and sapped their mother's strength; she deplored their selfishness and Sophia's inability to control them. Even during the best years of the friendship, from 1860 to 1864, Annie found the Hawthorne children a strain on her hospitality. She hid her feelings well, however, as Rose's recollection, written in 1897, shows:

> An oasis bloomed at remote seasons, when we went to visit Mr. and Mrs. Fields in Boston. My mother writes of my reviving, and even becoming radiant, as soon as a visit of this fragrant nature breathed upon me. (Lathrop 423)

Rose also provided a rare glimpse of the Fieldses at home:

> To tea we had Mr. and Mrs. Bartol, and Mr. Fields was so infinitely witty that we all died at the tea-table. Mr. Bartol, in gasps, assured him that he had contrived a way to save the food by keeping us in convulsions during the ceremony of eating, and killing us off at the end. Annie had on a scarlet coronet that made her look enchanting, and Mr. Fields declared she was Moses in the burning bush. (424)

Little wonder that so many found the Fieldses' house appealing.

James Fields had served the Hawthornes by providing advances; like other literary families of distinction, such as the Alcotts and the Thaxters, they did not live within their means, secure in the knowledge that someone would always rescue them. Fields had encouraged Hawthorne, a perpetual pessimist, to keep writing and snatched his work from him before his dissatisfactions made him withhold it. When Hawthorne became seriously ill in 1864, the Fieldses asked Oliver Wendell Holmes to observe Hawthorne and make an informal diagnosis to them and Sophia. When Holmes reported euphemistically that Hawthorne had "the shark's tooth upon him," the Fieldses persuaded Hawthorne to take a vacation with William Ticknor, who died unexpectedly during the trip. A second trip with his old school friend, Franklin Pierce, ended in Hawthorne's death. Sophia and the children became an even heavier burden for the Fieldses (Tryon 274–76; 342–46).

Sophia could not restrain her children's spending or keep track of her money, a problem which Fields aggravated by hiding the true state of her financial affairs from her in a well-meaning attempt to save her from worry. He often sent her money from royalties which had not in fact been earned. Resenting the fact that the family of such an author should struggle to make ends meet, Sophia had already become pathetic and belligerent when Mary Dodge provided Sophia Hawthorne with a target for her unhappiness.

By September of 1867, Annie had tired of Sophia's helplessness, her demands upon Annie's hospitality and James's pocketbook. She hoped the Hawthornes would act on a plan to go to Heidelberg, for her own sake as well as theirs. She wrote in her diary that

> Yesterday Mrs Hawthorne came to him [Fields] complaining of poverty. He has already given her 700 dollars above what he owes her and she has debts in Concord to the same amount, yet Julian lives at the Parker House and in spite of his mother's assertions to the contrary spends a great deal of money. She now says he is to enter the scientific school. It is sad to think that in 3 years Hawthorne's family should be virtually beggars.

The tone of Sophia's requests for money is injured, accusing, and whining, but at the same time, flattering and appeasing.[8]

Annie believed, as did most of the Ticknor & Fields writers, that Fields was the kindest and most generous of publishers. If he were not, he had fooled a lot of people. But Fields was a good businessman, too, which meant that he negotiated the most generous contracts with the best authors and less generous contracts with authors who did not sell. Hawthorne's books did not sell, and it would have been bad business to pay him royalties based on Fields's assessment of Hawthorne's greatness. Annie, like most other people, had no way of knowing whether Fields was really generous or whether he was merely just and affectionate. When Elizabeth Peabody later explored Sophia's financial dealings with Ticknor & Fields in detail, Ticknor & Fields's accounting proved to be so lax that the facts are difficult to prove one way or the other. It appears likely, however, that Fields had not overpaid Sophia to the extent he thought.

Annie felt very isolated at this time and had reason for feeling so. Dodge carried her grievance to their mutual friends, writing Sophia Hawthorne, Whittier, Longfellow, James Parton, and others. Even if Fields had paid her as small a copyright as he thought he could get away with—which is the worst he can be accused of—this hardly justified such malignancy. Nearly all the Fieldses' friends stood by them; Whittier later told Annie that he had reasoned with Dodge and tried to suppress *The Battle of the Books,* Dodge's thinly disguised account of the feud which she published herself.[9] Emerson "talked openly of the untruthfulness of the Peabodys." In October of 1868, the situation reached a crisis. Annie wrote:

> At night we heard, & we pray heaven it may not be true that Mrs. Hawthorne has sailed for Europe but has put her accusation against Ticknor & Fields into the hands of a New York lawyer—can such things be?

Whatever the source of that rumor, it proved not to be true. Annie and James had heard the last from Sophia herself. Yet the feud was far from over. Julian, who like Mary Abigail Dodge carried his complaint "into print," omitted all reference to Fields in his first book about his father and included only a negative (and erroneous, according to Annie) reference to him in his second.[10]

The Fieldses diverted themselves from the double grief of Dickens's absence and the Dodge-Hawthorne quarrel with an unusual amount of travelling. They pursued a long-standing interest in the Shakers, shared by many Victorians, by visiting Enfield, Lebanon, and Canaan, New Hampshire before making their usual spring trip to Willey's Farm in Campton, also in New Hampshire. Annie was disappointed by the mildness of the Shaker religious services after what she had heard:

> The motions of course are grotesque enough considered individually, but as these strange figures sway before your eyes with their countenances often full of ecstasy, always filled with solemnity, they produce the sensation which I am persuaded they feel of being possessed by an influence beyond themselves. I should not have been surprised to see any member step from the ranks and whirl away. But nothing of the kind occurred. They were mild in speech and behavior. (17 June 1868)

They also visited James's hometown, the Beals, and Mrs. Adams and Sarah. Both of them dreamed of rejoining Dickens in England, and when they returned to Boston in July the big event was a "Letter from dear C. D."

After a short stop in Boston, Annie and James went to Manchester, where their summer neighbors, the Bartols and the Danas, provided subjects for Annie's diary. She considered Cyrus Bartol a hypochondriac and the Danas elitist and aristocratic to such an extent that "The old man would be a monarchist if such a thing were not absurd." She later referred to Richard, Jr.'s inability to free himself from the "feudal elements" in his background.

In September their old friends Charlotte Cushman and Emma Stebbins paid them a visit in Manchester. Annie wrote of them: "Charlotte is a fine woman with true native genius in her. Emma shares her life." Another highlight was a visit to the Manchester beach by the painters Walter Gay and Winslow Homer, of whom Annie wrote, "They do the landscape no harm—" (20 Sept. 1868).

On 21 September they returned to Boston, and although the new furnace smoked and smelled and housekeeping was resumed, things seemed a little better. Mr. and Mrs. Leslie Stephen from England were visiting in Cambridge. The first Mrs. Stephen was Harriet Thackeray, Thackeray's younger daughter and sister of Anne Thackeray Ritchie, but more importantly, a good friend of Katie Dickens Collins. Annie added to her treasury of Dickens folklore by recounting in her diary that, according to Mrs. Stephen, "Katie has told her her mother did not drink but she is heavy and unregardful of her children and jealous of her husband." A little later, Annie wrote:

> Talked long with Harriet Stephen about Katie Dickens Collins—She [H. S.] . . . told me many things shedding side lights on Dickens's character & home—Of course intensely interesting to us who love him so much. We hear nothing from him lately but that his readings are beginning again, and this from the papers. (Oct. 1868)

The Leslie Stephens became friends with other Bostonians on this trip, notably Lowell, Norton, Emerson, and Holmes. As a result, when Leslie Stephen and his second wife, Julia Duckworth, had their second daughter in 1882, James Russell Lowell became godfather to the future novelist Virginia Woolf.

The second event which brightened Annie's life in the early fall months was Whittier's asking permission to dedicate his new book of poetry, *Among the Hills, and Other Poems,* to Annie.[11] After all her recent disappointments, she wrote of the dedication: "This 'sweetens toil' indeed." Finding a needed chambermaid quickly and receiving a compliment on her large garden at 148 Charles Street from a builder working nearby lifted her spirits considerably; she even made a new vow to keep a few hours each day for writing and keeping up with her journal. However, this enigmatic sentence followed all this cheerfulness and resolve: "Dear J. is going though a sad experience—It haunts him by day and by night" (Oct. 1868).

Day-to-day events gradually returned their lives to something of normalcy. Emerson consulted Annie about his new lecture series. She worked on a fair to raise money to aid blacks' integration into society and raised one hundred dollars for Mary Felton's industrial school for the Freedpeople, becoming involved in the personal problems of a black woman named Charlotte Forten, who had been a friend of Elizabeth Whittier's and was the secretary of the Freedman's Bureau:

> What increases [Charlotte's] difficulty is she became engaged to a white gentleman in Boston or vicinity whose family although they like her exceedingly, cannot make up their minds to receive her as daughter and sister. She refuses therefore to allow the matter to progress and things are suspended for the present. Poor child! She must feel how fruitful of discomfort and petty shame such a marriage must often be. Even Mr. Whittier thinks it a pity and wishes she might find somebody of her own color which would be clearly little less than a miracle. Beside unfortunately these two are in love. I cannot however help feeling that the man does not quite love her as he ought. . . . Charlotte is very sweet and attractive and unusually intelligent. (30 Dec. 1868)

Annie's interest in Charlotte Forten was typically personal; this incident is not widely known. Forten is known as the first Negro teacher of white children in Salem, Massachusetts and a Civil War teacher of ex-slaves on the island of St. Helena, located on the Atlantic coast between Charleston, South Carolina and Savannah, Georgia. Annie probably met Forten as a result of the *Atlantic* publication of her article "Life on the Sea Islands" in 1864. In 1878 Forten married Francis James Grimke, a minister of a Washington Presbyterian church who became a spokesman for blacks.

In December, at a dinner at the Fieldses' that included Lucy Larcom, Fields's partners Clark and Osgood, and Thomas Bailey Aldrich and his wife, the Fieldses heard that Dickens had put them in the "New Uncommercial," the latest episode of Dickens's series *The Uncommercial Traveller,* "by name." The Fieldses said it was "impossible," and bet a large turkey on their belief. The Fieldses' servant, Patrick Lynch, was sent out for the issue and the rumor proved to be true.

"Aboard Ship," which was written on the *Russia* just after Dickens left America, contains a one-paragraph imitation of *Tristam Shandy* with Fields called Eugenius and

Annie mentioned by name: "Eliza—or call her, Eugenius, if thou wilt, Annie—."[12] Annie was miffed by this liberty, and wrote in her diary,

> We laughed over it although I felt rather inclined to write Dickens "an imitation" in turn, saying, "and why, Ingenious, *quitting* these regretful shores . . . did you do it?" I was to tell the truth a little surprised. (10 Dec. 1868)

Another woman might have felt flattered, but Annie recoiled from all publicity. Dickens thought little of the incident, writing casually to Annie and James from Glasgow: "I trust, my dear Eugenius, that you have recognised yourself in a certain Uncommercial, and also some small reference to a name rather dear to you" (*Nonesuch* 16 Dec. 1868).

By mid-January, the year of separation drew swiftly to a close. Annie had invited twenty-seven-year-old Mabel Lowell, who had "a standard of excellence, a high tone, and an ideal which embues her with the poetry of womanhood," to accompany them to England (8 Jan. 1869).

Annie's comments on writers and guests at this time suggest that she and James had been permanently changed by their experiences with Gail Hamilton and Sophia Hawthorne. She wrote of Thomas Wentworth Higginson, one of Mary Abigail Dodge's mentors, that he was

> full of kindness and compliment & even at the last of tenderness. . . . It shows a grievous lack of something, let us call it culture, for a man to be so at fault for expression that he must press a lady's hand. I don't believe in such approaches. (30 Dec. 1868)

She was equally scathing in her comments on a Hungarian physician and linguist named Dr. Naphegyi, whom she described as "perfumed" and "dyed,"[13] noting that "He plastered me thick with flattery and Jamie also" (3 Feb. 1869). Annie was amazed that the doctor told them a story about smuggling gas into Spanish America without any idea that the Fieldses might disapprove.

Annie dreamed again of Dickens as their reunion approached. One night she dreamed that "in my joy at seeing him once more I did not faint but a fiery color suffused my whole face and I grew dizzy like one about to fall" (30 Dec. 1868). In her waking hours, Annie struggled to fit Dickens into his place in her life:

> Thinking of Dickens just now while I was dressing in the yellow afternoon sunshine I thought how like heaven it is to have known two such men, men whose sympathies stand ready to receive and love and forgive yet with minds to comprehend the difficulties by the way. It makes a new world at least to have had such an experience—. (23 Jan. 1869)

Dickens was the second, and last, man she loved in this way, and he may have precluded, for Annie, the possibility of ever loving another man.

On 28 April 1869, one year to the month after Dickens left America for England, Annie and James boarded the steamer Russia for England. On 11 May Annie wrote:

"Have seen Mr. Dickens! At last we can rest." The long year of separation was ended, and whatever emotions had driven Annie and James to Dickens were satisfied.

Almost immediately, Dickens took Annie and James on a tour of his private London. Annie described the first stop, the children's hospital Dickens described in "A Small Star in the East," in her diary:

Friday he came at ½ past 10 a.m. to go with us to the little hospital at Stepney "A small Star in the East." . . . He seemed altogether at home in this poor part of London and especially liked the young Dr. and his wife for the simple reverent earnestness of their lives. "How they bear it," he says, "I cannot imagine." My only answer was that they had been raised up to do the work and yet the wonder still remains that people so sensitive so alive to the suffering of others should be so little depressed by the dreadful scenes among which they live. . . . The doctor carried us before our return into one of the poor houses in the neighborhood. A mother father & 7 children in one room! And yet, he said, this was not an extreme case! But I shall never forget the look in the eyes of that woman nor her patient manner—

D. did not go up stairs with us—The sight of misery which cannot be relieved is too terrible to be sought often—but it was best for us to go and we went—. (May 1869)

A few days later Georgina took Annie to the Foundling Hospital and Dickens took James to see the "thieves of London." Jamie was

excited and depressed by the scenes he had witnessed—full of wonder too at the intimate knowledge the police have of these characters and [how] well officers & thieves understand each other. (April–May 1869)

They dined often at Leslie Stephen's and at Frederick Lehman's, where Robert Browning, Mrs. Rudolph Lehmann, Wilkie Collins, Mrs. Proctor, and the Leslie Stephens were guests.[14] Annie found much to criticize at this "London dinnertable of the first rank," and even though she could by now adapt to almost any social situation, this party made her uneasy: "This is the kind of life Dickens's children have known too much of since they have grown up—especially K. C. [Katie Collins]." Although Robert Browning was "like a piece of polished steel, receiving on his surface keen reflections of persons and giving back sharp points of light," Annie found him "scornful unsympathetic, powerful and swift." She complained that

Their jokes at table were bandied as often in French and German as in English. . . . They were all entirely at home but did not succeed in making us feel so—There is an ignorance of, and a subtle contempt of outsiders in such a company. (May 1869)

Other celebrities Annie met on this trip included William Morris, whom she described as a "maker of painted glass windows and objects of medieval Art—Poet also," and Algernon Swinburne. She spent some time talking with Swinburne, "a half mad poet, a half baked man," and recorded some of his speech:

"The four great poets who have espoused the cause of liberty in England, Landor, Byron, Shelley and (if I may say so) myself, belong to the haute noblesse[.] As to this low german family now upon the throne, I have studied there [sic] claims to aristocracy well, and they have not one, absolutely none at all."

Annie wrote that "He would shriek out as he talked, would twirl his hands nervously, would leap up and down and fling himself at times on the floor. A strange, gifted, weak, diseased, intense, vain, excitable angelic-devil man" (May 1869).

After a brief visit with William Allingham, Annie, James, and Mabel travelled to Farringford to see the Tennysons. More suspicious of new Americans since Bayard Taylor had allowed a description of his visit to be printed, Tennyson

> frightened Mabel at first until she actually cried though I think no one discovered anything beyond her distressed and frightened manner. He asked her if her father was a letter writer referring to Bayard Taylor's unfortunate half private epistle which leaked unhappily, most unhappily into print. He cannot get that out of his head and harks bitterly upon it continually. (May? 1869)

While at Farringford, the Fieldses met the great photographer Julia Cameron, Tennyson's neighbor and the sister of Virginia Woolf's maternal grandmother.

On the second of June, Annie, James (and presumably Mabel) arrived at Gad's Hill Place for the first of two visits. The house was full: Katie and her husband, Mary Dickens, and Georgina were all at home, and Annie recorded one of her most memorable passages about Dickens:

> It is wonderful the fun and flow of spirits C. D. has for he is a sad man. Sleepless nights come too often, oftener than they ever would to a free heart. But the sorrows of such a nature are many and must often seem more than he can bear—Mine has been a most exceptional lot to have known this great man so well—think of having sat by Shakespeare's side at dinner for weeks, and since Shakespeare there has not been a more various and dramatic and thoroughly human creature than Charles Dickens—. (2 June 1869)

Between visits to Dickens they returned to London, toured Abbotsford, Edinburgh, Glasgow, the Lake District, and Stratford, visiting, among others, Harriet Martineau, Edward Flower and his wife,[15] Charlotte Cushman and Emma Stebbins, Longfellow, the Macmillans, Alexander Ireland, Disraeli, Charles Reade, and the studio of Gabriel Rossetti. They also saw Katie Collins and her husband, of whom Annie wrote:

> I was struck by the sickness of his brain when I heard him say to the wondering Mabel that he hated physical competence in woman as he should hate the reverse in a man. (21 July 1869)

Revolted by this antifeminist view, Annie was particularly pleased by Charles Reade's "delicate courtesy" that "all women must appreciate . . . deeply" (29 Sept. 1869).

On their second visit in October Annie and James slept in Dickens's room and were haunted by his insomnia. Dickens called Fields down to his study and read him the opening chapters of *The Mystery of Edwin Drood,* which Fields considered a masterpiece and arranged to publish in America. There was much joviality at mealtimes; Annie wrote that Dickens

> laughed at me for the crusty way in which I replied "no thank you" to J.'s kindly suggestion that the apple pudding was nice and I should do well to have some of it— "I've seen her do it before on her own ground" he said half to himself and half amused.

After meeting Edward Lear and Dickens's friend John Forster, Annie and James departed for Liverpool, with Dickens to see them off at the train:

> A crowd had collected to see him by the time we started out he did not seem to see it and the blood rushed all over his face as the cars came— —and we were off—He ran forward a few steps and all was over—except eternity. (24 Oct. 1869)

Annie, James, and Mabel reached home on 7 November 1869, a week before the fifteenth anniversary of the Fieldses' wedding day.

Fields again became depressed when they returned to Boston. On 27 November Annie wrote, "Jamie has been ill and I 'enormously' *busy* of all weak naughty words the worst—," and on 7 December she added, "Jamie very sad.—he is too young for this—but" and her entry, not written very clearly, trails off into nothing. In January Annie wrote, "In the meantime my dear Love, formerly the lights and life of all— sweet, quick & loved by all is silent and sad—God only knows what next—" (31 Jan. 1870). On a page marked "Private" in a letter to her friend Laura Winthrop Johnson, Annie wrote enigmatically:

> All things conspire together for good I believe, dear love, as they ever have done but Jamie is not altogether well and you who have been through everything will understand my anxieties. I dare say they are ill-founded enough but he does not seem like himself. I try to keep the house as bright as I can and never a week passes without some cheerful fireside talk with invited friends—but—You will not remotely whisper a word of this to Lissie Adams not anyone, please, but I could not quite go on writing to you as usual without putting down a little of the weight—. (HL 31 Jan. 1870)

Fields's business was affected by an economic depression which threatened him with serious losses. Annie wrote in her diary that "Gold has touched 110—No man can see the end of this sudden downfall—The business world is sadly depressed and wavering—Men know not what to do" (May 1870).

Dickens was by no means forgotten; in February his name came up at a small dinner occasioned by his friend Charles Fechter's American tour:

> Mr. Longfellow spoke again of Mr. Dickens restlessness of his terrible sadness.—"Yes, yes" said Fechter "all his fame goes for nothing since he does not have the one thing. He is very unhappy in his children.["] (24 Feb. 1870)

The culmination of all this sadness was the news of Dickens's death. The entry in

Annie's diary reads simply: "June 10. Friday—our dear friend Charles Dickens died last night." Later she added the exact date and time: "June 9th at 6 o'clock." By 13 June she had recovered sufficiently to add a comment: "We cannot think of other things, his memory and the thought of those who loved him is never absent." Annie summed up the years from 1867 to 1870 in a single sentence: "It is doubly strange to us to remember the valley of shadows we have passed this winter and to discover it as leading to his tomb."

6.
Charity Work
"A Dangerous Eagerness"

The "valley of shadows" that preceded Dickens's death—James's depression and mysterious illness—was not yet over, nor would it be until he had relinquished completely the reins of his offices. James had ceased to enjoy the responsibilities of his editorial work when it no longer carried with it the universal high regard of his clients. Although James still depended on Annie for help with his writing and emotional support, his retirement from publishing and editing left her much freer to pursue her own interests.

Ironically, now that she had time for writing and study, she turned her talents elsewhere, perhaps realizing that literary success would require far more time and determination than she could give it. Annie rationalized her failure by talking about the doctrine of true womanhood and denigrating the quest for knowledge as selfish and un-Christian. She could mask her disappointment at the indifferent reception her poetry had received by telling herself that philanthropy was intrinsically suitable for a woman and more worthy of her energy.

In 1868 Annie began a new diary with an epigraph propounding this point of view:

"We have duties so positive to our neighbor," says Bishop Butler, "if we give more of our time and of our attention to ourselves than is our just due, we are taking what is not ours and are guilty of a fraud." (Jan. 1868)[1]

By persuading herself that writing was a selfish occupation, Annie was able to shift her priorities without a corresponding loss of self-esteem.

The part Dickens played in triggering Annie's changed priorities cannot be overestimated. Although Dickens's effect on Annie was unplanned and perhaps even unconscious, his few well-timed and well-chosen remarks turned a marginal interest into a career just at the moment when urban immigration, population growth, and industrialism were necessitating a worldwide change from private philanthropy to large-scale organized charity. His interest in charity in general and in the work of his friend Angelina Burdett Coutts in particular suggested a way to succeed outside writing, drawing together all of Annie's drifting energies and unfocused desires and providing her with a model. Numerous passages in Annie's diaries document Dickens's influence, such as this entry written after a successful holiday party:

Indeed . . . I could not help feeling proud I fear . . . but there is something else which will

. . . keep me from it, the knowledge of short coming and the slight value of the world's praise compared with true well-doing and the difficulty of it. For Mr. Dickens is very kind and we cannot help loving him as all must do who have the privilege of coming near him and seeing him as he is. (28 Dec. 1867)

The discontinuity of the passage and its apparent non sequitur reflect the connection in Annie's mind between "doing good" and Dickens. Her mind travels naturally from the pleasure she takes in Dickens's admiration to her desire to please him further by "true well-doing."

Dickens's influence can be traced more directly through an essay to which he specifically directed Annie's attention in a letter:[2]

As an instance of how strangely something comic springs up in the midst of the direst misery, look to a succeeding Uncommercial, called A Small Star in the East, published to-day, by-the-bye. I have described, *with exactness,* the poor places into which I went, and how the people behaved, and what they said. I was wretched, looking on; and yet the boiler-maker and the poor man with the legs filled me with a sense of drollery not to be kept down by any pressure. (*Nonesuch* 16 Dec. 1868)

Even before this letter reached her, however, Annie had discovered this piece herself and its powerful sentiment had done its work.

"A Small Star in the East" recounts a visit Dickens made to "the borders of Ratcliffe and Stepney, eastward of London," an extremely impoverished area of the city. The first part of the article describes four visits Dickens made to individual families in the area, the first to a dwelling where a young woman with lead poisoning lay with "her brain coming out at her ear." In the second dwelling lived the boilermaker Dickens mentioned in his letter, a man both deaf and simple whose wife acted as interpreter between him and Dickens. The third scene is about the "man with the legs," an out-of-work coal porter who unbandaged his swollen and ulcerated legs for Dickens's inspection. The fourth visit, described only briefly, was made to a tenement family consisting of a woman and five children all living on four shillings and five loaves of bread per week. None of the members of these families held full-time employment.

After visiting the last of these families, Dickens describes his journey back toward the railway, exhausted and depressed by what he had seen, particularly the suffering of the children. He encounters a sign reading "East London Children's Hospital" and crosses the street to visit it. There he found the young, well-educated doctor and nurse, husband and wife, running a charity hospital for the children of the area with the aid of only a few other young, dedicated, underpaid nurses—the hospital that Annie and James would later visit with Dickens.

This short but stirring article provided the final impetus for the change of occupation which Annie had been considering. She wrote in her journal on Christmas Day of 1868:

As for literature and that difficult thing knowledge whose glorious pursuit fires even my unworthy heart, the cares of the world have pushed lately out of my way every possibility of such delightful occupations.

> The truth is I have been truly fired by Dickens's last paper about the Childrens' Hospital[.] I lay awake at night to ponder of it and if I ever go to England I shall go there—In the meantime while I live here such children are my own—God help me!—.

An intelligent as well as a busy woman, she resented disrupting her leisure and wasting her time by going to church only to hear a poor sermon: Annie described one sermon by their minister and friend Cyrus Bartol as a "most puling and inadequate discourse too long by half since there was so little for him to say" (19 Jan. 1868). She also disliked the worshipful attitude toward ministers that she felt was entering Unitarianism (an attitude she associated with Catholicism and Anglicanism), writing that "I *know* societies are good for the sake of union in benevolent schemes but when it comes to making the preacher a figure to be worshipped—faugh!" Thus, Annie's irritation with going to church and her commitment to charity coincided; she came to feel that the true course of Christianity was to devote oneself to action, to fight directly the evils of this world as Christ had instructed. Here, too, she may have been influenced by Dickens (whose reverence she had defended to Tennyson in 1859), who did not support any established church.

Other forces combined with Dickens's timely influence to push Annie toward social work. Now a mature woman in her mid-thirties, Annie wanted to accomplish something on her own more fiercely than ever before:

> I am eager, eager to do something—a dangerous eagerness which analyzed may only show ambition in covert form—I *can* live the poem I would write—let me do it then and thank God! (18 Feb. 1868)

Unlike writing (especially undistinguished writing), social service brought with it the immediate, unconditional approval of the people who mattered in Annie's world. Both Annie's father and her teacher, George Emerson, had been deeply supportive of community service and considered it an appropriate role for women. Because charity work was a traditionally female occupation that served the goals of Christianity, it was easier to reconcile with societal notions of woman's duty than was the pursuit of knowledge and the ambition to write. It provided an important outlet for the energies of the intelligent, well-bred, well-to-do woman for whom few other careers were open. Charity work was less solitary than writing, less reliant on inspiration and concentration, taking Annie out of the house where she was less vulnerable to interruption by James, callers, and servants.

Social work drew on Annie's strengths—her intelligence, her organizational skill, and her ability to handle people—and minimized her comparative lack of imagination and creativity. Through a decade of forwarding her husband's business interests, she had learned to plan both social events and public events such as lecture series, helping to plan Emerson's last lecture series, Dickens's second tour, and a lecture series for women which was part of the movement for a women's college. Her experience in talking to writers had made her nearly fearless, and her writing experience was put to use in publicizing and raising money for her numerous projects. Social work was undergoing a complete redevelopment and new ideas and new faces were desperately needed, unlike literature, where one had to compete with Longfellow, Lowell, Emerson, and the recognized names of the previous thirty years. Her work for organized charity eventually required Annie to supervise others and manage an association much as a businessman would manage a business.

Prior to the 1870s, Annie's contact with the poor was minimal and sympathy came easily. In 1865 Annie and James gave over five dollars a day to charity, which Annie said would "not be too much if business increases as it promises but it is too much at present that is, it is more with our necessary expenditures than our receipts will cover" (Dec. 1865). The gift of nearly two thousand dollars a year explains the Fieldses' reputation as philanthropists when Annie began her charity work. In later years, she gave less money and more time, in accordance with the newer ideas about public welfare. Annie enjoyed watching "the working intelligent people" who lived on the other side of Beacon Street from her who "have a kindliness and warmth of exterior on a Sunday afternoon which you cannot find on Beacon St; they are [beaming] with the happiness of having nothing to do for a few hours" (1866). On one of her excursions through the poor districts seeking a child model for Lissie, Annie remarked that

> Such handsome dirt is not frequently seen by us. The Irish crowd tried to compete with the Italians, one mother catching her children and washing their faces, then asking us if they wouldn't do—but their washed out blue eyes and freckled pallid faces looked poorer yet by the side of the smiling olive filth of the Genoese and Tuscans[.]

Far from being indifferent to the inequities of society, Annie felt guilty about "wearing a satin dress with the beautiful gold locket containing the ancient gem which Mr. [William] Stillman sent me when I remembered [the people of Crete] had scarcely food enough to eat or room to be comfortable in." Her increased sensitivity to the problems of the working class led her to support labor organization and various kinds of working people's clubs. By 1875 she was in the front rank of those who were willing to expend time, energy, and money to alleviate the suffering of both native and immigrant poor.

The 1860s and 1870s were decades of learning for Annie; her mind became broader and her social awareness increased. The evolution of her attitude toward Roman Catholics is a typical example. As her journals from the 1859–60 trip showed, Annie did not much like papists or Romanists, as she called them. Her continued dislike is evident in her comments about the work of Boston Catholics who founded a home for "fallen women" that was operated by Catholic nuns:

> I am grateful for the institution whoever may start it but I feel as if in this home of Protestantism it was a wrong and a disgrace that such things must be left to this effete and decaying authority. It shows that . . . the organisation of the Church as a [family] contains a strong principle of life not the smallest feature of which is that it is a refuge for women and always ready to give them holy work adapted to their strength in which the sorrows of the world may be assuaged if not forgotten. (1 May 1867)

Annie's prejudice against Catholicism finally dissipated because of her charity contacts and the friendships she and Sarah Orne Jewett shared with two Catholic poets, Alice Meynell and Louise Imogen Guiney, the latter a young woman who helped to ease the loneliness of Annie's last years.

In 1870, Boston provided charity through a combination of private philanthropy by individuals and relief by churches for those of their faith or in their own neighborhoods. In the small communities which made up old Boston, discovering who needed help and providing it on a personal basis had been an easy matter. However, the influx of immigrants into the city, primarily Irish of the poorest class, caused large concentrations of the poor to live in areas of the city, the North End in particular, which were no longer inhabited by the middle class.[3] In addition, most of the immigrants were neither Calvinist nor Unitarian but Catholic, and the existing Catholic churches were not well equipped to distribute charity because they were small, few in number, and lacked wealthy parishioners. Thus, neither private gifts nor church relief worked adequately in the new situation.

The entrance of the city as a whole into charity was a new response. The ideas behind the movement toward organized charity were not new; they had developed in various parts of the world, including Boston, from the 1830s on. Because the older methods had still worked reasonably well, however, many innovative ideas had never been put into effect. Recent economic downturns had caused many private sources of charity to dry up and fewer funds were available. This created a new emphasis on eliminating double and triple donations to the same recipient and on helping the "deserving poor" who did not drink and were willing to work. A distinction was made between poverty, which was considered by many to be an ineradicable condition of the human experience, and pauperism, which was considered to be an evil resulting from ignorance and immorality. These different kinds of poverty were felt by the new reformers to deserve different approaches.

Another difference between the old private philanthropy and the "new" organized system was that the new system attempted for the first time an analysis of the sources of pauperism and ways to alleviate or to eradicate it. The new social workers thought about the reasons for poverty and its continued increase, and social work became much more scientific. Evolutionary theory; the new historical approach to theology; a more optimistic view of human nature and the "decline" of original sin; and the scientific attitude toward the home environment preached by proponents of domestic science all fed an evangelistic zeal to eliminate the slums and assimilate immigrants as quickly as possible (Ahlstrom 2:229–36).

Despite their "scientific" approach, the early social workers retained the religious context of earlier aid. Religious liberalism may have made the Charity Organization Movement possible, but both thrived among socially conservative and wealthy people who still believed that poverty resulted from laziness, moral turpitude, or shortsightedness (254). This manifested itself in their definition of poverty as possibly ineradicable and of pauperism as resulting from sin.

The later Social Gospel movement sprang from religious liberalism as well, but it took more from abolitionism, evangelicalism, and socialism. Eventually the Social Gospel called into question the free-market economy, the morality of Darwin's theories, and the Puritan ethic itself (256). Social Gospelers and Christian Socialists were open to ideas of redistribution of wealth and other radical action, while the Charity Organization Movement remained "more conventional and less imaginative," according to Nathan I. Huggins, author of *Protestants against Poverty* (12). The difference was partly generational and partly a matter of preparing the field: Annie was a charity organizer; William Dean Howells could be a Christian Socialist. Charity Organization, a primarily nineteeth-century movement, continued to look to God for its inspiration, while the Social Gospel, a primarily twentieth-century movement, transferred its hope for change to human beings (43).

Annie moved into charity slowly, a project at a time. The North End of Boston, the home of merchants at the beginning of the nineteenth century, was abandoned by the middle classes shortly thereafter. The well-to-do moved into the suburbs, first the South End, then South Boston, and finally Roxbury (where Annie's mother and sister Sarah were living in the 1870s) and Dorchester. The North and West Ends became low-rent districts, then overcrowded slums, the home of the immigrants. Since this area was close to the wharves and offered low rent, the poorest Irish immmigrants, those who could not afford to leave the place where they landed, settled here. The conditions soon approximated, if they did not equal, those of the London slums.

In 1845 Lemuel Shattuck, the leading authority on demography in Boston, said the North End of Boston could never accommodate more than 80,000 people; in 1855, 90,000 lived there. Each room of this area, including attics and basements, was lived in by a family. Many of the dwellings had inadequate light, no plumbing, and no sanitation or drainage. There were no arrangements for disposal of garbage; trash dumped outside caused diseases. Heat was expensive and ventilation nonexistent; fires started easily and were hard to extinguish. No wonder cholera, smallpox, and tuberculosis thrived.

In addition, the area had an extraordinarily high birth rate—52.87 per cent of the total births in 1850 in Boston were among the Irish. Intemperance, crime, and prostitution thrived. Irish men took to the bars because it was their tradition and because their homes drove them out, and unemployment and poor wages led to petty theft and prostitution. This was the situation that had existed for more than twenty years when Annie started visiting the North End.[4]

Beginning in the early 1870s, Annie went to the North End at least once and often twice a week, on Fridays and Sundays. Several Protestant churches had established "missions" in the midst of this Catholic ghetto; the one Annie supported was called the North End Mission. Since their work was unlikely to succeed on a solely religious footing, the church members brought nonreligious activities to their centers. A group called the North End Union operated a gymnasium; held classes in dressmaking, plumbing, and printing; provided playrooms, public baths, and reading rooms; and organized lectures and socials.

The activities of Annie's "mission" were undoubtedly similar. Annie herself taught Friday afternoon classes in French literature and other subjects to working girls. The North End boasted an Industrial School and Work Rooms where girls learned sewing and other domestic skills. Annie called upon her husband and friends such as Holmes and Whittier for Friday evening lectures and readings for mixed audiences. And gradually, as one writer puts it, "What had been salvation became social improvement or uplift" (Huggins 50). Her field work at the North End showed Annie what was needed and involved her in the massive task of charity organization.

Ideas came to Annie in swift succession, and she acted on them rapidly.[5] Her contact with Dickens suggested her first personal project, the establishment of coffeehouses in poor districts. In Boston, as in London, numerous alehouses were a problem. In Boston this was partly due to the large number of Irish immigrants. The public houses were the only warm, friendly meeting places open to Irish men. The new social architects, however, felt the pubs led to a number of evils, primarily drunkenness, which led in turn to physical abuse and the loss of jobs. In addition, drinking meant that the small amount of money earned was not wholly available for food, clothing, and education for wives and children. Since alehouses and drinking were perceived as a source of pauperism, Annie wanted to replace them with coffeehouses, which would be equally warm and inviting but sell inexpensive coffee instead of liquor. She began to think about the plan shortly after her return from England and named her coffee rooms the Holly-Tree Coffee Rooms after Dickens's Holly-Tree Inn.[6]

The coffee rooms absorbed Annie's attention from 1870 to 1872, and she never completely abandoned them. Fortunately for social historians, the evolution of the project is recorded both in her diaries and in her letters to her closest woman friend of the time, Laura Winthrop Johnson.[7] Annie first mentions her plan in her diary on 13 November 1870, when she wrote, "I am entirely filled with my endeavor to found a coffee-house to counteract whiskey drinking—God knows if I shall succeed." By Thanksgiving she had solicited funds from a number of her friends, and early in December she discussed the coffee room scheme with Whittier and others. By January of 1871 the city fathers of Boston had indicated that they supported her plan to "establish Coffee houses all over the city at '5 cents a cup'"; in June a neighborhood policeman dropped in to suggest a proprietor.

Finally, on 9 June 1871, the first anniversary of Dickens's death, Annie cut flowers for her first operating coffeehouse. Holmes and Whittier visited the coffee room to congratulate her. By October of 1871 there were plans for opening two or three more, one in Eliot Street, one in Lincoln Street under "Dr. Bowditch's reformed hole called Crystal Palace," a third in the Neponset district.

By early December of 1871 Annie noted two houses established and three under way. But the strain of organization was beginning to tell: "I shall be glad to get the Coffee Rooms fairly launched, because the responsibility weighs somewhat of course." She had lost two hundred dollars on one unsuccessful shop so far, but felt this to be a small failure only. She signed a Miss Potter to run the third Holly-Tree coffeehouse in early December.

While her coffeehouses were yet in the early stages, Annie had already chosen her second major project: a home for working women. She wrote to her friend Laura Winthrop Johnson about a new coffee room for sewing women which would have

> connected with it rooms, at cost also (lodging) for the same women. Such places are most helpful in preventing h[orror or horing] and usory. There should be many, in our large cities, where women *cannot afford to live honestly* on the sums they receive in the shops for work.

Annie understood the drudgery of working women's lives: "These poor creatures look back upon hours of crime with positive joy compared to the prison-like slavery they often fall into *afterward* to drag out their wretched days."[8] In January of 1872, she wrote a detailed account of Christmas dedication of the house to Laura:

> On Wednesday evening . . . my home for Working-women was inaugurated with simple services. The Sunday school children sang a Xmas carol, then Mrs. Caswell a lovely missionary . . . [read] a shorter prayer, after which portions of letters were read from Mrs. Livermore and Mr. Whittier, expressing their interest in the idea and their sorrow at being absent—then Mrs. H. B. Stowe read one of her own stories "Huldy's Housekeeping" . . . and to conclude (after another carol by the children and the singing of a hymn by Lucy Larcom written for the occasion,) we all dispersed to view the home and the Coffee Room.[9]

It is evident from this passage how many of Annie's old interests she brought to her new work; indeed, it is often hard to tell which Annie was more missionary to, religion or literature.

After decorating "her home," Annie was concerned that she may have made it so pleasant her friends wouuld nott donate the additional furnishings for it. She was also

> Myideas,nottohavethishouselookeduponasacharity.Iwisheverywomanliving theretofeelherowndignityassafeandfreefromfeelingofdependenceasifshelived inthewors[t]denoftheFivePointsonNorthSt.

Although Annie felt sure that her home would become self-supporting and successful, even before it had opened, she said its proprietor, Miss Philbrook, was not "immaculate," charged high prices, and did not run the restaurant well (25 April 1872). The home for working women failed to pay its expenses and eventually had to be given up.

The fires which plagued American cities at this time posed a different, more urgent problem. As a result of the crowded conditions and predominance of wooden buildings, fires occurred frequently and required a major effort from the developing network of social workers. Some fires, such as the Chicago fire of late 1871, demanded national cooperation. When Chicago minister Robert Collyer came to Boston to raise money for relief, Annie and her friends collected food, clothing, and money.

Then, in November of the same year, Boston was itself the victim of a major fire which struck the industrial district, leaving many of the poorest out of work (Huggins 57). As Annie wrote in her diary, "Alarms of fire are so continually heard in every quarter that a plague of fire seems to have fallen upon our devoted city" (Nov. 1872). Since the building occupied by Osgood & Co. was completely destroyed, Annie and James lost money.

As a result of the fire, Annie was brought into closer contact with the poor, visiting the homes of girls who had been thrown out of employment. In December she wrote, "Found several Irish women on my list who did not especially excite my sympathy, one bright girl must be taken care of." Stating what would become the guiding principle of Associated Charities, she said, "I shall however arrange for them to come to me as far as possible that I may understand them pretty well before giving money away" (1 Dec. 1872). Annie visited every day during this time of crisis, looking for those out of work.

By the first of February, she had succeeded in opening work rooms to employ twenty to thirty seamstresses whose workplaces had burned. She had organized the rooms partly out of frustration with the inadequacy of the City Relief Committee, which felt its work was "drawing to a close" after relocating people and finding food and clothing. Since the city did not feel her project worthy of its funds, Annie invested money which she had saved from various donations. The work rooms produced "women's suits, children's clothes, aprons, and useful articles *for the shops,*" and they were operated according to "cooperative principles" by a dressmaker who was "an old adherent" of Annie's (LWJ 9 Feb. 1873).

The Boston fire, the depression which followed it, and the worsening conditions of the North End intensified the need for organization of charity resources. In 1873 there were already several independent agencies for relief in Boston, among them Joseph Tuckerman's Society for the Prevention of Pauperism, founded in 1835, and the Boston Provident Association, founded in 1851. The Provident had urged citywide organization from the beginning, but when that proved unlikely, its plan to house societies in a single building where they could easily confer was put into effect with the construction of the Charity Building in 1869.

Motivated by her frustration with the existing organizations, Annie spent many hours at the Charity Building on Chardon Street learning all she could about current methods of charity administration in the city and all over the world. She was particularly interested in the "Elberfeld system," which originated in Elberfeld, Germany in the 1850s and was first described by an Englishman, Andrew Doyle, in 1871. In 1864 Octavia Hiill, the granddaughter of Dr. Southworth Smith, the English sanitary expert, had established a housing project and visiting system in the East London slums based on the Elberfeld plan. Annie wrote to Hill, who had written pamphlets about her work, but she received a noncommital and even curt reply.[10] She had better luck with Miss Schuyler, of the New York State Charities Aid Association, who had already travelled to England and Germany to observe their systems.

The product of Annie's research was a series of articles describing the Elberfeld system.[11] The main ideas of the scheme were the institution of personal visits by semi-professional agents, the prevention of duplication through assiduous record keeping, and the extension of work or other "constructive" aid (not money) whenever possible.

In the summer of 1875 Annie and her new friend, Mrs. James Lodge, made the next successful move in the drive for centralization of social services. Closeted together at the Fieldses' new Manchester cottage, the two women formulated the principles and structure of their new group, which they named the Cooperative Society of Visitors. With Mrs. Lodge as president and Annie as vice-president, the Society began immediately to implement the Elberfeld system, which entailed dividing the city into districts and recruiting volunteer "charitable visitors" and professional social workers to visit families in each district. The visitors did not have the power to grant aid but filed a report with the central administration, where a committee decided what kind of aid was appropriate and allocated it from a variety of resources. The Society lasted from 1875 until 1879, when it was absorbed into the more comprehensive Associated Charities of Boston.

By December of 1875 Annie had recruited forty-seven visitors, including herself, for her district (LWJ 12 Dec. 1875). They included her sister Mrs. Beal, Mrs. Robert Treat Paine, Alice Towne, Mrs. Admiral Stedman, Phillips Brooks, and William Dean Howells. Annie wrote twenty-five reports a week all winter as a visitor in addition to attending to her administrative chores. Some of the projects Annie and Mary Lodge worked on in 1876 were establishing a new work room that employed forty seamstresses, improving the women's prison in Massachusetts, and creating a home for "wandering girls." Annie also helped Robert Treat Paine with the Cooperative Building Society, presided over meetings of the Women's Mutual Benefit Association and the Women's Union, advised the Gwynne Home for children, and helped plan Sunday excursions to the country for city children.

Anyone who started up and took a hand in as many projects as Annie did was bound to have at least a few failures, and she did. Although Annie was always disappointed when a home, coffee room, or work room was forced to close, she and James had enough money to sustain the loss of some capital, and most of the funds invested were not their own. Some failures had more serious consequences because a member of the working class had invested his or her own money or given up a secure job to participate in one of Mrs. Fields's schemes. Such was the case with Mrs. Murphy, who had borrowed money from the Fieldses to establish a work room for seamstresses displaced by a fire in the garment district.[12]

When the business failed in the summer of 1874 and Mrs. Murphy found herself in debt (with a "hard husband"), she tried, as Annie said, "to extort money from us on the plea that I persuaded her into an unsuccessful business." Mrs. Murphy could repay neither the original loan from Annie nor the subsequent debts she had incurred, and she wrote Annie a letter "so full of hatred and trouble and threats" that it frightened her. She confided to her diary, "I could not tell what she might do. I thought of it by day and by night." James, however, did not believe there was any real danger from Mrs. Murphy.

Annie was reluctant to stay alone at Manchester, and, sure enough, one day when Mr. Fields had gone to the city, Mrs. Murphy appeared at the door. Annie hid in her room upstairs, leaving Mrs. Murphy alone in the parlor until James came home. She wrote, "I went up to my room and sat alone. I feared a violent scene, I could not tell what the end might be." When Fields arrived, he met Mrs. Murphy calmly and asked her to wait while he ate his dinner, then he extracted an apology from her, lent her more money, and sent her away. Annie was greatly relieved to have the matter settled.

Annie was profoundly affected by this experience, which disillusioned her about the extent to which her beneficiaries would be grateful. She wrote, "How strange it is that our best efforts may end in this!" and later she decided that she "had been too daring and headstrong in aiding and abetting her desire to undertake the business which turned out so fatally." She cited the opinion of her banker brother-in-law, with whom she seldom agreed, that "He had never known a single instance of money loaned in that way to do good." This experience undoubtedly had an impact on the policies of the Associated Charities, which some people felt were hard. Being threatened, frightened, and pursued by one of the people she was trying to help changed the way Annie thought about the poor.

Despite these temporary discouragements, Annie persevered, and her Cooperative Society of Visitors succeeded where other attempts had failed, largely because of her vigorous fund raising, organizational ability, and the same kind of publicity and management that helped make her husband such a success. She was essential to the formation of the first truly efficient large charity organization in the United States and was one of its "most active directors and creative minds" (Huggins 60).

Organized into conferences which corresponded to city wards, the Associated Charities brought together all the private and public agencies that were involved in relief in the city. Each conference was a little democracy with elected representatives to a central council. The Society employed both paid and volunteer visitors, and comprehensive records were kept for the first time. New York modelled its better-known Charity Organization Society on the Boston group two years later in 1881. Not only was Annie's group early on the field, it was better organized and more successful than its closest equivalents in Buffalo, Philadelphia, and Brooklyn (Huggins 62–63).

Naturally enough, the Associated Charities met with some opposition from existing groups, especially from Robert C. Winthrop of the Provident Society, who differed with the Associated Charities on several matters. Robert Treat Paine, the first president of Annie's group, was forced to carry on arguments with rival organizations for several years (Huggins 64ff.). However, because the friends of the Associated Charities "were so active as to sometimes be considered social nuisances," its views (and Annie's) prevailed.

It is ironic that Annie's first long publications in the leading magazines came only after she had set aside her literary ambitions to devote her major energy to charity. Annie's first article was in fact a letter to the editor of the *Christian Union* publicizing her coffeehouse scheme. From that point on, Annie skillfully used the press to publicize her projects and inform interested citizens about how they could help. In 1878 she published three major articles about the charity efforts in Boston: "Problems of Poor Relief," which appeared in a new magazine called *Sunday Afternoon,* and two articles in *Harper's,* given the joint title, "A Glimpse at Some of Our Charities." All were published anonymously and written in the third person plural; the text contains veiled references to a "friend," who is Annie's husband James.[13] The first of the two articles in *Harper's* opens with an homage to Charles Dickens and a description of the tour he gave James through the slums of London. After a general discussion of the "new" ideas of charity association, Annie described and commented upon particular organizations or projects, such as St. John's Guild in New York City, which she found inefficient and wasteful; her own Holly-Tree Coffee Rooms; Octavia Hill's Homes for the Poor in London and similar projects in Philadephia, Brooklyn, and Boston. The article ends with another reference to Dickens.

The second part of the article, called "The Employment, Education, and Protection of Women," illustrates Annie's interest in women of both the working and the leisured classes. She urges women to give real meaning to their lives by volunteering their services to aid their sisters among the poor and argues that women, often victimized by the fathers and husbands who should be supporting them, suffer most from poverty and need special institutions to aid them. She urges the education of women as "the only real safeguard" to keep women from pauperism, and discusses the work of the Association for the High Medical Culture of Women in trying to open medical school to prospective women doctors.

The culmination of Annie's writing about charity came in 1883 with the publication of her book *How to Help the Poor,* a semi-official guide to the philosophy of the Associated Charities of Boston. While the people who had direct contact with social-service organizations understood the benefits to be gained by centralization, many individuals and churches were ignorant of the advances that had been made. Increasing numbers of the poor had no association with churches, while others had discovered they could collect money from several churches, the city, and private individuals as well. The people who had come to know the problem of poverty, and thought they understood it, felt that the middle and upper classes needed to be educated before more headway could be made. Thus, Annie's book was an attempt on the part of the social-service workers to persuade the general public to give time as well as money, and to give money only through the central bureau to ensure that resources were distributed as fairly and intelligently as possible.

How to Help the Poor appeared in 1883 and it sold 22,000 copies in two years (Tryon *Not. Amer. Women* 1:616). The bulk of the book is aimed at prospective donors and volunteers, describing charity organization and how it works. The book takes us inside the complicated administrative network which Annie had helped to create and helped to run. It provides a fascinating glimpse into how Annie thought and her underlying sense of values.

Although she writes from a Christian point of view, Annie rejects the idea that poverty is a part of God's plan and should be accepted as inevitable. She felt that effectively combatting the growth in poverty called for new techniques and organizational principles. She organized her ideas around the anecdotal experiences of Mrs. X, a woman who, like Annie, after being inundated with requests for money and personal aid, finds herself frustrated by the inefficiency and duplication she observes in the help received by the poor. Like Annie, Mrs. X also learns about a city in Germany that had been divided into districts for the purpose of efficient investigation of each family's needs.

In the second chapter, Annie describes Boston's organizational plan, alluding to the *Handbook of Friendly Visitors among the Poor of New York,* a guide which preceded her own. According to the guides, churches should continue to provide relief to their own poor but were requested to record their almsgiving in the central bureau. Annie's organization was opposed to "out-door relief," the nineteenth-century name for public welfare. One reason for this was the widespread belief that it was the Christian—not civic—duty of each person who could afford to do so to give money for the sustenance of those less fortunate. If everyone gave money voluntarily there would, theoretically, be no need for taxation. Annie and her fellows believed that public welfare led to an increase of pauperism, largely because its impersonality ignored the causes of poverty and made no effort to eliminate the instigating problem.

Annie and her organization espoused coupling relief with work, except in cases where work was completely impossible. Even the aged who were on relief were encouraged to do something productive, such as take in an orphaned child, in return; this protected the pride of the aid recipient and motivated him or her to keep well and active too. Annie believed in providing, in addition to work, education—free general education for the children of the poor and industrial education for adults. She felt that a combination of relief, work, and education and a careful analysis of the underlying causes of poverty (intemperance, illness, refusal to work, lack of employment, inability to both work and take care of children) would be effective.

Annie devoted a special section of *How to Help the Poor* to the problems of children of the poor. She was particularly interested in the frequency of delinquency or "moral disease" in children, a subject she discussed in her letters to Abby Morton Diaz.[14] Just what moral disease meant to Annie is uncertain, but presumably it referred to chronic or habitual stealing, lying, insolence, truancy, and probably masturbation and fornication as well. Annie believed that moral disease could be eliminated by moral teaching in school, which was especially vital for the children of the poor, or children at risk, as we might call them today. Abby Morton Diaz thought the causes of moral disease were deeply rooted, perhaps even hereditary. Annie's conviction that environment was the crucial factor gave her an almost missionary zeal toward the children of immigrants; she believed a proper education would make such children "our useful and busy compatriots."

In her discussion of the care of the aged, Annie made a distinction between "worthy" and "unworthy" poor. People "infected with moral disease"—those who refused to work, refused to stop drinking (in cases where intemperance was the cause of poverty), or did not wish to become useful members of society—should be helped only in the almshouse and never given discretionary money. On the other hand, she felt that society should make it possible for an aged person who had lost money through misfortune or had earned too little to save to continue to live at home. Further, she felt that public funds should be used only when there were no friends or relatives to provide support.

Annie inserted a note of personal experience into a section about investigating the poor, stating that knowledge of the poor could be obtained only by skillful searching; she noted, "We have only to see how difficult ladies usually find the business of obtaining proper knowledge of the servants they engage, to understand how unfit volunteers often are for this business" (80). Annie was herself a visitor; it is regrettable that she did not record in her diary more of what she saw on her visits, for her impressions of these individual cases would make fascinating reading.

All in all, Annie's experiences with the poor of Boston had the effect of broadening her social view. She learned that simply attending church and giving money was of little use in a world where people lived in hunger and squalor. Her knowledge of the Vincent de Paul Society enlightened her about Catholics and caused her to compliment them on their handling of their poor. Although she did not advocate total abstinence, she understood the problems caused by liquor in poverty-stricken immigrant families and sought to provide alternatives. She learned about the role of tenement landlords who refused to improve living conditions in aggravating or creating existing poverty.

She came to believe that visitors should be paid professionals and that payment was essential to the dignity of labor, especially for women. She fought against using the position of overseer of the poor to reward political service.

Although *How to Help the Poor* was not published until 1883, it illustrates the maturity and authority that Annie gained through her charity work in the 1870s. For the first time, Annie was exploring new territory, not merely following the footsteps of those who had come before. Perhaps she was too much in awe of and too close to her literary fathers to see beyond them, but no such awe blinded her in the charity field. Annie would have defended Boston's close-knit literary circle to all detractors, but her partial dissociation from it is an unconscious acknowledgment that it may have been suffocatingly close. Viewed in this light, Annie's commitment to social work was a declaration of independence which enhanced her status and extended her sphere of influence.

Wedding portrait of Annie Adams Fields, age twenty. *By permission of Mrs. Benjamin P. Bole.*

James T. Fields at the height of his editorial career, probably in the 1860s. *By permission of the Houghton Mifflin Company.*

Daguerreotype of Annie, one of several similar poses taken by Southworth and Hawes within a few years of her marriage. *By permission of the Metropolitan Museum of Art. Gift of I. N. Phelps Stokes, Edward S. Hawes, Alice Mary Hawes, Marion Augusta Hawes, 1937.*

View of the Fields garden and the Charles River from the drawing room window of 148 Charles Street. *From W. D. Howells*, Literary Friends and Acquaintances *(Harper & Bros., 1901), by courtesy of Harper & Row, Publishers, Inc.*

The Fields residence, 148 Charles Street. *From Edward S. Payne*, Dickens Days in Boston *(Houghton Mifflin, 1927), by permission of the Houghton Mifflin Company.*

Sarah Orne Jewett. *By permission of Special Collections, Miller Library, Colby College.*

John Singer Sargent portrait of Annie Adams Fields at the height of her writing career near the end of the nineteenth century. *By permission of Boston Athenaeum.*

Annie *(left at window)* and Sarah in the Charles Street drawing room. *By permission of the Houghton Library, Harvard University.*

7.

Home and Family

1870–1881

Annie noted in her diary that James's depression and illness had disappeared immediately as a result of his retirement from Fields, Osgood & Co. in 1870 and the *Atlantic* in 1871. Although Fields was only fifty-three when he began arranging his retirement in 1870, his stressful experiences had aged him, and Annie confided to Laura Winthrop Johnson that she feared death could be near.

James had a decade of activity ahead of him, however, and Dickens played a part in inspiring it, as he had with Annie. Toward the end of his friend's visit, Fields had seized one of his manuscripts and read it to the gathering in Dickens's own manner. Delighted, Dickens predicted that Fields would follow him at the podium (AF/*JTF* 255–56). When Fields retired, he turned immediately to lecturing, almost as if he felt a compulsion to imitate, to follow in the footsteps of his dead friend. Although his charisma could not match Dickens's, Fields was a gifted and immensely popular speaker, the most successful in America since Dickens himself.

In 1871 Fields began to write the essays upon which his lectures would be based, a synthesis of his reminiscences of a fading literary era that audiences would find both educational and amusing. Annie helped him with the diaries which she had begun as a record of her husband's success and the literary life of the time. Fields's use of Annie's diaries in his lectures and articles was common knowledge among their friends, although never acknowledged in print. Annie and James had together written an *Atlantic* obituary of Dickens which bore James's name only, and they collaborated on his talks and other articles as well.[1] In this way she continued her role as editorial assistant and business partner.

At first James lectured close to home at schools, colleges, and town halls. However, by 1872 he was lecturing frequently in New York, Philadelphia, and all over New England. He wrote to Annie daily. His notes are loving and affectionate, expressing concern about her health and happiness. He wrote to her from Buffalo, "Don't be without some one near you of Woman Kind, to whom you can speak in the night if you wish to," and he urged her to ask Lissie to visit during his absences (HL n.d.). He worried whenever the mail did not bring his daily letter from Annie.

James's notes to Annie during these trips poignantly illustrate the happiness of their union. One note from Philadelphia, addressed "Dear Birdie," says, "Everybody regrets you did not come and so do I most of all" (HL n.d.). The same note alludes to a running joke which James and Annie shared, that Fields's audiences liked him so well because they mistook him for some other Fields, "Cyrus or Dudly or John F.!" Another note ends, "Only five days more! Wont I dance when I am [well] on my homeward way!" Fields decorated the bottom of the page with a little picture of a man leaping into the air with "148!" written below (HL n.d.). He sympathized from a distance with Annie's nervousness about public speaking: "I know you got handsomely over your talk to the ladies, for I felt it sure as I thought of it yesterday. Tell me all about it though, please."

Two of these notes are especially poignant. One was the letter James had written to Annie when she argued against his suggestion that her work at the North End was endangering her health:

> But my motive you say in your letter, is not a good and sufficient reason, and that it is "very very hard" for you to hear my request in this matter, so, my dear love, do not let me stand in the way of your happiness. . . . It is not for me ever to put a bar between you and inclination. It has always been my desire to see you contented and happy in your duties in life, and to help on so far as I could in wisdom in the helping. The Mission seems to be your magnet, and in God's name, I say, go on and do all the good you can, everywhere.

On their twenty-fifth wedding anniversary, 15 November 1879, only two years before Fields's death, James wrote to Annie that he had received her gift and sent his thanks:

> Thanks my love for all your tenderness and affection. We have been and always mean to be happy as larks. The little bird I sent, fat as [illegible], will tell & chirp and twitter twenty million loves to you. . . . God bless you dear Love & may we be "a long time" yet together is my constant prayer. Our lot is a happy one.

Unfortunately, not a single one of Annie's notes or letters to James survives. It is difficult to be sure without seeing the other side of the correspondence, but James's notes suggest that emotionally he was the more dependent member of the couple. Annie's independence in remaining in Boston, despite James's desire to have her with him, anticipates her later independence in her friendship with Sarah Orne Jewett. Annie occasionally accompanied James on trips of a few days, but except for two long trips west to Chicago and Iowa she usually stayed home.

There were several reasons for this. Annie was very much involved in her charity work, going to the North End on Sundays and Fridays and to the Charity Building at Chardon Street on Tuesdays. The lecture trips were strenuous, leaving James exhausted when he returned. The enervating conditions of travel had not improved since Dickens's trip: the trains were either stuffy and overheated or freezing cold; the food and the accommodations were poor. Despite his reluctance to be separated from Annie, the more James learned about the conditions of such travel, the less he wanted to subject Annie to them. Annie would sometimes stay with friends in Philadelphia when James travelled to his lectures there, but she soon decided that she would rather stay home.

Annie did accompany James on two long trips west in the 1870s. The first of these trips began in September of 1875 and took them through New York City, Rochester, Niagara, and Chicago, where they stayed at the home of Robert Collyer, the Chicago minister who had come to Boston to raise funds after the Chicago fire. With the Chicago rail system at the hub, they spun out and back to little towns and small cities in Illinois, Wisconsin, and Iowa, including such midwestern hot spots as Sterling, Illinois and Beloit, Wisconsin. In Evanston, Illinois, they received a telegram from Annie's brother claiming that their housekeeper had been caught stealing from them, but Annie did not take the accusation seriously, writing in her diary: "We do not believe it nor can we help it at this distance" (9 Oct. 1875). During one of their Chicago layovers Annie wrote a poem about Lake Michigan and sent out an article on charity.

Annie's account of their trip to West Lafayette, Indiana illustrates the conditions they frequently encountered. She vividly described their bedroom in the home of their host, a judge:

> We turned the water faucet and the water came like mud smelling wretchedly. There were 2 chairs in the room one of them was broken, 3 empty cologne bottles, a gas chandelier with a broken globe, a paper on the walls with a black hole broken through it into some mysterious blackness which had been pasted over and broken through the second time; a soiled tapestry carpet on the floor, a good mirror, a large bedstead and good bed covered with cotton sheets which had been torn and the slits run up, but the pillow cases and bolster cover were of fine ruffled linen upon which I found we were expected to sleep—. (24 Oct. 1875)

After characterizing the lady of the house as cordial but having an "undeveloped nature," the audience as being in a "comatose" condition, the refreshments as "indegestible [sic] wine jelly," and the water closet as a "portion of an Irish hovel," Annie surprisingly concluded that "the kindness and devotion of these good people cannot be overstated[.] Everything possible for them to do for our comfort was done." Little wonder that Annie declined to accompany James most of the time.

The summers of the 1860s stand out as a time of creativity and blessed escape from household responsibilities for Annie. Up until 1875 Annie and James boarded during the summer, which meant no supervision of servants, no guests, and plenty of time to write and read. Most of Annie's nature poems, about wildflowers and the ocean, were writtten on her walks in Mancheester. She didn't have to entertaiin her husband's clients and their many friends, supervisee aa single servant, or fulfiill herr moral duty to the poor.

Most middle- and upper-class Bostonians took long summer vacations at the various seaside resorts nearby. During the first years of their marriage, Annie left James in Boston and accompanied her family or friends to a cool ocean town; James slipped away to join her as business permitted. Their first summer spot was Pigeon Cove; later, they sometimes went to Rye Beach. They regularly spent several weeks at a farmhouse near Campton, New Hampshire, where they boarded with the Willey family and took long walks every day. The charm of this spot was that none of their acquaintances were there; this became an increasingly important criterion for vacations. Annie's mother and sister Sarah went to North Conway in the summers, and Louisa and the Beals went to Nahant, which was always full of neighbors from Boston and Cambridge, notably Longfellow. Annie and James paid brief visits to relatives but eventually chose for their own summer home the less populous village of Manchester,

Massachusetts, a little fishing town just north of Salem, Massachusetts. Manchester was also the summer home of the Bartols, with whom the Fieldses had gone to Pigeon Cove; the James and Dana families; and a number of Boston's resident actors and actresses, including the Booths.[2]

Annie and James boarded with the same woman every summer in what Annie called "Manchester-by-the-sea." She kept telling Jamie that if they built their own house, their pleasant summers would end; family and friends would expect to be invited, and soon their Manchester life would be just like their Boston life. Knowing that James could not withhold invitations, she wanted to protect both of their vacations.

In Manchester Annie walked on the beaches alone or with James, strolled through the Bartol woods with a book, sat and sunbathed on the rocks, searched for wildflowers, went swimming. Annie often posed for the artist daughters of summer neighbors, Elizabeth Bartol and Elizabeth Greene. Annie often recorded her love for the country and her wish to live there. She liked to think of herself as a child of nature, a Romantic or a Transcendentalist, although in fact she lived her entire life in Boston. Pigeon Cove, Campton, and Manchester were the sites of many of Annie's happiest days.

Annie's reluctance to own a vacation home was justified. She wrote in her diary, "I confessed to R. H. Dana [Jr.] . . . my enjoyment at floating about here without thought of ownership—Ah! Said he, 'My father has but one objection to this beautiful place and that is he owns it'" (22 July 1871). While boarding, Annie was able to relax and to read and write without thought of supervising meals and servants. She knew that housekeeping was inimical to her writing (and any other improving activity), and though she was resigned to it for most of the year, in the summer her time was her own.

The Fieldses had considered renting the Bartols's house in the summer of 1872 before discovering that the rent would be one thousand dollars. Annie was relieved when they decided to board again; after helping her sister Louisa put her house and garden in Nahant into shape for the season, she commented, "What a job! Blessed be nothing!" (May 1872). The summers passed peacefully until 1874, when James purchased a site and they "Talked and thought and examined cottages. Came up with Mr. Cabot the architect, a good man, whose kindness and interest pleased me well" (14 June 1874).

The building process was finally set in motion by a sequence of disasters that took place at their boarding house. On 11 July, they arrived at the house to find everything changed:

> We found Mrs Dame our landlady very ill-disposed to receive us as her only maid a kind
> of adopted child Mary, a good little soul as ever breathed [was] at the point of death from
> hemorrhage[.] Our reception and the lack of home feeling about the house has quickened
> our desire to have a house of our own into a necessity. I am really thankful for this because
> I have resisted as long as possible the idea of a second house however simple, for two
> people. (12 July 1874)

By 18 July, the Fieldses had inspected their site, the highest hill in the area, only about a quarter-mile from the beach and a half-mile from the village. The house would sit with a short hill at the front and a long steep hill at the back, where Annie would plant rock gardens that kept six gardeners busy.[3]

The crisis at Mrs. Dame's, the Fieldses' disagreement with the Darrahs over the allocation of rooms, and Mrs. Murphy's harassment convinced Annie and James that a cottage of their own was now a necessity. By August, they had named their site Thunderbolt Hill and were proceeding with preparations. They furnished the house with "old furniture" (antiques) for less than a thousand dollars. On 31 August stone cutting for the foundation of the house was begun.

Because James was home so seldom in 1874 and 1875 the task of supervision fell entirely to Annie. They corresponded about the project, but James was content to leave everything to Annie, telling her that "I am sure what you have done about the house matters at Manchester will be all right" (HL n.d.). Later, in regard to the purchase of a dining room carpet, he wrote, "Always your judgement is better than mine & you must get what seems best and all" (HL n.d.). But Annie wrote to her friend Laura:

> I do not like building—I knew I should not. We neither of us have any time which we wish to give to it and the architect and builder instead of settling things for us, keeps asking us questions. . . . This is but a mood, of course, but "J." is away and wishes me to decide—. (26 Oct. 1874)

The house, which was built among large boulders at the top of a hill overlooking the sea, was ready by July of 1875. The site was originally bare, but Annie covered it with trees and shrubs; it is now nearly a wilderness. Although the house with a gambrel roof was called a cottage (as people in the Adirondacks called their summer houses "camps"), it would be considered a large family home today. The Fieldses used untrimmed trees for the pillars of the front porch, having surrounded three sides of the house with huge porches.

Downstairs are a library, parlor, dining room, and kitchen, although the kitchen was originally in the basement. The second floor contains four bedrooms, one known to have been Annie's and two assigned by tradition to Sarah Jewett and Willa Cather. On the third floor under the slanted roof are a kind of bunk room for servants and two tiny rooms for the cook and another servant. The back slope has remnants of beautifully designed rock gardens and paths with strategically placed benches for the uphill climb. Annie brought many cuttings for this garden from England and spent hours working in it alongside a number of gardeners she hired locally.

On 5 July Annie wrote in her "own little book-room" for the first time. She was pleased with her efforts and more optimistic about the house:

> We cannot recover from the wonder of it, and the beauty of it too. It is an ideal country house to look at and I shall try to make it such in reality—a place where dear "J." shall find leisure and I also for he wil [sic] not be happy without this—I shall soon take to the comfort of having a housekeeper as the duck takes to water I see that. (5 July 1875)

Things did not turn out as expected. Laura Winthrop Johnson came to visit right away and Annie found that owning a summer home obliged her to entertain overnight guests.

Her time for reading and writing was lost in "long wasteful sessions of talk." She suffered from "utter depression of spirit" as she saw "the precious time going going" (19 July 1875). One day the servants overslept and all quit when Annie reprimanded them. "Servants do not like it" [in Manchester], she said, "the solitude & silence seem to weigh upon them" (31 July 1875). Even James found it "impossible to write here, he says—He feels the care and responsibility much more than I wish he could—. . . . It is not a profitable thing for us to waste ourselves and our substance in receiving company all summer" (24 July 1875).

But receive company all summer is exactly what they did. Besides Mrs. Lodge and Susan Hale, who came to work with Annie on their new charity plans, they had an almost unbelievable number of visitors, and Annie (bitterly) listed in her diary those who stayed for one night or longer in the summer of 1875. The list includes, in addition to Laura Johnson and her daughter, Elizabeth Stuart Phelps, James Freeman Clarke, Frederick Lehmann, Anna Leonowens, Mr. and Mrs. Andrew Lang, Bayard Taylor, Whittier, the senior Henry Jameses, Osgood, Bret Harte, Lucy Larcom, and numerous relatives. Annie wrote to Laura that despite "the loveliness of our surroundings . . . I wish I were brave enough to sell the place but I fear that Jamie will be sorry" (20 July 1876). Annie's 1876 list was nearly twice as long, adding the Collyers; Dickens's illustrator, Sol Etyinge; the sculptor Anne Whitney; Dinah Mulock Craik's husband; Celia Thaxter; and the governor of Michigan, who came to talk charity.

Despite the extraordinary number of visitors and the extra work, the house proved to be a success and Annie spent nearly forty more summers there, most of them with Sarah Orne Jewett, who first visited the Manchester house, briefly called Gambrel Cottage, in 1879. Annie spent so much time there that some scholars have assumed she moved there.[4] She left Thunderbolt Hill to her nephew Boylston, and although it is no longer in the family, the house stands as a monument to Annie's taste and judgment.

Although Annie had changed her priorities from writing to charity work, her diaries during these years still reveal her "conflict between the desire to know and the desire to do," as Annie phrased it:

> Have read a brilliant article by H. James Jr. in which he says of Gautier, he learned one thing from his career: notably this, that a man's chief purpose in life is to learn to play his intellectual instrument and to bring it to the farthest point of perfection—!! . . . Let us see this intellectual instrument brought to its greatest perfection; if the instrument belongs to a writer it is surely true, if he be a musician it is equally true, why not if he be a philanthropist or even a woman!!! . . . the instrument may be tuned in various ways and may be kept in tune in other ways than by the study of books. (6 April 1873)

Annie applied this analysis to her friend Mrs. Caswell, a missionary who worked with Annie among the Boston poor. Annie described Mrs. Caswell as "a distinct case of the intellectual instrument being brought into its finest perfection by continual use . . . for a moral purpose." By honoring the missionary, Annie seemed to be closing the door on perfecting one "intellectual instrument" and opening the door to perfecting another.

Annie felt so strongly about the need to achieve personal perfection that she struggled continuously to clarify and define the philosophies she lived by. One of her diaries begins with an epigraph from Goethe's *Wilhelm Meister:*

> I reverence the individual who understands distinctly what he wishes; who unweariedly advances; who knows the means conducive to his object, and can seize and use them. How far his object may be great or little is the next consideration with me. (Howe *Mem.* 132–34)

She was also struck by Aristotle's statement that "Virtue is concerned with action, art with production." But according to Annie, "The problem of life is how to harmonize the two—either career must become prominent according to the nature of the individual." Thus Annie was led to write down "what I wish to do in life":

> I discern in myself; 1st, the desire to serve others unselfishly according to the example of our dear Lord; 2nd, the desire to cultivate my powers in order to achieve the highest life possible to me as an individual existence by stimulating thought to its finest issues through reflection, observation, and by profound and ceaseless study of the written thoughts of the wisest in every age and every clime.

This order of goals clearly reverses Annie's priorities of the previous decade. She went on to describe what she considered her three duties in life, inadvertently revealing her continued ambivalence toward them:

> As a woman and a wife my first duty lies at home; to make that beautiful; to stimulate the lives of others by exchange of ideas, and the repose of domestic life; to educate children and servants.
>
> 2nd, To be conversant with the very poor; to visit their homes; to be keenly alive to their sufferings; never allowing the thought of their necessities to sleep in our hearts.
>
> 3rd, By day and night, morning and evening, in all times and seasons when strength is left to us, to study, study, study.
>
> Because I have just put this last, it does not stand last in importance; but to put it first and write out the plan for study which my mind naturally selects would be to ignore that example of perfect life in which I humbly believe [Jesus], and to return to the lives of the ancients, so fine in their results to the few, so costly to the many. But in the removed periods of existence, when solitude may be our blessed portion, what a joy to fly to communion with the sages and live and love with them!
>
> I have written this out for the pleasure of seeing if "I distinctly understand what I wish."

Mrs. Fields continued to "fly to communion with the sages" in the time which remained to her after taking care of her husband and home and ministering to the poor.

As a result of her charity work, Annie settled into a more comfortable relationship with literature. Her friendships with the Ticknor & Fields authors became less intense, and Annie grew closer to women like herself. Although she had befriended women clients of Ticknor & Fields such as Rebecca Harding Davis, she had had little opportunity to get to know some of the active, but less exclusively literary, women of Boston. In the 1870s, Annie began the close identification with women which dominated her life from 1881 on. She began to champion women's causes and became much more aware of the political and social injustices that limited women. In 1871 she attended a meeting to determine the best way of using a sum of money given to Massachusetts for the higher education of women. Annie, who wholeheartedly supported the idea, was amused by the misgivings of two famous advocates of domestic science:

> Mrs Stowe and Miss Beecher are both filled with alarm at the maidenly scholar guiltless of all a maiden needs to know in her career as a woman which the present colleges and schools are developing and the question is cannot education in the training of young children, in the making of garments, care of a garden & in short the care of a home be included as a highly independent [adjunct?] of a woman's university? (Dec. 1871)

In April of 1872 Annie noted only that "the Women's College stands still," but in fact she had been busy. Annie's contribution to the plan involved setting up lectures and eventually a lecture series on English literature for which her husband was the main speaker.[5]

These talks were intended to gauge the number of women who would enroll in a university, and perhaps to test their faithfulness as well. A large number of women attending a series of lectures that was advertised as a preliminary to a college course would help to sell the idea to those in authority. The women involved were aiming high: they wanted Harvard to admit women, and it was toward this end they worked.

James's lectures succeeded but progress toward the women's college was slow. In September of 1876 James Freeman Clarke, one of the first elected trustees to support co-education, told Annie that "President Eliot [of Harvard] though opposing the education of women was gradually admitting them to the college classes." Mr. Clarke thought that "In the end Harvard also would be emancipated from prejudice" (26 Sept. 1876). In February of 1877 Annie reported going to "the State House to assist in the Incorporation of the Boston University Women's Education Assn." The Harvard Annex (later Radcliffe) opened in 1879, but nearly a hundred years passed before Harvard admitted women on an equal footing with men.[6]

In late 1876 Annie took an important step in bringing together a number of the Boston women for whom writing was an important, but not full-time, occupation. Annie wrote to Laura Winthrop Johnson:

> I have had no very new experience except the starting of a small club of ladies interested in literature to read and discuss tentative work, if I may call it so, by way of distinction from work positively launched or ready for the press, I think we shall have a very good time together. Elizabeth Phelps began by reading a portion of a new and unrevised story. I must tell you more of this another time. (26 Jan. 1877)

The club had ten members and met at Charles Street every Tuesday. Annie proudly listed the members of the 1877 group and their contributions, noting that Elizabeth Phelps had named the club "the Pandora," probably a tribute to Annie, whose major effort was the translation of Goethe's "Pandora" which she read to the group on 30 January 1877. The list gives a good idea of the kinds of talent present in Annie's circle:

1 Mrs K[ate] G[annet] Wells—did not read
2 Mrs Helen Bell   Sang her own music
3 Mrs Julia Ward Howe   Read Western Tour and Poems
4 Mrs Diaz   Sketches of Country Life
5 Mrs Martin   Emanuel Deutsch and "Mordechai"
6 Miss Maria Weston Chapman sent a sonnet but could not leave home
7 Miss Townsend   Greek Theatre
8 Mrs Fairchild   Strolling Players of England
9 Mrs Dresel   Critique from German on Goethe's Pandora
10 Miss Larcom   83 Waltham St   She came but twice
11 Miss Manning   Description of Couture[7]
12 Miss Whitney   Dissartation [sic] on French art
13 Miss Preston   27 St James Av   story (did not read[)]
14 Miss E. S. Phelps   story and poem
15 Annie Fields   translation of Goethe's Pandora

Annie's notes indicate that she also intended to invite Mrs. Apthorp, Miss Palfrey, Miss Frothingham, Mrs. Goddard, Lucretia Hale, Mrs. Waterston, and Mrs. Clement.

As Karen J. Blair has noted in her book *The Clubwoman as Feminist,* literary clubs like this one helped many women work their way into the mainstream of society— from literary clubs they went on to found political organizations for women and to become board members of previously all-male groups. Annie mentioned an instance of this in a letter to Laura a year after the club began: "Miss Preston read us one night a portion of a new story and Mrs. K. G. Wells a paper on Libraries She having been chosen on the Public Library Com. The first woman in the country who has had that honor!" (2 Feb. 1878). In 1878, the group added Celia Thaxter, Miss Hawes, Miss [Susan] Hale, and Mrs. Eichberg, and its contributions included the paper on libraries mentioned above, a translation from "the Russian of Tourguenieff," and "a paper on Liszt."

Sharing her work with her peers helped Annie rebuild confidence in herself as a writer. She had continued to write poetry in the first years of the 1870s and occasionally mentioned in her diary a poem in hand or recently completed. She noted proudly that Longfellow liked "Little Guinever" and that James read her long poem on the Shakers, *The Children of Lebanon,* to a group of friends at Manchester. More often, however, she expressed her frustration with her work. James was evidently too honest a critic or too experienced a reader to supply the kind of praise Annie needed. She was disappointed with his response to a long narrative poem called "Miriam's Life," which she had been working on for months:

> Jamie read Miriam's life—and finds it *pleasant!!* After all the work I have put in it this is indeed damning with faint praise! Doubtless it is all it deserves and on the whole I thank God! Success I fear would make me unbearable. Failure with its endless striving, endless reading, will doubtless carry me beyond this present—. (9 Sept. 1876)

Annie wrote a few other narrative poems, such as "Alice of the Hills," but except for her first romance about the young Shaker lovers who were forced to leave their home, none of them was published. During the years of the women's literary club, Annie concentrated her energy on translations rather than original work, perhaps because she was trying to learn German. The more casual environment of the literary group enabled Annie to see writing as a pleasure rather than a chore; as she wrote to Laura Winthrop Johnson about the Pandora: "It is a very agreeable Club. This is my diversion—The visiting is my occupation" (2 Feb. 1878).

The decade of the 1870s was marked by a number of scandals and tragedies that affected the Fieldses through close friends. In September of 1869 the *Atlantic* published Mrs. Stowe's article "The True Story of Lady Byron's Life," which exposed Byron's philandering—including his passion for his half-sister Augusta—to the public for the first time. Howells had printed the story while the Fieldses were in Europe, and the *Atlantic* lost thousands of subscriptions as a result. In 1874 the Fieldses awoke one morning to the discovery that their home had been burgled the night before; a silver tea set which had been a wedding present was stolen and a number of sculptures were broken. Far more serious was the scandal involving Henry Ward Beecher, Harriet Beecher Stowe's brother. Beecher was accused of committing adultery with a married woman in his parish.[8] Since Annie had been convinced of Beecher's innocence and defended him in her letters to Laura Winthrop Johnson, her faith in human nature was sadly shaken when she came to believe that Beecher was guilty.

Annie helped Celia Thaxter endure a series of misfortunes throughout the decade. Her marriage grew increasingly unbearable and because her eldest son, Karl, was mentally ill and difficult to care for, she felt compelled to spend most of her time in near isolation on Appledore Island in the Isles of Shoals. Because she saw few people outside her immediate family, she developed a close relationship with a group of five Norwegians, two men and three women, all related by either blood or marriage, who settled on neighboring Smutty Nose Island. In 1875 a man who had fished with and worked for the Norwegians rowed to the island on a night when the men were away, intending to rob the house while the women slept; when one of the women awoke and recognized him, he brutally murdered her and another of the women with an ax which happened to be lying nearby. The third woman escaped. Celia was deeply affected by this tragedy and eventually wrote an account of it for the *Atlantic*.

And, if that were not enough, it remained to Celia to discover the body of artist William Morris Hunt in a shallow pool not far from her home on the Isles of Shoals; his death was presumed to be a suicide. Annie and James had purchased several of Hunt's paintings and befriended him and his wife, Rooshue, both eccentric and difficult human beings. A fire in Hunt's studio had destroyed much of his life's work in 1872, and the Hunts's marital problems eventually forced a separation. Annie had mentioned Hunt's despondency in her diary not long before his death.

Then, early in January of 1877, Annie's mother became seriously ill. Annie visited her mother daily throughout January, but late in the month she seemed to recuperate. In February Annie wrote to Laura that

> The truth is mother's condition is so critical, yet she remains so nearly the same that we
> forget to count the time. My sister Lizzy is here and with two sisters and the nurses all

the time there is little remaining for anybody really to do, but her disease is chiefly of the nerves and her nights have been painfully restless. (26 Feb. 1877)

A Dr. Nelson, apparently a hypnotist, came at night and was able to calm Mrs. Adams without the use of drugs. In early March Annie wrote that "while my dear mother is so ill every extra thought and moment is directed her way if I am not by her side" (7 March 1877). A few weeks later she recorded an emergency summons by her sister: "Sarah came down to say mother is delirious—She and the nurse are very tired and they need assistance. They particularly wanted J. so he has gone" (21 March).

On 29 March, in a wobbly handwriting that reflects her distress, Annie wrote, "Mother died this morning at 6 a.M. [sic] at this writing (early in the afternoon) it already seems an eternity—so surely is time marked by feeling & experience and not by deeds done or moments counted." Eloquently, she left a page blank, and although she wrote to Laura in the interval, the next entry does not appear until 11 April, when Annie recorded spending the day at the Chardon Street office. She wrote enigmatically, "How strangely certain experiences bring you nearer or distance you utterly from former relatives." Annie spent time with Celia Thaxter and worked on her dramatic poem about the mother-daughter relationship of Demeter and Persephone, commenting that "Now and then I work upon *Demeter* and ponder it deeply" (11 April 1877).

Although Annie had seldom mentioned Mrs. Adams in her diary or in her letters, she was deeply grieved by her death. She struggled to complete "The Return of Persephone," which she dedicated to the memory of her mother. In the poem Annie dramatizes the intimacy of the bond between mother and daughter and the conflict which arises when the rival for her daughter's love appears. By late December of 1877, Annie still felt forlorn, and she wrote to Laura: "My sisters are so scattered now, that when he [JTF] is away I feel quite alone in the world—only in a narrow sense however, for I feel the warmth of love my friends hold for me wherever they are." Annie's loss is reflected in this comment about her friend: "Celia Thaxter has just lost her loving mother—the one being who could never turn or be swayed in her love towards her."

Annie's connection with illness and loss was just beginning. A few months after her mother's death Annie noted in her diary that James was ill. Her anxiety, although decreased, was still apparent when she wrote a few weeks later, "We are very happy—J. is pretty well—that is enough for me" (19 July 1877). But Annie's diaries offer no eyewitness account of her feelings, because the long, uninterrupted sequence of blue books, begun in 1863, ends in August of 1877 with the account of the Fieldses' last month of the summer at Manchester.

James had been the victim of a variety of illnesses throughout the 1870s. In October of 1873 he had "water-on-the-knee" and was forced to sit idle and wear a wooden splint. The following January, he had "a bad cold on the lungs" which lasted through February. In March he suffered from neuralgia. By April he seemed to be back to normal and between 1874 and 1877 he travelled constantly, mainly to eastern cities and towns, including New York, Philadelphia, and Baltimore.

By 1877 Fields's health was again precarious; he suffered from headaches, exhaustion, and colds during his travels. The lameness in his knee returned and his wrist became lame as well. A sore throat and weakened lungs plagued him constantly. Then, in May of 1879 the first serious sign of trouble appeared: on an overnight lecture trip to Wellesley College Fields suffered a brain hemorrhage and collapsed. Annie was telegraphed for and she brought him home, but a second hemorrhage occurred during a trip to Manchester to rest. Annie wrote later of the joy she had experienced during the long days she spent reading to him during his recovery.

A year later, in the spring of 1880, Fields felt well enough to give a few lectures but a third hemorrhage followed. In early 1881, a few days after a lecture, he suffered a massive heart attack. Annie stayed home with him and read to him once again. He appeared to recover and in April he began to go out, drive with friends, and visit his old offices.

On Sunday, 23 April 1881, Fields visited the Aldriches, who lived across the street, and accompanied Annie to her sister Louisa's for tea. During the evening visit of a Mrs. Giles Lodge[9] and Celia Thaxter, a fire alarm and the nearby fire brought Fields to the front window of the library. Aldrich waved at Fields from the street. Suddenly James collapsed and had to be helped back to his chair. Annie began to read in an effort to calm him, but he suffered another attack, fell forward, and died with Annie by his side. He was sixty-three years old.

When Whittier heard of the death of his friend Fields, he wrote to Annie:

> I have just got Celia Thaxter's telegram—the second one—and my great fear is realized, I am stunned; my heart is too full; I cannot write what I feel. No man has been to me what he has been. He has been my best friend—kind, helpful, generous, always: What a happy, genial temperament he had! What a capacity for enjoyment and making others share it! How all the sweet breezes of life seemed to blow over him! (WL 3: 434; 25 April 1881)

The Boston newspapers provide accounts of James's funeral and of the many tributes which were paid to him. The Boston Mercantile Association, whose membership contained hundreds of his friends, held a separate memorial service to pay him tribute. The funeral itself was held at the church of the Fields's friend and Manchester neighbor Cyrus A. Bartol. Although many called at 148 Charles Street to express their condolences, Annie saw only the oldest and dearest friends. Celia Thaxter came to stay with Annie immediately after James's death; other friends who called at this time included Longfellow, Holmes, Whittier, and Sarah Orne Jewett. Annie's sister Lissie probably came from Baltimore, and her sister Louisa Beal and brother Boylston lived close by.

On 16 May 1881, Whittier wrote to Annie again, saying:

> But does it not seem to thee that God has been exceeding good to thee in giving thee so much love, and so much love in return for so large a portion of thy life?—Blessed among women, the sweetest and truest earthly happiness has been thine. (WL 3:435n)

Immediately after James's funeral, Annie plunged herself into writing a memorial for Fields. By August, the biography was well under way, and Longfellow mentioned the project in a letter to Elizabeth Stuart Phelps:

> Mrs. Fields you have doubtless visited this summer. How lonely she must be, and how happy it is for her that she can devote herself to writing a life of her husband. I am truly glad of it, both for her sake and for ours. The work could not be in better hands. (WL 4:728; 21 Aug. 1881)

Annie asked her publisher, Thomas Bailey Aldrich, to set her draft in type before he read it. She emphasized her desire for a truthful account of any improvements which could be made:

> I should like to have three copies struck off because I am going to ask Dr. Holmes to look at it. I shall of course ask from you dear Mr. Aldrich the greatest frankness feeling sure that you would consider it an unkindness to *him* rather than to me to allow me to print anything too much, anything in bad taste, or any slips of grammar and construction.
>
> I believe the faults I fear, take rank in my mind as I have instinctively placed them above—
>
> First; I fear too much material; to put in unnecessary matter. I should prefer to strike out whole pages to having redundancy anywhere, or repetition of his own work in less worthy form.
>
> Second: bad taste in saying things which are either put in a bad manner or better not be put at all—
>
> Third slips of all kinds—I am very careless—, not willingly but sometimes putting off the evil day of corrections—or much worse failing to see them altogether! (19 June 1881)

In her anxiety, Annie sent Whittier a copy of Holmes's comments about the book and asked his advice about the mode of its publication. He responded:

> I do not doubt the book will be one of interest to the public generally: but if there is any hesitation in thy mind respecting it[,]—it would be safest to print a limited number of copies for private circulation at first. I, for my part, should unhesitatingly trust the matter to thy own judgment. I know of no one who could better decide what should be published and what omitted.
>
> Our friends Aldrich and Whipple would be safe counsellors if thee see fit to consult them. But, I do not see why thy own sense of propriety and fitness is not better than theirs. (WL 3:440; 27 Sept. 1881)

While to Elizabeth Stuart Phelps, Whittier wrote:

> I think Annie Fields cannot yet bear to talk of her great sorrow and loss and is nervously afraid that her old friends will speak of it or allude to it even remotely. I can understand it. I have felt just in that way. The heart knoweth its own bitterness, and, at times, neither friend nor stranger can intermediate therewith. (WL 3:444; 23 Feb. 1881)

When finished, Annie's book was called *James T. Fields: Biographical Notes and*

Personal Sketches, and it had appeared by November of 1881. A four-page review of the book in the *Dial* (by the Fieldses' friend Robert Collyer of Chicago) was favorable but more in the nature of a belated eulogy than a review. Collyer praised Mrs. Fields for having written a biography, not a "threnody," and for her tact in refraining from mention of living friends. Of the presentation of Fields's character, Collyer found this fault:

> We do not find any adequate emphasis . . . of the rugged strength, as of granite or Swedish iron, which lay within the man whose life, to the apprehension of those who could merely see what lay on the surface, was only sweet and refreshing as a queen's garden. (203)

Entirely different was the review of the English journal, the *Athenaeum.* After praising Fields's memoirs, *Yesterdays with Authors* (1872), the journal commented that beyond these memoirs there

> is not much that the public cares to know. The sensible thing would have been to reprint that book with an introductory biographical sketch and a portrait. As it is, this book is a biography with much that would have really been of value omitted, and much that is of no value at all inserted. (440)

After inferring that the anonymous author was Mrs. Fields, the reviewer remarked acidly: "In any case no one can think it well done" (440). Specifically, the reviewer criticized the inclusion of irrelevant passages from the letters of famous authors and of unedited quotations from diaries which he found "trivial and unworthy of being printed." While justified in his statement that the book is "weakened and injured by . . . unimportant matter," the next complaint, that Mrs. Fields printed a letter from "poor Mrs. Hawthorne on her husband's death which the public had no right whatever to see," is harder to understand. The fault lay not with Mrs. Fields but with the extravagance of the letter itself, which had "an unnatural exultation of feeling with which it is difficult to sympathize."

Although Howells had been planning to write a review for the *Atlantic,* he was ill when it was needed and despite his belief that the review had been assigned, none appeared. He wrote only briefly of the book: "The reading gave me a sad but constant pleasure: it kept dear Mr. Fields continually before me; I saw him, I heard him speak and laugh. Could I say more in praise?" (*Sel. Letters* 2:301; 10 Dec. 1881).

The question of whether Annie's book was an adequate biography, as opposed to a sentimental memoir, is touched upon by Longfellow in a letter to George Washington Greene. Longfellow had applauded Mrs. Fields's decision to write a biography, and seemed to have felt that she would do well; yet, in this letter, written after the book was published, Longfellow was undoubtedly expressing his belief that another, more professional biography should be written:

> I do not know who is to write a life of Fields. No letters ever passed between us, only little notes.

Howells has been ill with a fever, but is recovering. He would be the best man, if he felt like it, for a biography of Fields. Mrs. F. has already published her "Reminiscences," which are very interesting, and written with good taste and judgement. A difficult task, well done. (*Letters* 6:750; 28 Nov. 1881)

To what extent was Annie's book an adequate biography, not in terms of modern standards of scholarship, according to which it is certainly badly flawed, but in terms of the standards of her own day? In all respects, she was in tune with the standards for biography of the time, which held that authorial modesty and respect for living friends and authors were of foremost importance. Since Fields was among the first of his group to die, avoiding all mention of living friends and authors inevitably resulted in distortion. Annie herself had contributed significantly to James's success, yet conventional modesty prevented her from mentioning herself.

It must be admitted that Annie was not equal to the task of presenting such a massive amount of material. Her letter to Aldrich accurately describes the book's failings and she sought help from numerous advisors (Whittier, Holmes, Whipple, and Aldrich), but none of them had offered to take the book in hand, almost as if everyone assumed a lack of professionalism. In its favor, the book contains a wealth of information about Fields, is no worse than the vast majority of similar "life and letters" volumes, and was superior to some; as a reviewer commented, Mrs. Fields's ability to confine herself to one volume instead of two was almost by itself an indication of merit.

Biography was more a matter of sentiment than of scholarly value in those days and wives often undertook biographies of their husbands, despite Edmund Gosse's observation that the wife as biographer is "the triumph of the unfittest."[10] For Annie the roles of wife and biographer were especially difficult to separate. Her marriage to Fields had paradoxically both propelled her into the literary world and kept her aloof from it. His death made it possible for Annie to become a fully participating member of the "little world of Boston letters."

The years between 1870 and 1881 had been a decade of change and separation for James and Annie, but they had also been happy years. They had worked together on James's successful memoirs, published in 1872 as *Yesterdays with Authors,* and on his essays, published in 1877 as *Underbrush* and dedicated to Annie. They had gained new friends in the Clemenses, the Aldriches, and Sarah Orne Jewett and had continued their friendships with the Emersons, the Howells, the Stowes, Whittier, Celia Thaxter, and many others. The success Annie achieved in her charity work must have been gratifying to James as well as to Annie. They had taken long trips together in the middle of the decade and enjoyed vacations in Campton, the White Mountains, the Shaker villages, and other rural spots as well as Manchester. Annie became a widow in the midst of her life, after twenty-seven years of rich love; one is almost grateful that Annie's intimate feelings about this time were either unwritten or destroyed. All she allowed to remain of her and James's correspondence were some forty short love notes.

With James's death, Annie, at forty-six, ended one era of her life and began another. She had been blessed with one deeply satisfying relationship and would have another.

But in the interval, this note to Laura Johnson, written on her forty-seventh birthday, probably expressed the isolation she must have been feeling:

> I feel as if it were impossible for me to write to anyone just now & I see no one. I am packed up for Manchester whither I go on this my birthday! My tender love to you all—Your Annie Fields. (6 June 1881)

8.
A New Kind of Partnership
1881–1886

Childless and too independent to live with relatives, Annie undoubtedly found herself lonely after James's death. That changed in the winter of 1882 when Sarah Orne Jewett came to live with Annie in Boston; Annie was forty-eight and Sarah was thirty-three. Jewett's story "Mr. Bruce" had been accepted by William Dean Howells for the *Atlantic* in 1869, and she had probably met the Fieldses not long after that. Since she lived in South Berwick, Maine, less than sixty miles north and slightly east of Boston as the crow flies, Sarah was close enough to visit Boston often for social and literary events.

Although Sarah Jewett may have been invited over initially as a matter of routine hospitality, she was a young woman of unusual charm. Her manner retained much of that of a child, and she was a person who quickly became friends with kindred spirits of any age. Fields would have liked her immediately, and his jovial, warm, gregarious manner would have pleased Sarah, who was shy but always ready to find father figures or brothers in such unintimidating men as Fields and Whittier. By 1881 Sarah was the author of three books of stories, including the novel-like *Deephaven,* but she was still a comparative newcomer to Boston literary society.

No one knows exactly when the friendship between Jewett and the Fieldses became intimate, but Annie wrote to Sarah in 1877 during her mother's illness and Sarah came to Manchester to visit in the summer of 1879. It is possible that even from the beginning Sarah's feelings toward Annie were intense. Since her adolescence Sarah had shared close, companionable friendships with a number of women friends, and Annie was in many ways her ideal. Intelligent, talented, and influential, Annie would have appeared to Sarah much as James must have appeared to Annie at the time of their marriage. Sarah was more than willing to abandon, at least temporarily, her Maine home to share 148 Charles Street with Annie Fields.

The passage of time has made it difficult to remember that in 1881 Annie held a far more prominent position in Boston literary life than Sarah. The pre-eminent literary hostess of the day, Annie could introduce Sarah to all the writers she admired, including Tennyson, who disliked American literary tourists. By living with Fields, Jewett enjoyed the advantage of conversation with and exposure to the best creative minds of the time. She also benefitted from the advice, both editorial and practical, of a woman who, although not a successful writer herself, was extremely knowledgeable about many aspects of both magazine and book publishing.

Yet, as became increasingly clear as the years went by, Sarah had a great deal to offer Annie as well. While Sarah may have been Annie's protégée initially, she gained confidence in herself while living in Boston and developed as both a writer and a critic. Sarah proved to be a stabilizing influence of the sort that James had been: an anchor from which Annie could safely depart to do her work every day. At a time when it was more difficult for independent women to find satisfactory relationships with men, social mores made it easier for adult women to be friends.

The friendship seems, at first, a more natural one for Sarah than for Annie. Except for her father and nephew Theodore, most of Sarah's important relationships had been with women. Her father was her first love, a genial doctor who took her with him on his calls and made her his companion when she was too much of an invalid to attend school. Even as a child, Sarah had suffered from the arthritis (she called it rheumatism) which continued to plague her throughout her life. Sarah's father instilled in her a love of books and reading and of the simple country folk about whom she would write.

Sarah knew early in her life that marriage and a family were not what she wanted. Instead she developed with girls and women a series of close friendships of the schoolgirl kind, but more passionate. Many of her books, including *Deephaven, Betty Leicester's Christmas,* and *Country of the Pointed Firs,* document the importance of women friends in her life and her sense that the conventional destiny of heterosexual marriage was not suited to her. Whether one chooses to call Jewett's sexual orientation "lesbian" depends largely upon one's definition, but the word seems inappropriate and part of a later era; the earlier terms "romantic friendship" and "Boston marriage" seem more apt. And if the modern term seems inappropriate for Sarah, it is even more so for Annie. Even so tame a description of a lesbian as that of Blanche Wiesen Cook—"Women who love women, who choose women to nurture and support and to create a living environment in which to work creatively and independently"—cannot be applied to Annie Fields at the time of her husband's death.[1] While Annie later came to be "woman-centered" to a large extent, even at the end of her life she welcomed young writers of both sexes with equal pleasure.

For Annie, sharing her life with Jewett was more an accident of congeniality and fate than a conscious or radical choice. The most important people in Annie's life prior to 1882 were her husband and Charles Dickens, followed by Laura Winthrop Johnson, Celia Thaxter, Harriet Beecher Stowe, Whittier, and Longfellow. An intimate friendship with a woman was not inevitable for Annie as it was for Sarah, but nevertheless it is easy to understand in the context of her previous friendships and of the choices available to her. Annie and James were true companions throughout their married life; the high degree of satisfaction Annie had found in her first marriage and the Victorian suspicion of remarriage might have made her reluctant to marry again.

Remarriage might have proved difficult, however, if she had wanted it. There were fewer men in Annie's generation as a result of the Civil War, especially in the abolitionist circles in which Annie moved. And whom could she marry? Her standard would have been high, a synthesis of James, Charles Dickens, and other men she liked such as Whittier, Longfellow, James Parton. The living men she admired were either much older, already married, or confirmed bachelors. Men her own age would inevitably seem like sons to her; she had acted as mentor to Howells and Henry James, only a few years her junior.

Annie felt her loss deeply; she needed companionship now, not in several years. Sarah comforted her, loved her, and helped her recover. She was sisterly in a way that Annie's sisters were not. Annie and Sarah suited each other well as companions and since their arrangement proved more than satisfactory, there was never any reason to change it.

Although James's death had come as a shock and grieved Annie deeply, she now had more time to pursue her personal goals. Annie and Sarah's relationship was more reciprocal than Annie's marriage had been; in it, Annie received as well as gave the kind of emotional support which she had given James. Because Annie's writing created no dilemmas for Sarah, as it had for James during his tenure as publisher and editor, Sarah's encouragement was more wholehearted and unambivalent. She and Annie became advocates for one another, encouraging each other's projects, doing what they could to create an audience for one another. The second half of Mrs. Fields's life was, indeed, what Mark DeWolfe Howe called a "union—there is no truer word for it."

When the manuscript of Annie's biography of her husband was finished and sent to the printer, she was free to embark on a European trip that is usually described as an effort to recover from her husband's death. By the time she left, however, more than a year had passed and her friendship with Sarah Orne Jewett was well established.[2] Sarah had never been to Europe, and Annie, with her experience of travel and her many friends along the way, was the perfect person to initiate her. The two set off in May of 1882, and Whittier, who would become very close to both women in the last decade of his life, wrote a poem to wish them "Godspeed." In it, he called Annie "her in whom / All graces and sweet charities unite, / The old Greek beauty set in holier light"—references to Annie's work with the Associated Charities of Boston and her Greek-influenced poetry and Greek beauty. Sarah he described as "her for whom New England's byways bloom, / Who walks among us welcome as the Spring, / Calling up blossoms where her light feet stray."

The two women visited Ireland, England, Norway, Belgium, Italy, France, and Switzerland. Energetic travellers, within a few days of their landing they had visited Cork, Glengariff, Enniskillen, Portrush, the Giants' Causeway, Belfast, and Dublin; Sarah sent her grandfather a long letter (CL 48). Annie and Sarah took up the literary circuit where Annie and James had left it. They visited Annie's favorites, who soon became Sarah's favorites too: the Tennysons, Charles Reade, Anne Thackeray Ritchie, and the family of Dickens.

Upon their return in October of 1882, Sarah paid a quick visit to her family in Maine before rejoining Annie in Boston. As she wrote to T. B. Aldrich, now editor of the *Atlantic*, "I was only at home overnight to get a bigger trunk and some more clothes, and tell my family I was still very much attached to them" (Matthiessen 74). This separation of one night was also the occasion of a letter to Annie:

Here I am at the desk again, all as natural as can be and writing a first letter to you with so much love, and remembering that this is the first morning in more than seven months that I haven't waked up to hear your dear voice and see your dear face. I do miss it very much, but I look forward to no long separation, which is a comfort. (AFL 16–17; 6 Oct. 1882)[3]

Twenty years passed before illness caused Jewett to return home to South Berwick as a permanent resident. Boston was undoubtedly attractive to a young writer who had lived her whole life in a small Maine village, and 148 Charles Street was the ideal address. Although Annie had struggled in years past to make the household run smoothly, she was now an experienced housekeeper. For Sarah, this meant a home similar to those in fairy tales where meals were magically cooked and served, clothes were picked up, paper appeared on the desk, and inkpots were silently refilled.

Annie and Sarah now began a pattern of companionship which continued with little alteration for the next twenty years. Jewett spent most of the winter in Boston and usually visited her family in Berwick in the late spring or early summer. Annie often visited Maine briefly en route to Manchester for the summer. Then Sarah accompanied Annie to Thunderbolt Hill for the remainder of the summer; in September Annie returned to Boston to reopen the Charles Street house. Sarah followed after paying a brief visit to her family, and the seasonal cycle began again.

The events of Annie and Sarah's week, or at least weekends, were partly organized by the "at homes" they attended. Annie and Sarah held "Saturday afternoons," which were among the most popular and prestigious of literary gatherings. They attended Louise Chandler Moulton's "Friday evenings" and the Whipples' "Sundays." Annie and Sarah poured tea at the unveiling of Sargent's famous portrait of Isabella Stewart Gardner in the late 1890s. Then, of course, there were the club activities: the Pandora continued intermittently, and Annie attended a women's lecture club, the Saturday Morning Club. During the week an atmosphere of work prevailed. Sarah, a late sleeper, lay in bed while Annie got up early and organized her household. Sarah wrote letters in the morning and worked on her stories after lunch. The extent of Sarah's integration into the Charles Street household is indicated by the fact that the second small study off the library, which had belonged to James, became hers.

Annie divided her day among the business of running the house, working a little on poems or essays, and her most time-consuming work at the Associated Charities. As an officer and chief fundraiser, she must have spent some time every day at the Chardon Street headquarters or in paying calls and writing letters from home. She returned in the late afternoon in time for tea or supper with Sarah.

Annie's charity work continued to be exhausting. As James had worried about her in the past, Sarah worried about her now, remarking acidly in a letter that Annie was like "the monkey and the jack-in-the-box" about her meetings (AFL 13). Charity work was the one unshared aspect of Annie and Sarah's life together. Both doctors' daughters and writers with a shared literary taste for the classic in literature, they wrote, read, published, attended the theater and concerts, went for drives, visited and entertained in tandem. The communion between them was even closer than it had been between Annie and James, perhaps because they shared femaleness as well.

Although Annie now kept her diary only when travelling, many of the letters exchanged between her and Jewett survive. Scholars who have become aware of the Fields-Jewett correspondence in recent years have been fascinated by the puzzling use of nicknames, private and apparently childish diction, and enigmatic expressions of physical affection that the letters contain, all of which are illustrated in this letter written by Sarah about 1886:

> Dearest Fuff—I am sorry that this letter will not get into the morning post and so you will not have a word from your affectionate and lazy Pinny this rainy day. I long to see you and say all sorts of foolish things, and to be as bold a Pinny as can be! and to kiss you ever so many times and watch you going about and to be your own P. L. (1886?)

Such letters led Jewett scholars of an earlier generation, notably Eugene Hillhouse Pool, to conclude that Jewett remained a child in her emotional relationships.[4] These critics avoid potentially embarrassing interpretations by seeing Annie Fields as an older, parental figure in Jewett's life, an assumption which is only partly excused by the fifteen-year age difference between them. Henry James employed this assumption as a diversionary tactic when he called Jewett a kind of "older adoptive daughter" of Annie's in his article "Mr. and Mrs. James T. Fields." James reveals his awareness that such an interpretation is inadequate when he adds that "nothing could have warmed the ancient faith of their confessingly a bit disoriented countryman than the association of the elder and the younger lady in such an emphasized susceptibility." This deliberately enigmatic statement is obviously a reference to the ambiguous nature of the friendship. James was not naive; his sister, Alice James, shared what was called a "Boston marriage" with Katherine Loring, one of many similar relationships in Annie and Sarah's circle.[5]

Recent feminist critics, such as Lillian Faderman and Josephine Donovan, have focused on the emotional intensity of this relationship and considered it essentially lesbian in nature.[6] This point of view has led to a number of excellent articles about the relationship. However, both this interpretation and that of the earlier critics impose too conventional a structure on the Fields-Jewett relationship and finally lead to stereotyping. A careful reading of extant correspondence reveals a complex relationship in which there was an easy exchange of roles that fostered both freedom and security for the two women. The letters reveal a lack of fixed roles and a dynamic, highly reciprocal union that cannot be characterized by any single label such as "parental," "lesbian," or "Platonic."[7]

The letters establish that although Sarah was the more experienced and successful writer, she was more dependent on Annie's physical presence than was Annie on Sarah's. In 1882 Sarah wrote Annie:

> I have not been getting on very well without you, and I had to hear from you just as often as I could. . . . I wanted an armful of little books[8] dreadfully sometimes and I thinked and thinked about them! and I am sure you know just as well this minute, as if I could really put my head in your lap and tease you as you set [sic] at your desk—It is just like being with you still—I believe every thing of me but my boots and clothes, and the five little

stones and the rest of the things in my pocket, and the hairpin—all goes back to Charles St. and stays with you half a day at a time.

Fields's replies to Jewett's letters suggest that Sarah often pleaded with her friend to come stay with her during her visits home. But after spending twenty-five years giving someone else's interests precedence, Fields clung to her independence. She spent time daily at the Associated Charities, enlisting volunteer visitors, raising money, and lecturing at small meetings as well as conventions. She wrote *How to Help the Poor* (1883) and articles on the improved methods of assisting the needy and solving the problems of the city. Fields staunchly refused to give up any of her work for Jewett. As she wrote in an undated letter, probably from the early 1880s:

> My dearest dearest child; Your dear letters & urgings are hard to resist but I really have too much to do to be able to get away. My Boston business is enough for one person but added to that comes all my private affairs—you see I have the work of two people to do in the world while I stay now—.

In an 1888 letter, responding to a gift of claret from Sarah, Annie wrote: "Of course I wish we were together, but I feel as if my life were here and my *purpose*. By and by I will come to you O so gladly—." Unlike Jewett's, Annie's expressions of love do not seem to have included requests for Sarah's prompt return, and she did not dwell on their separation in her letters:

> My dearest child: How I wish for you all the time! I get quite tired sometimes making decisions and looking about things when you are not here. But this cold and changing weather has been rather difficult to bear.

When Sarah expressed guilt over her absence, Annie reassured her that she understood:

> O it is quite worth-while for you to be at home; entirely the thing to do just now. I am really very little alone; and when there is other company there are often steps to be taken and talk to be carried on at greater length than I can always manage alone and I am grateful for the assistance.

Although neither of the women enjoyed their separations, Annie approached them philosophically.

Those familiar with Jewett's correspondence or recent articles about her are aware that she frequently used nicknames when referring to herself, Annie, and other friends.[9] A careful reading of the letters shows that Jewett's use of these nicknames is an important key to analyzing the nature of the Jewett-Fields relationship. Sarah uses primarily one nickname for herself, Pinny, a childhood nickname describing the smallness of her head in proportion to her stature and broad shoulders. An important variation of this name, Pinny Lawson or P. L. for short, is a reference to Sam Lawson, a character in Harriet Beecher Stowe's *Oldtown Folks* and *Sam Lawson's Oldtown Fireside Tales*. Sam Lawson is the "village do-nothing" in the books, a lazy, talkative, shiftless storyteller and much-beloved rebel against Oldtown's Puritanical ways. Annie, Sarah, or both noticed a resemblance (or a playfully attributed resemblance) between Sarah (in certain moods) and Sam Lawson, and so the nickname was born.[10] Annie became T. L., a character who functions in Jewett's letters as the more responsible member of the Lawson family, perhaps modelled on Hepsy, Sam's waspish wife.[11]

What the letters make clear is that Jewett used these nicknames to correspond to different roles in which she saw herself and Annie. But instead of identifying each woman with one consistent role, such as parent/child or male/female, Jewett used the nicknames to create two different sets of almost diametrically opposed roles. The different names thus imply a relationship in which the women's roles were highly flexible and interchangeable. Pinny Lawson is, in fact, a well-developed character, an irresponsible scamp who needs to be prodded to work and can't resist leaning out of the window in Charles Street to watch the fireworks. When Sarah is P. L., Annie is T. L., a foil to Sarah's scamp, a conscientious monitor who encourages her to settle down and get to work. In one letter, Sarah refers to T. L. as P. L.'s "doctor." An early letter shows Sarah talking quite seriously about her lack of industry, then moving playfully into her "Lawson" self:

> I have had a hard time of worry and hard work since you went away on Monday. I wish I could be idle all the rest of June, that is not feel forced to do things. But I suppose it cannot be and the only thing possible in a busy life is to rest *in* one's work since one cannot rest *from* it. I think a good deal about the long story but it has not really taken hold of me yet—I do feel so impatient with myself dear Fuffy, I'm always straying off on wrong roads and I am so wicked about things. This is one of the time's [sic] when I think despairingly about my faults and see little chance of their ever being mended—But Fuffy to have patience with Pin and Please to love her!— . . . [(] Oh Pinny to go to work! An idle and thriftless Pinny to whom the rest of the Lawsons are industrious). (n.d.)

Another letter further illustrates the child/adult, patient/doctor dynamic which is operating in this set of nicknames:

> Pin wasn't going to tell this, but can't keep anything from T. L.—she runned against a door in the dark last night and banged her head shameful! She was so frightened of T. L., afterward because T. L. scolds she for banging she's head—It was on her eyebrow the blow fell, and after that recovered itself, and Pin composed herself to sleep, her dear nose suddenly began to ache worse than the other and she confidently expected a black eye but she is not at all out of repair this morning.

Jewett's use of nicknames is invariably accompanied by childish diction, a kind of dialect that sounds fearfully close to baby talk. Sarah's use of such language led Jewett scholars of an earlier generation to declare that Jewett had no mature sexual relationships and that the Fields-Jewett relationship was like that of a parent and child.[12] Sarah's declaration when she was forty-eight to her friend Sara Norton that "This is my birthday and I am nine years old" lends support to those who would argue that Sarah functioned as a child in her relationships (AFL 125). While it is undeniable, on the evidence of the letters, that Sarah enjoyed playing the role of a naughty child or tomboy in her relationship with Annie, it is equally true, on the same evidence, that this was not the only role she played.

Sarah called Annie by a variety of nicknames in addition to T. L.—Fuff, Fuffy, Fuffatee, Mouse, and Mousatee—none of them names one would normally associate with a stern parental figure. The context in which these nicknames appear suggests that Sarah used them when taking a protective role toward Annie, a role often in direct contradiction to her role as P. L. (although Sarah is still, confusingly, called Pinny). The protective (and adult) Pinny uses childish diction at least as much as the scamp P. L., which seems strange until one remembers that it is the parent who uses baby talk to the child, thus aligning Jewett with the role of parent. In her introduction to her edition of Sarah's letters, Annie showed that she understood Sarah's use of this language; alluding to the letters that Swift wrote to Stella, Annie wrote:

> The same handling of "the little language" is here; the same joy and repose in friendship. This "little language," the private "cuddling" of lovers, of mothers, and children, since the world began, was native also to her. (AFL 6)

Sarah's letters to Annie reflected this variety of roles. When Sarah addressed Annie as Mouse, she sometimes took a playfully superior tone:

> I remind myself constantly how good all this work is in every way—and how thankful I shall be to have done it when I go to England again—I shall be able to improve an ignorant [in tiny writing] mouse's Mind. (1885)

Many of the letters reflect a picture of Annie as a cute, diminutive, cuddly creature who required the protection of a tougher, more worldly Sarah. In a letter from Jewett to Fields after a big storm, she wrote:

> I hope my darling Fuff didn't go blowing along Charley St and get lodged poor little thing! in one of the trees or telegraph wires. Oh I *must* go and tend to her! I am her most loving and anxious Pinny. (n.d.)

Sarah's characterization of Annie as "mouse" makes her seem not only weak but also frivolous: "I hope now that you will have a quiet Sunday I think such a giddy mousatee must need it" (1889?) Sarah was not above using her nickname for Annie as the occasion for a pun reminiscent of Annie's earlier nickname, given her by the Hawthornes, "Mrs. Meadows": "Deep snows are hard on the mice—poor little field mice—(cousins of a dear friend!)" (1884).

The success of this relationship for both their personal and their professional lives lay in its complete reciprocity and in their ability to create for themselves a form of marriage in which all roles were interchangeable and neither partner was limited by the relationship. The fitness of their relationship extended beyond a conventional use of the term "marriage," with its implied roles of husband and wife, or "Boston marriage," which simply refers to a congenial arrangement of two women joining households. Both women brought to their union an understanding of how to make a relationship both intimate and unconfining. Annie had firsthand knowledge of the perils of traditional marriage because of her life with James. Sarah also understood the danger posed by any assignment of roles; in a conversation with Whittier, she is reported to have said that she had no intention of marrying and had more need of a wife than a husband (Matthiessen 72).

Jewett's interest in role reversal has been critically discussed only very recently. In her book *A Country Doctor,* Sarah rejected marriage for her heroine, Nan Prince, because being a wife precluded the possibility of simultaneously pursuing a career.[13] In addition, one of Jewett's most interesting but little-known stories, "Tom's Husband," published in 1883 in the volume dedicated to Annie, provides concrete evidence of Jewett's insight into marriage and her belief in the limitations of inflexible roles.[14]

In "Tom's Husband" Tom and Mary fall in love and marry despite Mary's unusually independent nature and Tom's lack of interest in the male world of work. Since both had independent incomes prior to their marriage, both stay at home and Mary takes over the housekeeping while Tom pursues his various hobbies. After a goading letter from Tom's sister, who lives in Japan, Mary persuades Tom to allow her to reopen a factory which he has inherited but has no desire to run. Although Tom thinks people will call him a fool, he admits that he had enjoyed running the house before his marriage, thinks he can do it better than Mary, and lacks interest in the factory himself. With Tom's somewhat grudging permission, Mary successfully manages the business.

At first this open-mindedness pays off but eventually it causes problems. Tom and Mary find themselves lapsing into the stereotypical behavior associated with the roles they have adopted: Mary becomes distant and condescending, brings people home for dinner without warning, and is too tired to be a companion to Tom in the evenings. Tom becomes obsessed with household details and feels humiliated when a neighbor calls to borrow some yeast at a bad moment. In the story, their difficulties are resolved, first, by their becoming aware of them, and second, by Mary's agreeing to set aside the business for six months so they can take a trip to Europe together and renew their relationship. Presumably, they will return to the jobs they prefer with a new understanding of the limits and dangers of any fixed role. In the story, Jewett makes it clear that role reversal is not in and of itself a solution to the role problem. In a successful relationship, both partners must refuse to be limited to any single role, whether conventional or not.

This story can be loosely read as a description of the Fields-Jewett relationship with its situation springing from Sarah's belief in the necessity of flexible roles in any intimate arrangement. The radical nature of their partnership (radical in a sense other than lesbian) has been overlooked because of inadequate or, in Annie's case, nonexistent biographical studies. Both Annie and Sarah possessed the experience and insight necessary to make their partnership work. Annie's successful, though limiting, twenty-five year marriage; her intelligence; her skill with people; and her insistence upon her own career were her main contributions, while Sarah had observed closely different kinds of marriages and households, including those involving two women. Their correspondence, especially Sarah's letters with their initially puzzling private language, documents the complete reciprocity and successful transcendence of stereotypes they achieved.

One of the effects of Annie's friendship with Sarah was a new intimacy with John Greenleaf Whittier. Whittier was perhaps the only one of the male writers from James's circle—if, in fact, he could be said to have belonged to James's circle—who was as much Annie's friend as her husband's. Whittier's unique position as a friend of women was not a matter of patronage, as it was with T. W. Higginson or with Fields himself, but a matter of personal preference.

After James Fields's death, Whittier welcomed the friendship of the two women and became a member of their household in spirit, if not in body. Whittier may have felt an even greater affinity with Sarah than with Annie; he sometimes referred to her as his "adopted daughter Sarah" (WL 3:573; 6 Jan. [1890]). Even in the 1870s he knew Sarah well enough to ask if she had ever been in love. Annie and Sarah frequently visited Whittier at his homes in Amesbury or Danvers, and Jewett often stopped by herself on her way to or from South Berwick. They also visited him on his birthday whenever possible. As Whittier's circle of contemporaries dwindled, Annie and Sarah increasingly came to stand between him and a lonely old age.

The three friends shared many interests. Annie relied upon Whittier to advise her about her poems, and Whittier frankly admired and criticized all he was sent. About one poem he wrote:

> I thank thee for sending me that grand awful and yet, all hopeful sonnet—a masterful verse which recalls Dante and Milton.
>   Of course thee do not mean in the last line but one of the poem to say that the *flight* was *unstained*. (WL 3:577; 3 June 1890)

He also read and praised everything of Sarah's that she sent him in manuscript or in print, and he particularly enjoyed her Irish stories such as "The Luck of the Bogans."

Annie shared with Whittier an interest in political events, particularly those which affected blacks, immigrants, and the poor. Whittier supported Annie's coffeehouses and other charitable projects, and she told him what might be called an Associated Charities joke:

> Mr. [Phillips] Brooks is very enthusiastic about India though when I asked him about the Mystics—he said—it was a nation of mystics and you soon ceased to be surprised. "When people come to a higher spiritual development in Boston you know they join the Associated Charities, when they come to the higher enlightenment in India they go and sit under a Bohen tree!!"

In her letters to Whittier Annie expressed her views on such diverse topics as prohibition (Annie espoused a "temperate middle course"); Edward Bellamy's utopian novel, *Looking Backward* (she asked, "Is there the root of a great tree in it?"); and the possibility of establishing a medical school that would admit women at the Johns Hopkins Hospital. But they wrote about less lofty topics as well, such as the surprising news of Elizabeth Stuart Phelps's engagement at age forty-four to Herbert Dickinson

Ward, a man seventeen years her junior. Upon receiving the news from Phelps, Annie wrote immediately to Whittier:

> It is a great mercy to me that my Sarah has gone to Berwick for I much fear I could not have held my tongue until tomorrow as she [Phelps] requests. I know you can't get this before the papers will have the news so I take great comfort tonight in talking with you about it on paper. (19 Oct. 1888)

She added, in regard to Phelps's well-known insomnia and frequent ill-health, "No wonder she is cured by him if he has given her Love's philter. . . !" Whittier replied, "How the wicked world will laugh over it! But if she is happy what will she care for the world?" (WL 3:559; 21 Oct. 1888).

Both Annie and Whittier shared an interest in Spiritualism and believed that communication was possible between living beings and the spirits of the dead. Not quite a year after James's death, Annie reported to Whittier "an interview" with her husband that had been conducted through a medium. Whittier confessed having communicated with both his sister Elizabeth and friend Phebe Cary by similar means, but told Annie that "I had a feeling that it was not safe or healthful for mind or body to yield myself to an influence the nature of which was unknown" (WL 3:445; 24 March 1882).

Their friend Celia Thaxter, however, evinced a more active curiosity. In response to Annie's description of an "unearthly" experience which she and Sarah had shared with Celia Thaxter, Whittier replied, "I am sorry that C. T. is yielding herself so unreservedly to the baffling and unsatisfactory experience" (WL 3:491; 1 Dec. 1884). Celia was evidently in frequent contact with a medium, Miss Rose Darrah, and in December of 1884 a seance was held at 148 Charles Street. According to Celia, she, Sarah, Annie, Mrs. Lodge, the medium, and Sarah's Irish setter, Roger, were arranged around the fire when the apparition of a young blond man elicited a growl from the dog. In a letter to Whittier, Celia quoted the words spoken by the medium as spirits appeared:

> "Now two shapes come from the little room and slowly past the piano, one, a tall, slender, graceful lady with light reddish hair, and the other, a man, I think it is Longfellow"—after a minute—"no, it is a larger, fuller, younger man, with a fine presence," she described him—she had never seen James, nor any picture of him she said, "he has straight dark hair, darker than his beard and *tumbled at the parting*" (you remember how he always did that?) . . . in short she described him perfectly and he spoke so that she could hear and repeated what he said, all beautiful and what you would expect from him, she spoke of the arch, merry, *human* expression . . . till we were all sobbing, Annie and Mrs. Lodge and I, and Pinny too was touched to tears. (WL 3:494n; 12 Jan. 1884)

Then, according to Celia, she herself felt a hand brush her cheek and the medium declared Celia's mother to be standing by her chair. Although Annie evidently accepted this experience as genuine at the time, she must have confided her later skepticism to Whittier, who declared himself "pained but not altogether surprised" about rumors of Miss Darrah's untrustworthiness (WL 3:498; 16 April 1885).

Annie continued to believe in the possibility of communication with those who had passed beyond, and one of her letters to Whittier sounds like the beginning of an article on the subject:

> The striking feature of today is the wide-spread interest in what we have called the supernatural. I am truly amazed at the new people and the new kinds of mind engaged in solemn consideration of this subject, since men of science have refused to scoff any longer but have joined the ranks of investigations.

Annie went on to talk about a convert:

> Mrs. Goddard came up here in one of those *glowing* sunsets and got talking with some earnestness about it [Spiritualism]. She has read all the books! as she says, but I'm glad to see some deeper interest awaking for I am sure she will find light in it and no one can need it more. I did not relate to her any personal experiences because she is not yet ready to receive them, but I can see something dawning in her mind where formerly all has been so dark. (9 Oct. 1884)

In late 1885 the niece who had been living with Whittier in his home married and moved away. Whittier could no longer live alone but he dreaded leaving his home to live with relatives, and he probably confided this regret to Annie. She responded with an invitation to become a member of the Charles Street household. Although the prospect was appealing, Whittier felt obliged to decline. He declared himself "unable to bear the excitements of city life" and uncomfortable with strangers because of his deafness. He was afraid that if he moved to 148 Charles Street his admirers would seek him there and "It would be like having a waif from Barnum's Museum shut up in your library, and people coming to see what it looks like" (WL 3:508–09, 2 Oct. 1885).

The next year, during one of Sarah's visits to Whittier, the conversation turned to Annie and the invitation. Sarah told Annie all about it in a letter:

> We went over Julian Hawthorne and Lowell . . . and I don't know what or who else except Fuff and her dearest one, for he talked about you both in a heavenly way, of your friendship and how much he owed to you—He said once when we were talking about you alone that he had no such reverence for any friend, that nobody knew what an inspiration you had been and were, You were "not like other folks but *just right*"—you must imagine him saying this things [sic] with his peculiar emphasis—and I cannot tell you with what feeling he told me that he did not dare to go to stay long with you for he could not bear having to come away. We had a good talk afterward about his not coming last winter—He said he could not be persuaded by either of us that it was not for his sake ("pity for *me*") that we wanted him to come and with all your cares, he had not the heart to be another thing to think of—He wanted to and thought a long while about it and gave it up. I did not press him about coming though I spoke earnestly to make him feel as you did about it, and we had a dear time. I cannot begin to tell you all—.

Whittier showed Sarah an old photograph of Annie which she had never seen before:

Dear Mouse when did she have a picture taken in a fluffy white dress holding out her hand to a little barefooted child? So sweet a mouse that I was taken with a sad attack of longing to see you again and even borrowed it off thy friend though he made me promise over and over again to give it back! In some ways it is liker you than anything—it perfectly fascinates me—do tell me all about it—It would be just like you to have a blessed hoard of one or two, and if you haven't, I must get this copied, that is all! Who is the Pinny? Oh dear I do want to get hold of you so when I look at it! (AFL 128; 1897?)

When Annie and Sarah travelled to Europe in 1892 they sent Whittier many letters describing the places they saw and people they met. When he died shortly after their return, it was for Sarah and Annie like losing a member of their family.

Although Jewett is known for her fiction she wrote poetry as well, much of it love poems written to her women friends. In her article "The Love Poems of Sarah Orne Jewett," Josephine Donovan has discussed the likelihood that many of these poems were written with Annie in mind. Nearly all of Jewett's letters to Annie could be called love letters as well. Early in their relationship, probably in 1883, Sarah came upon a box of Annie's letters and reread them. She wrote:

Oh my dear darling I had forgotten that we loved each other so much a year ago—for it all seems so new to me everyday—But a year ago last winter seems a great way off for we have lived so much since—.

The two women came to know each other so well that every habit was familiar. Sarah wrote to Annie from Berwick:

I can't help worrying because you directed some letters with a pencil yesterday which usually means that poor little Fuffs have colds! but I hope it was only that she had made a nest and had a pencil by her!! On such things hang our happiness! (n.d.)

Even in Annie's more reserved letters, their intimacy emerges. In response to a question from Sarah about the accessories for a dress, Annie wrote:

A belt suits your "big" style so much better than ribbon dear that I am inclined to prefer it—but if a sash I think one tied at the side is much prettier—and yet with *Punch* "agin" me I am ready to be voted down—especially as the soft lace and sich [sic] may need the flappiness of the bows to make the back quite large enough. (n.d.)

As the years passed, Annie and Sarah developed strategies for coping with their separations. Annie, for example, wrote to Sarah that she "had to talk with you a great deal while I was dressing this morning." And Sarah, always lighthearted, was comforted when Hannah, a member of the household staff, changed from singing "a high slow measured air" to "the *Girl I left behind me* which is very much more cheerful besides being appropriate to the occasion of poor Pinny" (n.d.)

Sarah's perception of the different selves contained within herself and Annie led to an apparent disjunction between personal and professional lives. When Sarah felt like

Pinny Lawson, she found it hard to deal with Annie in her persona of poet and scholar. After rereading *Under the Olive* (1881), Annie's first long book of poems, Sarah commented that the idea of "dear little Fuffy" writing such a book "seems quite amazing":

> It is like remembering that I have dared to talk nonsense and hug and play generally with something that turned itself into a whole worldful of thoughts and sights and beautiful things—Fuffy and this poet are a funny pair to live in the same skin you know, ladies! (1883)

When it came to writing, however, Pinny and Fuffy disappeared, and Jewett's most mature, intelligent, and authoritative self was in command.

9.

The Developing Writer

1883–1895

By the time Annie and Sarah had returned from their first trip abroad together Annie was a year short of fifty. While many of the friends Annie had made as a result of her marriage were approaching old age or already elderly, her most productive years as a writer were just beginning. Fields's death in 1881 was closely followed by those of Emerson and Longfellow in 1882 and that of Charles Reade in 1884. Although the 1880s passed without additional deaths among Annie's friends, by the late 1890s most of the old circle was gone. And Annie, who had wanted to be a poet and had recorded the incidents of Boston literary life chiefly for her husband's use, became a writer of memoirs.

Soon Annie found herself relying on Sarah, who clearly possessed greater authority where writing was concerned, for help and encouragement. Her support was invaluable to Annie, still smarting from her early failures. Sarah's acknowledged superiority as a writer balanced Annie's age and position of leadership in the Boston community. Sarah clearly played a crucial role in in Annie's blossoming career.

Prior to *James T. Fields,* Annie had published only three long poems, all privately printed, and a volume of classically inspired lyrics, *Under the Olive,* published by Ticknor & Fields's successor. Annie's poetry was received with respect by her friends and the press; a review of *Under the Olive* compares "her thought" to that of Mrs. Browning and describes the poems as "the type of the Tennyson—Swinburne—Rossetti poems." Of one poem, "The Lantern of Sestos," the reviewer declares that "Outside of Hyperion, Keats himself, we think, never wrote anything finer." The reviewer had not entirely lost perspective, however, as this comment reveals: "It can hardly be said that the treatment of the themes is strong and vigorous enough to offset the great disadvantage under which the author labored in selecting hackneyed classical themes."

Although the slight attention the volume received was polite and even complimentary, up to and including *James T. Fields* Annie was not taken seriously as a writer. That began to change for several reasons: Annie directed her writing energy into personal essays rather than poetry; she did not attempt another long, unwieldy project until the late 1890s; and she now had Jewett to advise and encourage her to write.

In the years between 1883 and 1895, the year of *A Singing Shepherd,* Annie published more than twenty articles, some quite long, all significantly better than her earlier work, but not as good as *Authors and Friends* (1896). Thus, these years served as Annie's continuing education, or perhaps apprenticeship, in writing.

In 1883 Fields published her first memoir, "Mr. Emerson in the Lecture Room," which paraphrases Emerson's 1870 lectures at Harvard University. Annie's "prose transcriptions" were written from memory, since, as she pointed out, Emerson did not like his audience to take notes. "Mr. Emerson" appeared in the same issue of the *Atlantic* as Act III of Henry James's dramatization of *Daisy Miller* and Jewett's story "A Landless Farmer." Jewett wrote Fields to compliment her on its appearance and initiate her into the mysteries of reprint rights:

> I have been looking over the Atlantic and liking it very much—only I think it was an outrage to have filled so much space in three numbers with Daisy Miller's Dramatiza-tion—and I don't see how Mr. James could bear to waste his time over it—Oh, dear Fuff, the cheque for your article will not come until the first day of June, so dont be looking for it in vain before that time. thinking about there being any trouble about your doing it, but I think there couldn't be for they could use it in a book if they liked just as well as ever. I should never have a fear of it. Pin always said so. (n.d.)

Insecurity about her writing was not the only reason Annie entertained doubts about the very nature of memoir writing itself. She expressed disapproval of many such projects in her diary while noting with interest the routine destruction of correspon-dence by Harriet Martineau, Dickens, and Whittier. As a result of her uncertainty, she carried circumspection to an extreme. When Annie had written a second article on Emerson, she asked Whittier to approve the manuscript, calling upon him because Sarah had known Emerson very little. She wrote Whittier twice to thank him for his help; in the second note, she told him: "It is a weight off my mind to think you like it, because one may so easily make a slip in such a paper" (Jan. 1884).

Because of Annie's insecurity and native delicacy, Sarah's expressions of con-fidence and reassurance were crucial. The following note probably refers to the second Emerson article, "Glimpses of Emerson" (1884):

> My dear little Fuff I am so glad about it—Didn't I always say you would have more lovely things to say? Not to be a keeping-still Fuff—but I know the thing—that Pintoe bursted its dear self with pride—it hoped you would excuse it, but it could not contain even one of Pin's feets when she was so proud. (1883?)

Another note refers to one of the lectures on charity work which Annie gave at this time:

> Dear Mouse So you are a-writing too! Good luck to you then—and Pinny to be there to hear the paper please Ladies—and to tell Fuff it is good because she will think it isn't, she always does, you know—Now be like Pinny-a-bragging of her success as a historian. (n.d.)[1]

The next essay which Annie wrote to commemorate a friend was "An Acquaintance with Charles Reade," started shortly after his death in 1884. Annie had found Reade charming during her visits to England and was angered by the press's harsh treatment of his irregular "marriage" to Laura Seymour, an actress who had died in 1879. Annie rose to Reade's defense as she had to Dickens's, explaining the situation to Whittier and no doubt others in this manner:

> Charles Reade is gone, I send you the Tribune with the first *just* paragraphs concerning him I have ever seen—He was all that is said of him here but there was a conventionality of the middle [a]ges bred in him and a lack of religious development which led him into strange ways. He was never married being bursar of Magdalen College Oxford and born to high degree but he fell in love with an actress many years ago and she was really his wife only he did not acknowledge her. He was entirely happy with her and devoted to her and died partly I am sure from sorrow and solitude. It is a strange story for the 19th century.

Sarah was, of course, busily publishing also, with a collection of her stories coming out in 1881 and two novels in 1884 and 1885. Annie and Sarah now consulted each other frequently, not only about the contents of their writing, but also about payments, and neither Annie nor Sarah chose to acknowledge the fact that Sarah was still a better and more sought-after writer. The women's demand for equal rights at the publisher led them into trouble, however. Annie had been receiving ten dollars per page for her prose and discovered that Sarah received thirteen. When Annie sent the completed Reade article, which had been accepted by Aldrich, to Horace Scudder, then a sub-editor, she asked to be paid at the higher rate which Sarah received. After consulting with Mr. Houghton, whose publishing firm now owned the *Atlantic,* Scudder refused to pay Annie more than ten dollars per page (Ballou 377–79). When Annie reported to Sarah how much she had been offered (and evidently accepted), Sarah became indignant:

> (I felt much disturbed about the Reade paper, and was going to have something done about it right away; I wish you had put your price on it—and I wonder they could offer you less than you had for the other—the Longfellow. That was such a silly reason they gave but we shall grow wiser and wiser and I am afraid never grow any richer writing for the magazines—I imagine Scudder sneaking and asking some Century person how much they paid you. I wish you would ask the Editors to please not mention the price to anyone as it is less than you have—but I dont know whether it would be wise). (1883?)

Annie must have withdrawn the article as a result of Sarah's objections. Scudder sent a snide note to Aldrich, saying that he regretted the loss of the paper and blaming Mrs. Fields. The piece appeared in *Harper's* in 1884 in the same volume as Howells's *The Rise of Silas Lapham.*

This incident was the beginning of a serious quarrel between Scudder and the Charles Street ladies. Scudder succeeded Aldrich as chief editor of the *Atlantic* in 1890; rumor had it that Aldrich was asked to resign because of conflicts about editorial policy with Houghton. Annie and Sarah were very friendly with the Aldriches at this time and were not kindly disposed to Aldrich's successor. For two years, 1892 and 1893, neither Annie nor Sarah sent a single contribution to the *Atlantic.* Although

Jewett's relationship with Scudder had been long and fruitful, she was reported by Robert Underwood Johnson to have said, "What a strange world this! full of scudders and things" (CL 80). In addition, a riddle about the new editorial slant of the *Atlantic* became current: "Why is Horace Scudder greater than Moses? Moses dried up the Red Sea once only; Scudder dries up the *Atlantic* monthly" (Ballou 437). Though the breach was eventually healed, Scudder was never completely restored to Annie and Sarah's good graces.

After the publication of "Glimpses of Longfellow in Social Life" (1886) in the *Century,* Annie turned her attention from memoirs and tried out some new ideas. She still went regularly to the Chardon Street headquarters and she had become a fairly outspoken critic of the established policy. She wrote two letters to *The Nation* in 1886 and 1888, one protesting against the inhumane conditions of asylums for children, the other suggesting that work done by prisoners be given to "honest paupers" instead.

She also helped to launch two new magazines, both edited by friends. Annie contributed the lead article to the first issue of *Lend a Hand,* a new social-work journal edited by Annie's friend and co-worker Edward Everett Hale. In "Lend a Hand, for 'Pain Is Not the Fruit of Pain,'" she described the work of the Associated Charities and supported the new journal. The second new magazine, *Wide Awake,* was aimed at children and adolescents and was edited by Annie's old friend Miriam Pratt, one of Rufus Choate's daughters.

The four short articles that Annie wrote for *Wide Awake* (which later merged with *St. Nicholas*) reveal as much of Annie personally as any of her writing and mark a new stage in her development as a writer. "The Poet Who Told the Truth" describes a young girl who hopes to do some great work in the world and patterns herself after such women as Felicia Hemans, Elizabeth Fry, and Lydia Maria Child.

The second article, "Noble Born," is based on a story by Walter Besant called "The Children of Gideon" about two girls raised together, one of noble birth and one of humble origin. When they grew up, both were taken to see the wretched home where one of them had been born; one girl shrank from the misery, but the other returned to live with and help the impoverished family. The girl who lived among the sewing girls proved to be the girl of noble birth, from which Annie drew the moral "that real nobiity is not afraid to look misery in the face, nor to do hard work" (342).

Sarah suggested another topic for Annie in a note she sent her after the publication of the first piece:

> Dear Mouse the little paper in *Wide Awake* is very sweet and full of a vague personal sweetness that I can't find words to describe. I don't know that I have ever found so much of yourself in any bit of prose that you ever wrote. I hope you will do some more for Mrs. Pratt—you know you held out hopes to Pinny of speaking of clothes and their expressiveness. (n.d.)

Annie's third article, "About Clothes," reflected upon the money and time that women invested in their clothing and examined the philosophies underlying clothing selection. Annie drew up four principles that girls should follow:

Simplicity is beauty in itself; and as rare as it is beautiful. . . . Rich materials are seldom in good taste for young women. . . . Discover as soon as possible the style best suited to yourself and . . . use the favorite old [dresses] as patterns. . . . A sense of neatness and order is essential to good dressing. . . . (87)

"A Helping Hand," Annie's fourth article for *Wide Awake,* is closer to a short story than anything else Annie published. The story is a parable urging young women of the upper and middle classes to do something constructive for their less fortunate sisters by creating schools and social clubs for mill girls and young men of the working classes.

Although Annie devoted most of her writing energy to essays in the later 1880s, she continued to write and publish poems in the *Atlantic, Harper's,* and *Scribner's.* Despite the greater success of Annie's essays, she always felt uncomfortable writing prose and thought her true gift was poetic; as she wrote to Sarah:

I am so pleased and "set up" because you like the bit of prose—only I can never do it again—I have the asses gifts of slowness and dulness with prose I fear generally—. (n.d.)

Annie also sent poems to Sarah and confided to her the uncertainty she felt:

It was so strange and good that you should have felt as you did about the latter lines in the first half of Chrysalides![2] I too had my suspicions in that direction—There was something much larger there, and something which I do not seem to find at all satisfactorily in the lines was in my mind to say further, so I believe I shall cut the passage quite out. Whatever can be spared in a poem certainly, should be omitted. But wasn't it interesting that you and I had thought it together. (n.d.)

On an occasion when Annie had praised one of Sarah's poems, Sarah deftly turned the compliment back to Annie:

My dear Fuff you are so good about the verses but when I get thinking about your Orpheus as I did today—*I* think that is the top thing and I am so proud of it and so thankful that we went to Richfield[3] for the writing of that if for nothing else—I want to hear it again when I come, if we get time, and we *will* you know!

Annie worried that the unfinished poems she sent Sarah would turn up after her death, and she asked Sarah to destroy them. Sarah's response to these requests was sometimes uncooperative:

What a Fuff to say that I must destroy the Pearl St—Fuffy poem!![4] I *won't!* so you may expect vast naughtiness on that point. I love them very much and you are not to be low about them or about your work or your own dear self—I wonder if you are skipping your claret for lunch or misbehaving yourself any way—Pinny to come and tend to you awfil! [sic] (1889)

Annie finished the decade with two papers on charity that appeared in 1889, "The Aged Poor," which appeared in the *Chautauquan,* and "Special Work of [the National Conference of] Associated Charities [and Corrections]," which appeared in *Lend a Hand.* She had also written and published two sections of *A Shelf of Old Books,* which would be published in book form in 1894, and numerous poems. Annie had already published in this decade more than twice what she had published in the 1860s and 1870s combined, and the 1890s would be even more productive. Jewett published four new books of stories, a history book for young people, and a girls' story in the years between 1886 and 1890. Then, probably feeling that they deserved it after a decade of hard work, they took a vacation.

The first years of the 1890s were spent in relaxation and travel to St. Augustine, Florida; the Chicago World's Fair; and Europe, where they finally met Mme. Therese de Solms Blanc in 1892 after eight years of correspondence (AFL 91). Blanc was a French admirer of Sarah's work who wrote for the *Revue des Deux Mondes* under the pen name "Th. Bentzon." During the second of Blanc's trips to the United States, in 1897, she described Mrs. Fields's Boston salon in a series of articles on the life of American women.[5]

Annie and Sarah wrote often to Whittier, who was increasingly isolated because of his health and deafness, when they were away. Annie tried to cheer him up by offering to translate an essay Mme. Blanc had written about his work. Whittier wrote another poem for Annie after missing her and Sarah during a brief trip to Boston:

> I missed the love-transfigured face,
>   The glad, sweet smile so dear to me,
>   The clasp of greeting warm and free,
> What had the round world in their place?
>
> O friend! whose generous love has made
>   My last days best, my good intent
>   Accept, and let the call I meant
> Be with your coming doubly paid!

(WL 3:530; 12 Oct. 1886)

Whittier's death in 1892 left a painfully empty space in Annie and Sarah's lives.

By 1894 Annie had spent forty years trying to establish herself as a writer—not as a full-time professional, but certainly as more than a dilettante. Now sixty, Annie was picking up steam. These were the years when she came into her own as a person and a writer. The writing which she finally settled down to do—memoirs and biographies—skipped over the last twenty years and relied on her memory and notes of her services to literature as a hostess and patron.

Neither Annie nor Sarah published much in the first few years of the decade, although both women produced their best work in the 1890s. In 1892 Annie published an interpretation and translation of French poet Maurice de Guerin's "Le Centaur," which George Sand had published in the *Revue des Deux Mondes* after Guerin's death in 1840. After the deaths of Tennyson and Whittier in 1892, Annie wrote memoirs about them which appeared in *Harper's* in 1893. "Tennyson" was reprinted in *Authors and Friends* (1896), and "Whittier: Notes of His Life and Friendship" appeared as a book in Harper's Black and White Series (1893). Annie published seven other books between 1890 and 1904, including biographies of Whittier (1893), Hawthorne (1899), and Charles Dudley Warner (1904); an edition of the letters of Celia Thaxter (1895); a long biography of Harriet Beecher Stowe (1897); another volume of reminiscence, *A Shelf of Old Books* (1894); and two books of poetry, *The Singing Shepherd* (1895) and *Orpheus* (1900). Annie's only other book publication was the *Letters of Sarah Orne Jewett* in 1911.

Annie's memoirs and biographies are her most interesting work, from the perspectives of both her own time and eighty years later. The shorter pieces are most appealing and successful. The larger the amount of material Annie had to organize, the more trouble she found herself in; her memoirs work well when she followed the natural flow of her thoughts but falter when she accumulated a large mass of material and tried to process it logically. Although her short biographies of Hawthorne and Charles Dudley Warner were never collected, most of her best pieces appeared in two books, *A Shelf of Old Books* (1894) and *Authors and Friends* (1896). Anyone wishing to evaluate her contribution to literary history must give these books a serious reading.

The stories Annie told about her subjects give a bird's-eye view of them from a perspective entirely her own. If she did not know her subject, she based her interpretation on stories told by his friends or the opinion of her husband. If Annie did know her subject, she based her interpretation on an intimacy which few biographers have the opportunity to experience; she knew how her subject treated his or her friends, spouse, and servants.

An admirable generosity of spirit is evident in every sentence. Armed with the kind of knowledge a writer of a later generation might have used to annihilate, Annie Fields chose simply to characterize. Without gossiping or exploiting her friend's failings, she stated outright her subjects' flaws—and allowed them to become motifs that are threaded through the essay: Dr. Holmes's egotism, for example, or Mrs. Stowe's absentmindedness and disorganization. Having acknowledged these flaws, however, she focused on her subjects' common humanity and showed how they rose above their weaknesses. Her admiration for her subjects was sometimes extreme, but she did not overestimate literary worth. Annie wrote with an awareness of her own fallibility and of the fickleness of fame.

A Shelf of Old Books, Annie's first collection of essays, was published by Scribner's in 1894. The first words of "Leigh Hunt" set forth Annie's premise:

> There is a sacredness about the belongings of good and great men which is quite apart from the value and significance of the things themselves. Their books become especially endeared to us; as we turn the pages they have loved, we can see another hand pointing along the lines, another head bending over the open volume. A writer's books make his workshop and his pleasure-house in one, and in turning over his possessions we discover the field in which he worked and the key to his garden of the Hesperides.

The idea of writing an essay in which books are the vehicle for propelling discussion of famous writers had been used by James Fields, although it certainly didn't originate with him. Fields had become friendly with Leigh Hunt during his two trips to England; Annie met Hunt in 1859, a few months before his death at age seventy-five. Still in England when Hunt died, Fields purchased the whole lot of Hunt's books—a collection marred by poor condition and missing volumes—at auction and shipped them to Boston.

Annie's essay is a combination of literary anecdote, myth, and love of books and literary mementoes. Fields gave away or sold about 250 of the original 450 volumes. Among the treasures of Hunt's library were first editions of his own work and books he had loved and covered with marginal notes: his Boccaccio; his commentaries on the Italian poets; his volumes of Shelley, Keats, and Milton; his copy of Diogenes Laertes; a rebound volume of Coleridge, Shelley, and Keats; a much-thumbed copy of the *Arabian Nights*; Plato's *Republic*; Emerson's *English Traits*; Carlyle's *French Revolution*. To Annie, part of the charm of Leigh Hunt and his books was his proximity to greater poets, who seemed to have lived so long ago because they had died so young:

> It seemed the most natural thing possible to hear Leigh Hunt talk of Shelley and Keats as if they had just closed the door by which we had entered. There was the very couch, perhaps, where Keats lay down to sleep. . . . (13–14)

Curiously, Hunt was for Annie the same kind of touchstone that she became for later generations of writers, someone who had sat down to dinner with Hawthorne and Dickens.

The Fieldses' admiration of Leigh Hunt had a personal basis, since both had met him and been welcomed as his friends. But Annie's estimate of his reputation was perceptive as well as generous:

> That Hunt's gifts were second to those of Keats, no one can deny; but that they were second-rate powers in themselves, the record which he has left in his Autobiography and other works must forever disprove. (57)

Annie alluded to the two-year prison term which Hunt had served for libelling the Prince Regent in 1813 and pointed out that unlike his friends and poetic superiors, Hunt had "what they had not, a hand-to-hand fight with poverty from the beginning to the end of his long life" (66). Perhaps Hunt's friends were fortunate to have died young, she implies, and escaped drinking "the bitter cup of existence to the dregs" (67).

According to Annie, the misfortunes and hardships which Hunt suffered make it an even greater pleasure for a reader "to discover a few beautiful and enduring poems which will embalm his name forever; and still further, to recognize his leadership in letters, by which other men are brought to the fountain of inspiration and sustainment" (67). The essay provides new insight into the Fieldses' motivations in befriending and patronizing (in its former sense) writers such as Hunt, Walter Landor, Celia Thaxter, and Harriet Beecher Stowe. The essays reveal that despite Annie's personal enthusiasm for her subjects, who were in fact both authors and friends, she was well aware that not all of her subjects were the great writers of their age. She asked her readers to evaluate her friends, and by implication, herself, not only in terms of the quality, consistency, and craftsmanship of what they produced, but also in terms of their humanity and their service to the field of letters. According to these criteria, Annie's own writing takes on added value.

The subjects of "Edinburgh" are less familiar to contemporary readers than those of "Leigh Hunt": Dr. John Brown, David Douglas, John Wilson ("Christopher North"), DeQuincey, Robert Burns, Allan Ramsay, and Sir Walter Scott. Annie had met Brown and Douglas in 1860; James had known DeQuincey and Wilson as well. Her discussion is based on anecdotes Fields told and on the books themselves—first editions and copies with manuscript notations. Despite this diluted source material, Annie brings the Edinburgh circle to life and uses it to reveal some of her own interests and crotchets also. For example, she quotes John Wilson in praise of women memoirists:

> I have a great faith in the memoir-writing powers of women—witness Lady Holland's life of her father, Sydney Smith, and the sketch of Lord North by his daughter in Brougham's "Statesmen of the Reign of George III." (101–02)

She quotes her husband on DeQuincey, defending the high value her age placed on the personal characteristics of its writers:

> He seemed to me to have accomplished nothing with his pen, great as his achievements have been, compared to the eloquence and greatness of his spoken words. (115)

Of another writer, Allan Ramsay, Annie said that he "stopped a gap before the time of Scott and Burns" and "established the first circulating library ever seen in Scotland, and many sins should have been forgiven him for that" (123–25).

At the end of this long essay, Annie relates an anecdote about Scott which Dr. John Brown had told. One day when Scott and a number of his friends sat down to dinner, they were interrupted by Marjorie Fleming, a young girl Scott called "Pet Marjorie," of whom he was very fond. Rather than frighten her by bringing her into the dining room full of strangers, he brought his friends into the lobby one by one to meet and welcome her. Of this innate consideration, Annie wrote:

> Surely it is this gift above all the rest which makes us value the least trifle with which he had to do, the gift of which Matthew Arnold has said:
>
> > "For will and energy, though rare,
> > Are yet, far, far less rare than love." (140)

The great distance between Annie's and the present age is once again revealed; our own is slower to praise, readier with cynicism, and more fearful of expressing sentiment.

The point that Annie Fields was trying to make in these rambling essays is that personal greatness adds an important dimension to a writer's work and increases the value of his contribution to humanity. Annie believed that a writer should be judged as a human being, not merely as the author of his or her books. A corollary point is her conviction that greatness as a writer could compensate for flaws as a human being, as in the case of Dickens, but here, her emphasis is on the former. Annie quoted approvingly from Lowell's introduction to Milton's *Areopagetica* in the third and final section of her book: "Milton is not so truly a writer of great prose as a great man writing in prose, and it is really Milton we seek there more than anything else" (146).

Three of the final subjects of "From Milton to Thackeray"—Mrs. Proctor, "Orinda," and Thackeray—show Annie at her best, with congenial material at hand. The prolonged discussion of Anna B. Proctor, "Barry Cornwall's" wife, gives us an opportunity to see how Annie handles a discussion of a woman whose place in literary society was not unlike her own. Like Annie, Anna B. Proctor entered literary society through marriage, though in her case it was the marriage of her mother to Basil Montagu before she herself married "Barry Cornwall." Annie quotes the *London Academy*:

> By her mother's marriage she was brought, when quite a child, into contact with Lamb and Coleridge, Keats, and Leigh Hunt, and other men of note, who frequented the houses of the editor of Bacon, and she speedily learned to hold her own among the wits, her masterful and clear intellect early asserting itself. (189)

Like Annie, Mrs. Proctor knew several generations of authors, the friends of her stepfather, the friends of her husband, and a younger generation that included Thackeray, Dickens, Tennyson, and Browning. Dickens said of Anna B. Proctor that "no matter how brilliant the men were who surrounded her—and they were all that London had of the best—she always gave the last and wittiest rejoinder" (188). Annie quoted again from the *London Academy*:

> Not that Mrs. Proctor was at all a mere repository of reminiscences. She took a keen interest in the topics of the day, and her talk was admirable, both for what she said and the way in which she said it. She held strong opinions of her own on most subjects, and about most people, and often her expression of them was more emphatic than cautious, and this earned her a reputation for bitterness she did not deserve, for she was essentially kind-hearted. (190)

In this portrait of Anna B. Proctor, Annie may reveal her own secret aspirations as an editor's wife and the way she hoped to be seen by the later generation of writers, such as Mark DeWolfe Howe, Louise Imogen Guiney, and Willa Cather.

Annie regretfully noted that Mrs. Proctor had been "so shocked by the posthumous publication of Carlyle's 'Reminiscences' that she destroyed all diaries and correspondence in her possession" (190). Noting that James Russell Lowell had said a biography of Mrs. Proctor should be written, Annie agreed and suggested for the job a writer who would later become one of her own memoirists:

Unless Mr. Henry James can do it for us, we now seem to lack the mental camera which will throw on paper the portrait of this distinguished woman as she moved through a long half-century of London society. (192)

Annie wrote a long digression on "The Matchless Orinda," Katherine Philips, who wrote poems which describe (according to Annie) "an apotheosis of love between man and woman" (201), although other readers believe her work describes love between women. Then Annie presents a rare glimpse of herself in her section on Thackeray. Like Dickens, Thackeray had been persuaded by James to give a lecture tour in America; Annie had been married only a short time and was not yet accustomed to entertaining the great. She wrote, "I can recall his goodness to one who, although married already, was hardly more than 'a slip of a girl,' and very much afraid of him." However, as Annie says,

> He took it all in at a glance, and sat down by the window and drew me to him and told me about his "little girls" at home . . . and how they were the dearest girls in the world, and when I came to England I should find them more like two old friends, and should have somebody, I am sure he thought, "to play with," though under the circumstances he could not use just those words! (205–06)

Her anecdotes include a description of a segregated *Punch* dinner that Annie attended in England where she and Thackeray's daughters were relegated to a small table out in the hall but were frequently visited by Thackeray to make sure they were having a good time (212).

In 1894 Annie and Sarah were grieved by the death of their friend Celia Thaxter. Annie published an obituary in the *Boston Transcript*; it was reprinted in the *Atlantic* and eventually published as the introduction to the *Letters of Celia Thaxter,* which Annie edited with Rose Lamb, as well as in *Authors and Friends*. The essay on Thaxter is one of Annie's best and is still an important source of biographical information about Thaxter.

In 1895 Annie's second collection of poems, *The Singing Shepherd,* was published to mixed reviews. The *Overland Monthly* declared that while Annie's Civil War poems may have "ranked well with the average songs of that day," the poems now had to be compared with the best poetry of the Civil War, written by Whittier, Mrs. Howe, and Longfellow, and "in this light, Mrs. Fields shows painfully weak" (59). The *Atlantic* concentrated on positive aspects of the book, accurately declaring:

> It may be said with some confidence that the most winning beauty of the book is to be found in the poems which seem to have sprung most directly from human intercourse and the memory of it. This may be only another way of naming the verses into which the element of immediate personality has entered most strongly. (269)

As this review suggests, *The Singing Shepherd* is more interesting than *Under the*

Olive because it depends less on classical themes and is more personal—personal in a Victorian sense.

The philosophy of the poems is Transcendental and Romantic, and they reflect the influence of Wordsworth, Keats, and Emerson as well as Tennyson, Swinburne, and Rossetti. The poems reveal an intimate knowledge of wildflowers, birds, bees, crickets, and other residents of woods, fields, and shore. The poems' interest is threefold: first, they reveal Annie's intellectual influences and her reading; second, they offer some insight into her feelings and her inner life; and third, the poems provide a reading of Annie's aspirations, her goals for herself, and her view of the poet as the highest human interpreter of life's mysteries, a view she shared with many of the men and women of her circle. It was this view of the poet as interpreter of the divine, so different from current thinking, that allowed Tennyson and Longfellow to attain their status as demigods of Victorian culture in England and America.

In "Song, to the Gods, Is Sweetest Sacrifice," Annie creates a dialogue between Criton (Crito), who voices Platonic scorn of the poet, and the common citizens who look to poetry to show them the meaning of life:

> Is this all?
> To fade and die within this narrow ring?
> Where are the singers, with their hearts aflame,
> To tell again what those of old let fall,—
> How to decaying worlds fresh promise came,
> And how our angels in the night-time sing.

In Annie's writing, nature, religion (belief in a divine power, an afterlife, and Christian principles of living), and poetry itself form a trinity of hope.

Poems on the role of poetry and the poet, poems on classical subjects, and poems on personal subjects share roughly equal space in this book. Of these, the poems about nature are most successful. "Blue Succory," "Herb Yarrow," "Ros Solis," "Sweetbriar," and "The Cricket" are charming, if minor, poems which anticipate William Carlos Williams in their simple use of a single natural image as a metaphor for human life.

The personal poems include a number of lyrics dedicated to Annie's friends, living and dead. In addition to a birthday poem to Laura Winthrop Johnson, there are poems to "A. D. T. W.," "G. D. H.," "I. S.," and in memory of Dickens ("Threnody"), Otto Dresel, Celia Thaxter, Tennyson, and Elizabeth Whittier. "The Soul of the Poet" suggests Emerson, and "The Singing Shepherd" Whittier or Longfellow. These poems are all conventional memorial lyrics: the most interesting are "Winter Lilacs," which seems to be about the Fieldses' friendship with Dickens and the subsequent friendship between Annie and Georgina, and "Elizabeth's Chamber," a memorial to Whittier's sister. "River Charles" describes what living near the river had meant to Annie and to the poets of Cambridge. Only a handful of poems seem to refer to Annie's major relationships with Fields or Jewett. "Upon Revisiting a Green Nook,"[6] a poem which Whittier said "blends so beautifully with the two worlds, the seen and the unseen," returns Annie to a spot in Manchester that she and James had often visited together

(WL 3:584; 6 March 1891). "Tides" is about the gap left in her life by James's death, and its prompt filling by Sarah, and "To ———, Sleeping," is probably about Annie and Sarah's friendship. Annie drew upon her experience as a charitable visitor in a poem called "The Ruined Home," in which she attempts a Frost-like narrative about a home destroyed by alcohol.

Although Annie published many individual poems and several volumes of poetry, she achieved little success as a poet. Her omission from the anthologies of her time, even anthologies of women poets, shows that she was not taken seriously as a poet. This is not to say that the poems are bad by the standards of her day; they are competent, carefully written, coherent poems free from the sentimentality of the popular poets and the sing-songy rhythms that many better poets, such as Poe and Longfellow, occasionally overused. Her poems appeared in the best magazines next to the work of the best writers; most of the other writers whose work appeared with that of Longfellow, Henry James, and Howells have been forgotten as well. It is sad that Annie, who wanted so badly to be a good, if not a great, poet, and who felt that writing poetry rather than prose was her native gift, never rose above competence and conventionality in her poems.

lls w/ Sarton,
also lost at memoir

10.

Success

1894–1902

Both Annie and Sarah did virtually all their best work in the two decades between 1881, when their life together began, and 1902, when a carriage accident ended Sarah's writing and her life in Boston. The peak of both women's careers occurred in 1896, the year that Fields's *Authors and Friends* and Jewett's *Country of the Pointed Firs* came out. With the exception of *How to Help the Poor, Authors and Friends* was Annie's most popular book and the book most interesting to readers today.

Authors and Friends collects Annie's best essays about her native literature and the American writers she knew well. With the exception of the two short final pieces on Tennyson and Lady Tennyson, the subjects of *Authors and Friends* were members of Annie's social circle, neighbors, and other intimates: Longfellow, Emerson, Holmes, Harriet Beecher Stowe, Celia Thaxter, and Whittier. There is no essay on James Russell Lowell, who died in 1891, probably because she never wrote an essay that she could not write with a generous spirit.

Why did Annie never write an essay on Lowell? She never warmed to him; his biting manner and egotism never charmed her, as did the manner of another egotist of warmer personality, Holmes. In a letter to Whittier about a number of mutual friends, Annie remarked:

> What a blessing it is to keep one's intellect to the end. Lowell complains I see that he has to look out words in the dictionary! But does he expect to be *more* than mortal! (1887)

Annie's remarks about Lowell from her letters and diary, many of them uncharitable, were never collected.

Other omissions are explained by the fact that nearly all of Annie's essays were essentially elegiac. The prohibition against writing about living authors explains why so few women are subjects of Annie's writing; Whittier, Holmes, Emerson, and Longfellow belonged to James T. Fields's generation and died before her, while her women friends were mostly her age or younger. As a result, it was they who would write about her, as did Elizabeth Stuart Phelps, Louise Imogen Guiney, and Willa Cather. Annie left unfinished articles on Elizabeth Stuart Phelps and Sophia Hawthorne among her papers at her death. But in the case of Phelps, Harriet Prescott Spofford, Abby Morton Diaz, Rebecca Harding Davis, and others, what might have been an important source of biographical information was lost because of Victorian convention.

The essays in *Authors and Friends* contain Annie's best sustained writing. The first essay, "Longfellow: 1807–1882," makes use of an embedded two-part structure which Annie used in other essays as well. The first half of the essay assesses Longfellow as a man and writer. Annie brings together her memories of Longfellow, stories she heard others tell of him, and stories he told about himself to create a sense of Longfellow as a human being. She intersperses bits of circumspect biography among the anecdotes, just enough to provide the reader with a skeletal chronology of Longfellow's life. The essay proceeds partly in chronological order and partly according to free association; Annie moves backward or forward in time to make a thematic connection. In the first half of the essay the sense of a benevolent consciousness, controlling and shaping the material, is never lost.

In the second half of the essay, Annie turns to excerpts from diaries, occasionally Longfellow's or James Fields's, but primarily her own. Some of these chronological excerpts touch only slightly on Longfellow; others are long and dull. The effectiveness of the second half of the essay is marred by poor editing.

Annie began her essay on Longfellow with the image of lilacs, one of his favorite flowers that bloomed near his home:

> It was the most natural thing in the world that he should care for this common flower, because in spite of a fine separateness from dusty levels which every one felt who approached him, he was first of all a seer of beauty in common things and a singer to the universal heart. (4)

Longfellow was all that Annie felt a true poet should be—a person both above the common and yet of the earth, at one with nature and ordinary men. This paradox of aristocrat and peasant joined in one—perhaps a reflection of the Christian mystery of Jesus as God and man—explains why Annie and her contemporaries raised this poet above all others. Unlike Holmes or Lowell, Longfellow was without egotism; although religious, he was neither as unworldly as Whittier nor as political. His political opinions were not as central to him as they were to some others, as was appropriate for a poet: "He was a tender father, a devoted friend, and a faithful citizen, and yet something apart and different from all these" (4).

Annie both admired and envied Longfellow's knowledge, in particular "his power of acquiring language [which was] most unusual." Throughout her life she struggled to acquire a limited mastery of languages and was awed by the man who could still speak fluent Spanish thirty years after learning it. Longfellow's perseverance also impressed her:

> The single aim of Longfellow's life, the manner in which from his earliest days he dedicated himself to Letters, would prove alone, if other signs were lacking, the strength of his character. (9)

From a letter Longfellow wrote to his father when he was seventeen, Annie quotes the lines which described her own fierce longing as well: "Whatever I do study ought to be engaged in with all my soul,—for *I WILL BE EMINENT* in something" (11).

Like James T. Fields, Longfellow had yearned for domestic life, and after the early death of his first wife he married Fanny Appleton. After too few years of happiness, Fanny died after her clothing caught fire in her home. Annie alluded to but did not discuss Longfellow's bereavements. Early in the essay, she noted that "his history is not without its tragedies" (15), and later, she said of the effect of Fanny's death on Longfellow that "Ever after . . . he was a different man. His friends suffered for him and with him, but he walked alone through the valley of the shadow of death" (36).

At this point in the story of Longfellow's life, Annie's diary, begun in 1863, caught up with her narrative, and although the anecdotes that fill out the rest of the essay are individually interesting, the continuous narrative flow of the earlier portions is missing. Many of the anecdotes concern the trials which Longfellow endured as the result of his enormous popularity. He was constantly sent manuscripts with the request that he give his "real opinion" of them, something that, as he told Annie, he could not possibly do. And there is the story about the autograph seeker who wrote to Longfellow that he "loved poetry in most any style, and would he please copy his 'Break, break, break'" for him (35). Despite its organizational lapses, inevitable at a time when many biographies consisted of little more than strings of expurgated quotations from letters pasted together with a little text, Annie's essay creates a vivid picture of Longfellow as he appeared to his friends and neighbors.

At the beginning of the second essay, "Glimpses of Emerson," Annie tried to articulate her sense of why biography, and its special branch, the personal memoir, satisfied a human need. Annie herself had always been fascinated by the lives of the great and good, and biographies, autobiographies, letters, journals, and diaries always headed the list of her reading. According to Annie, the reason that the lives of the great are important is that

> the perfect consistency of a truly great life, where inconsistencies of speech become at once harmonized by the beauty of the whole nature, gives even to a slight incident the value of a bit of mosaic which, if omitted, would leave a gap in the picture. (67)

If every "slight incident" helps to create a complete picture of an admirable person, and this picture can become a powerful inspiration or influence toward good, then it is the special mission of those who have lived in proximity to the great to gather the tiny bits of the mosaic together and to shape them into a comprehensible form. The result of such an action is that

> in so far as such fragments bring men and women of achievement nearer to our daily lives, without degrading them, they warm and cheer us with something of their own beloved and human presence. (67)

The act of writing a memoir was full of meaning for Annie, and writing about Emerson, the prophet of her generation, was especially so.

The first part of the essay focuses on Emerson's perfectionism, which was illustrated by his reluctance to include in his edition of Thoreau any work he believed to be inferior. Emerson is reported to have told Thoreau's sister, when she insisted on a more inclusive edition, "You have spoiled my Greek statue" (69). Annie tells how Emerson had edited the poems of an unnamed writer on the way to publication and asked the publisher (Fields?) to allow the author to think the changes had been made by the compositor. Emerson applied these same standards of perfectionism to himself, for Annie noted with chagrin that he went over his manuscripts so many times that it was "almost impossible to extort a manuscript from his hands" (71).

Annie told readers about Emerson's declared inability to read either Goethe's *Faust* or the *Divine Comedy,* two classics which Annie had struggled to read in the original and believed every educated person should read. She was uncomfortable with Emerson's dismissal of a writer in the Fields circle (unnamed) "whom we all knew and valued for extraordinary gifts." Emerson said of him: "——— is irreclaimable. The sentimentalists are the most dangerous of the insane, for they cannot be shut up in asylums" (81).

In her diary Annie had recorded the problems caused by Emerson's increasing infirmities; sometimes he couldn't prevent the loose pages of his manuscript from flying off the podium, and occasionally his eyes refused to focus and made it impossible for him to read the text of his speech. In "Glimpses of Emerson," Annie omitted such specific details and referred only obliquely to Emerson's declining powers: "The day came, alas! when desire must fail, and the end draw near." For Annie, the lesson of Emerson's life was "the righteousness and beauty of his personal behavior" (106).

The next essay, "Oliver Wendell Holmes: Personal Recollections and Unpublished Letters," focused on two of Holmes's characteristic traits, his gregariousness and his egotism:

> Dr. Holmes's social nature, as expressed in conversation and in his books, drew him into communication with a very large number of persons. It cannot be said, however, in this age marked by altruisms, that he was altruistic; on the contrary, he loved himself, and made himself his prime study—but as a member of the human race. (110)

Annie's perspicacity and forthrightness here are surprising, relating as they do to the man who was her neighbor and friend for many years. Although he was never a personal friend in the sense that Whittier was, Annie genuinely liked and admired Holmes. Annie was never very close to Holmes's wife, Amelia, whom she regarded as unduly self-sacrificing: "His wife absorbed her life in his, and mounted guard to make sure that interruption was impossible" (110). Annie and Holmes existed on a footing of mutual sympathy and respect, and her knowledge and analysis of his character were based on the observation of many years.

After visiting and admiring the Fieldses' classically styled townhouse on Charles Street, Holmes had moved into a similar house just up the street. Thereafter it was only a short walk to breakfast at the home of his publisher, where Holmes's insatiable sociability was fed through conversation with visiting authors. Such breakfasts occurred as often as two or three times a week among notable company: "There were few men, except Poe, famous in American or English literature of that era who did not appear at least once" (129–30). Annie attributed the success of her years as a literary hostess to the quality of her guests rather than to any gift of her own:

> For a brief period Boston enjoyed a sense of cosmopolitanism, and found it possible, as it is really possible only in London, to bring together busy guests with full and eager brains who are not too familiar with one another's thought to make conversation an excitement and a source of development. (130)

Annie said that Holmes was not driven by "a determination to be cheerful or witty or profound" but by a childlike ability to be "always open to the influences around him, and ready for a 'good time'" (110). Although Annie had occasionally been annoyed by his monopolizing the conversation at dinner, she admitted that "the wise guest . . . usually led Dr. Holmes on until he forgot that he was not listening or replying" (111). Holmes's "power of sympathy" was so strong that Annie described it as a kind of telepathy which allowed Holmes "to understand what his companion would say if he should speak, and made it possible for him to talk in a measure for others as well as to express himself" (111).

Despite his egotism, Holmes was unfailingly modest about his own accomplishments and proud of the successes of his friends and classmates. In reply to a compliment on his lyrics, Holmes said, "there is something too hopping about them. To tell the truth, nothing has injured my reputation so much as the too great praise which has been bestowed upon my 'windfalls'" (132). Annie noted dryly that "Dr. Holmes had never known any very difficult hand to hand struggle with life, but he was quite satisfied with its lesser difficulties" (139).

Annie greatly admired Holmes's sense of humor, especially his ability to laugh at himself. When Holmes's hearing had declined and his eyes were developing cataracts, he quoted to Annie part of an 1879 poem, "The Archbishop and Gil Blas," which gently satirized the elderly:

> *Can you read as once you used to?* Well,
>   the printing is so bad,
> No young folks' eyes can read it like
>   the books that once we had.
> *Are you quite as quick of hearing?*
>   Please to say that once again.
> *Don't I use plain words, your Reverence?*
>   Yes, I often use a cane.

Holmes said that his cataracts "increase so very slowly that I often wonder which will win the race first—the cataracts or death." The year before he died, he told Annie, "I gave two dinners to two parties of old gentlemen just before I left town. . . . our baby was seventy-three!" (147).

Holmes was lonely in his last years; his wife and his daughter predeceased him, and he was disabled in hearing, sight, and locomotion. One has a sense that his life dragged on longer than was comfortable for him. Annie's essay unconsciously imitated his life, as if after considerable discussion of his infirmities and the loneliness of his old age, she was surprised that she had not yet come to the end of his life. Quoting Holmes on the sad fate of the person who has outlived his generation, a fate which was hers as well as his own, she wrote:

> One that remains walking . . . while others have dropped asleep, and keeps a little night-lamp flame of life burning year after year, if the lamp is not upset and there is only a careful hand held round it to prevent the puffs of wind from blowing the flame out. That's what I call an old man. (155)

"Days with Mrs. Stowe" appeared in the *Atlantic* in 1893 and was collected in *Authors and Friends*. The essay exhibits an extravagance of rhetoric not found in the other essays, perhaps because their shared womanhood permitted a closer friendship than was usual between a woman and a man. Annie's identification with Stowe is immediately apparent. Few subjects elicited this kind of passion from her:

> Her heart was like a burning coal laid upon the altar of humanity; and when she stole up, as it were, in the night and laid it down for the slave with tears and supplication, it awakened neither alarm nor wonder in her spirit that in the morning she saw a bright fire burning there and lighting the whole earth. (160)

From this fiery beginning the essay turns to a description of the prosaic events of Mrs. Stowe's daily life, describing the hardships she suffered while rearing her family and the events which led to the visit to Kentucky on which *Uncle Tom's Cabin* was based.

Annie brought to her essay on Stowe an effective combination of perception and restraint. For example, when recounting Stowe's well-known statement that God wrote *Uncle Tom's Cabin,* Annie noted that Stowe had made this statement "late in life (when her failing powers made it impossible for her to speak as one living in a world which she seemed to have left far behind)" (176). Annie evidently believed that Stowe's colorful assertion of divine inspiration stemmed from the senility which overtook her at the end of her life.

Despite her skepticism, Annie knew that even before Stowe's mind was affected, she always "behaved as if she recognized herself to be an instrument breathed upon by the Divine Spirit" (167). As a result, according to Annie, Stowe was capable of highly subjective and controversial convictions which "absorbed her to the prejudice of what appeared to others a wholesome exercise of human will and judgment" (167–68). This remark was Annie's gentle reference to the attack on Byron and defense of Lady Byron which had alienated a large portion of Stowe's public, an attack Annie disapproved of because she believed Byron a great man in other respects.

Like Holmes, Mrs. Stowe was a great talker. Though gregarious, she felt herself to be too dependent on the opinions of others, stating in a letter to her brother that "This desire to be loved forms, I fear, the great motive for all my actions" (173). Her desire to please may have contributed to the tendency to overreach herself, which Annie referred to with regret, saying that if Stowe had not begun *The Pearl of Orr's Island* before finishing *Agnes of Sorrento,* both would have been better. Perhaps basing her judgment on the opinion of Jewett, Annie recognized the superior potential of the Maine story.

Her admiration for Stowe did not prevent Annie from acknowledging the disorganized work habits and uneven writing of her subject. In *Literary Friends and Acquaintance,* Howells made this point bluntly: "Her syntax was such a snare to her that it sometimes needed the combined skill of all the proofreaders and the assistant editor to extricate her (118–19). Stowe's childlike faith in humanity permitted her to call upon not only her editors and her publisher but on Annie as well. Despite her knowledge of Annie's busy life, Stowe asked Annie to finish research, revise proofs, and perform a variety of other errands on occasion; in one letter she told Annie, "I want to get one or two special bits of information out of Garrison, and so instead of sending my letter at random to Boston I will trouble you (who have little or nothing to do!) to get this letter to him" (199). Stowe was sometimes so exhausted by her household responsibilities, the pressure to earn money with her writing, and the struggle to write itself that she came to Boston to recuperate.

Her misfortunes were made no lighter by the fact that many, including Annie, thought she never matched the achievement of her first great book:

> The woman who had written "Uncle Tom" was not to continue a series of equally exciting stories, but she was to bear the burden and heat of much everyday labor with the patience and the rejoicing of all faithful souls. (179)

Annie's assessment of her friend's contribution to literature was understanding but frank. She wrote:

> On the whole we may rather wonder at the high average value of the literary work by which she lived, especially when we follow the hints given in her letters of her interrupted and crowded existence. (186)

Annie quoted from a few of the letters she would use later in her biography of Stowe describing the author's attempts to dictate a novel, instruct a cook, nurse a baby, and care for a toddler or two all at the same time. As a result of the obstacles in Stowe's path, she was destined to "fall short in ability to accomplish what she undertook . . . but the elasticity of her spirits was something marvelous and carried her over many a hard place" (190).

Annie had been disappointed in Emerson's inability to read Dante and Goethe, so her statement that "the writer of one of the greatest stories the world has yet produced . . . was not a student of literature" is not unexpected. While Annie saw literature as a great continuum, a tradition into which the best writers try to fit themselves, Stowe valued books for other reasons:

> Books as a medium of the ideas of the age, and as the promulgators of morals and religion were of course like the breath of her life; but a study of the literature of the past as the only true foundation for a literature of the present was outside the pale of her occupations, and for the larger portion of her life outside of her interest. (193)

The fact that her writing was not always an artistic success probably did not bother Stowe much; her priorities were not the priorities of Hawthorne, Longfellow, or

Lowell. In a letter to George Eliot, Stowe wrote that "After all, my love of you is greater than my admiration, for I think it more and better to be really a woman worth loving than to have read Greek and German and written books" (212). Such a statement illustrates the emphasis on human qualities that separated many nineteenth-century women writers—even women of genius—from the emphasis on art and style which inevitably dominated the now "classic" writers of the age.

If Stowe's belief in the primary importance of the human being was shared by a majority of the women then writing, it is not hard to see why the style and structure of so much of their work compares unfavorably with that of men. Annie Fields may never have written the kind of poetry, fiction, or essays that undergraduates read in college because she was not sure she had a *right* to be an author, to make writing her first priority. Harriet Beecher Stowe was not crippled by ambivalence, as her statement that it was "more and better to be a woman worth loving" reveals, but her priorities kept her from reaching her potential.

"Celia Thaxter" first appeared after Thaxter's death in 1894 and was later used as the introduction to the *The Letters of Celia Thaxter* (1895), edited by Annie and Rose Lamb, an amateur painter who worked primarily in watercolor (CL 97n). The lives of Stowe and Thaxter contain some parallels, yet two more dissimilar lives can hardly be imagined. The life of Harriet Beecher Stowe was laborious but seldom beautiful; though gifted, Stowe never lived gracefully. The life of Celia Thaxter, however, was artistic and picturesque at every turn; though her trials were more difficult than Stowe's, Annie's essay gives us the sense of a life that was beautiful even when it was tragic.

Thaxter was brought as a young child to live on the Isles of Shoals, a group of bleak, semi-inhabited islands to which her father fled after a disappointment in his career. Celia was very young when she married Levi Thaxter and the marriage did not prove fortunate. According to Annie,

> Their natures were strongly contrasted, but perhaps not too strongly to complement each other if he had fallen in love with her as a woman, and not as a child. His retiring, scholarly nature and habits drew him away from the world; her overflowing, sun-loving being, like a solar system in itself, reached out on every side, rejoicing in all things. (240)

Annie held herself in check to describe thus a man she loathed and a marriage she knew was a prison.

But Celia's life had a beautiful side as well. She knew flowers and plants intimately and painted delicate and exact portraits of them on porcelain and paper. She created unique copies of her book for friends by painting flowers in the margins. She knew birds and mourned those that died by flying into the lighthouse beam. In her youth Celia herself had been beautiful:

> She was slighter in figure then, and overflowing with laughter, the really beautiful but noisy laughter which died away as the repose of manner of later years fell upon her. I can remember her as I first saw her, with the seashells which she always wore then around her neck and wrists, and a gray poplin dress defining her lovely form. Her sense of beauty, not vanity, caused her to make the most of the good physical points she possessed;

therefore, although she grew old early, the same general features of her appearance were preserved. (236)

Thaxter became stout and wore her pure white hair in a bun, but pictures taken late in her life, among the beautiful gardens she planted at the island home where artists and writers came, suggest the great beauty she must have possessed.

In writing of Thaxter, Annie again showed an interest in the circumstances of women's lives that often prevented them from reaching their potential. Annie wrote of Thaxter:

> Every year we find her longing for large knowledge; books and men of science attracted her; and if her life had been less intensely laborious, in order to make those who belonged to her comfortable and happy, what might she not have achieved! Her nature was replete with boundless possibilities, and we find ourselves asking the old, old question, Must the artist forever crush the wings by which he flies against such terrible limitations? (251)

Annie wrote that "this careless happy creature possessed the strength and sweep of wing which belonged to her own sea-gull" (240)—an image surprisingly similar to that used later by Henry James in writing of the relationship between Annie and Sarah. Annie would not have compared her own life to those of Stowe or Thaxter in hardship or sadness, but she used the vehicle of the biographical memoir to express the frustration that she and many more of her women friends felt at their inability to devote their lives fully to art.

Annie's essay on Whittier focused on his singularity, the ways that he differed from the other men in Annie's circle. His Quaker beliefs formed the basis of this difference:

> His lithe, upright form, full of quick movement, his burning eye, his keen wit, bore witness to a contrast in himself with the staid, controlled manner and the habit of the sect into which he was born. (265)

Despite his religion, however, he shared with non-Quakers of his time the ideals common to New England philosophy. Annie wrote that "he made one course with Garrison and Phillips, Emerson and Lowell, Longfellow and Holmes. His standards were often different from those of his friends, but their ideals were on the whole made in common" (266).

Whittier's preference for rural life and his dislike of social events singled him out in a society of visitors. He avoided all but a few, which made possible his intimate friendships with Annie, James, and Sarah. Annie noted that because of his headaches and invalidism, his letters did not measure up to the high epistolary standards of the day:

> His correspondence suffered from a literary point of view, but his letters were none the less delightful to his friends. To the world of literature they are perhaps less important than those of most men who have achieved a high place. (267)

Whittier's unusual relationship with the women writers of his time is now well known, but Annie may have been the first to mention it:

> His sympathy with the difficulties of a literary life, particularly for women, was very keen. There seem to be few women writers of his time who have failed to receive from his pen some recognition. (272)

Sarah Orne Jewett was one of Whittier's favorites even before she and Annie, another, joined households. Lucy Larcom and Lydia Maria Child were two more of his women friends; although Annie does not mention Mary Abigail Dodge, she was close to Whittier as well.

Whittier's life changed when he moved from his home in Amesbury, where he had lived with his niece, to live with his cousins at Oak Knoll, Danvers. He returned to his family home occasionally and sometimes stopped with other cousins in Newburyport. But as he grew older, Annie implies, his lack of a fixed home and inability to live alone plagued him more and more. Because of his keen interest in Spiritualism, even when he was alone, "A host of friends, friends of the spirit, were . . . forever clustering around him, and what a glorious company it was!" (331).

Annie concludes this essay with reference to the etymology of the word "sage," remarking that Whittier "brought the antique word into use again and filled it with fresh meaning for modern men" (334). She notes that death "is far less dreadful" to us than old age, which "appears in comparison to every other stage of human existence as a most undesirable state," words which reflect the pain she must have felt as many of her friends faded into infirmity, decrepitude, and finally death (334). Annie Fields, of all her generation, had perhaps the largest experience of death to prepare her for what lay ahead.

The two short essays on Tennyson and Emily, Lady Tennyson, which close the book, differ significantly from the others for several reasons. Unlike the other subjects of *Authors and Friends,* the Tennysons could not be described as intimate friends. They seem to have more in common with the subjects of *A Shelf of Old Books,* who were removed by nationality and nearly a generation of time. Indeed, Annie began her essay on Tennyson by relating an anecdote about herself as a young child reciting "The Lady of Shalott" in the classroom. And yet, Annie came to know Tennyson well, well enough for him to have revealed to her, on a country walk, the crevice in a summer house where he hid small bits of paper and pencil to write on when away from home.

Annie seems to have known Lady Tennyson less well, although she must have spent more hours in her company than in Tennyson's. A reserved woman who was absolutely devoted to her husband, Lady Tennyson "was ready to sympathize with every form of emancipation; but for herself, her poet's life was her life, and his necessity was her great opportunity" (352). Annie recalled Elizabeth Barrett Browning's statement that Lady Tennyson indulged her husband too much and did not criticize him enough. Annie, who perceived a basic lack of sympathy between the Brownings and the Tennysons, answered Barrett Browning's remark with the words of Lady Tennyson: "It is a mistake in general for [Tennyson] to listen to the suggestions of others about his poems" (353).

Indeed, the essay provides Annie with an opportunity to express her preference for the Tennysons and her dislike of Robert Browning. When Lady Tennyson remarked to Annie that Browning would not come to visit them at Farringford because "we are too quiet for him," Annie "remembered the fatuous talk at dinner-tables where I had sometimes met Browning, and thought of Tennyson's great talk and the lofty serenity of his lady's presence" (354). To Annie, the Tennysons were something above and apart from the rest of the world, and she saw in Lady Tennyson an ideal, and perhaps a type, that she realized was fast disappearing. She concluded: "The memory cannot be effaced of one lady who held the traditions of high womanhood safe above the possible deteriorations of human existence" (355).

Authors and Friends is not only Annie's best book, it is a good book. Her characterizations of her friends are always complex, fair, and insightful. These essays are not mere eulogies to friends who have died, they are also analyses of what made them great and what made them human. Although contemporary memoirs of this era have largely been displaced by up-to-date biographies, there is value in reading these notes written by a woman who had such a close view of her bit of American literature and wrote about it with such care and considered opinion.

The Country of the Pointed Firs, now universally acknowledged to be Jewett's best book, also appeared in 1896. The book has the same innovative form that Jewett used in *Deephaven,* a sequence of related incidents bound together by place, time, and a central relationship between two women. However, *The Country of the Pointed Firs* is more successful than the earlier book in style, structure, plot, and characterization, especially in the vivid portrayal of the two main characters both as individuals and in relation to one another.

The novel takes place in Dunnet Landing, a coastal New England settlement inhabited by sailors and fishermen. The village is slowly dying because its youth prefer to move to the cities and enter industrial life. But while the book is about the decay of a way of life, it is also about the relationships among its characters, primarily between Mrs. Todd and the unnamed narrator, a writer who has come from the city to improve her health. Mrs. Todd's relationships with her family and the narrator's relationships with the inhabitants of Dunnet Landing are also important. Because the central friendship between Mrs. Todd and the narrator is the heart of the book, it is natural to look for ways in which the Jewett-Fields relationship might have influenced Jewett's masterpiece.

The key to an understanding of the fictional relationship in the book can be found in the flexibility of the Fields-Jewett relationship as it is reflected in Jewett's use of nicknames. This passage from one of Sarah's letters shows the ease with which she could move from one role to another, in this case from the tomboyish Pinny to a romantic lover:

> I think of you at the lecture and I wonder who went too! Pinny to want to go dreadfully ladies (on account of going with Fuff! as much as anything)—. . . Oh Fuff I always hold

you so close to my heart in these early November days! I wish I could always spend them with you! (n.d.)

In *Country of the Pointed Firs,* Jewett illustrates her characters' flexibility by showing their ability to change themselves in a variety of ways but especially within their relationships to others. Most of Jewett's characters are either middle-aged or elderly—as were she and Annie by 1896. Numerous passages in the book describe the characters' ability to alter themselves in some way, often by becoming youthful; this metamorphosis happens most frequently with Mrs. Todd, Mrs. Blackett, William, and Esther. These references to girlishness or boyishness do not mean that Jewett and her characters longed for childhood or were reluctant adults; rather, they demonstrate a chameleon-like ability to become what one is not, to change roles. Jewett is simply varying the classical themes of metamorphosis and androgyny.

Both Jewett and Fields had the experience of living with a member of an older generation, and both had many younger friends. Annie Fields turned sixty in 1894, two years before *Country of the Pointed Firs* came out, and she was as energetic as, and more productive than, she had been at thirty. When Mrs. Todd says, "Keep me movin' enough, an' I'm twenty year old summer an' winter both" (131), she is describing agelessness and adaptability, not a longing for childhood. When Jewett's narrator says about William that "Once I wondered how he had come to be so curiously wrinkled, forgetting, absent-mindedly, to recognize the effects of time" (118), she was reflecting a natural indifference to aging in a person one loves.

The inhabitants of Dunnet Landing have the ability to play different roles in their relationships with others as well. The most notable examples of this are Mrs. Blackett and Mrs. Todd, who regularly exchange the roles of mother and child. There are numerous examples of role exchange or reversal: William, Mrs. Todd's brother, is both "son and daughter" to Mrs. Blackett (42); Mrs. Todd sends the doctor on vacation; Elijah Tilley in some sense "becomes" his wife after her death by keeping the house just as she left it; when Mrs. Todd goes to visit poor Joanna, she mothers the older woman, who then reverses the situation and comforts Mrs. Todd. Mrs. Todd says that William resembles Mrs. Blackett, while she herself takes after their father, and on several occasions she proves to be a better man than the man; she knocks down the minister, for example, to keep him from capsizing her sailboat.

The bond between Jewett and Fields appears in more definite form in the relationship between the narrator and Mrs. Todd. Although the intensity of feeling between the two women has been evident to feminist critics for some time, the obvious lack of resemblance between Mrs. Todd and Annie Fields has deterred anyone from attempting to compare the two relationships in any specific way. However, when the obvious disparities in appearance and occupation are set aside, there are a number of remarkable parallels between the Jewett-Fields relationship and that of the narrator and Mrs. Todd. First of all, Mrs. Todd is repeatedly spoken of in classical images, such as the sibyl and the caryatid; at one point the narrator says of Mrs. Todd, "She might belong to any age, like an idyl of Theocritus" (56). While Jewett might certainly be expected to have knowledge of classical Greek images, the emphasis suggests Annie's poetry that was so often based on classical myths and historical figures. *Under the Olive* is entirely composed of poems on Greek subjects, including a tribute to Theocritus, one of her favorite poets. Jewett refers to her admiration of this volume more than once in her letters to Fields. Thus, Mrs. Todd and Annie Fields are linked by classical allusion at the outset.

The first key to the parallel appears in the first sentence of the second section, when the narrator says of Mrs. Todd's house, "There was only one fault to find with this choice of a summer lodging place, and that was its complete lack of seclusion" (13–14). There follow a number of parallels between Mrs. Todd and her house and Annie and 148 Charles Street. Jewett, like the narrator, is a writer who intellectually desires seclusion so that she can write, but both found themselves drawn to a house that was constantly flooded by visitors. These are Mrs. Todd's customers, seeking herbs and spruce beer, for the narrator, while they are the throngs of friends and writers who called at what Henry James called the "waterside museum" on Charles Street, for Sarah. The narrator becomes a "business partner" in Mrs. Todd's absences (16); Jewett became Fields's co-hostess at Charles Street. Mrs. Todd went "afield" every day to gather herbs; Annie went to work at the Chardon Street headquarters of the Associated Charities, leaving Sarah to deal with callers.

Like the narrator of her story, Jewett needed resolution to withdraw to get her writing done. Although she did write while in Boston, going home to South Berwick was Jewett's self-imposed exile from Fields and sociability. But, just as in the novel, "Mrs. Todd and I were not separated or estranged by the change in our business relations; on the contrary, a deeper intimacy seemed to begin," so, too, Annie and Sarah were never distanced emotionally by their separations, but carried on an intimate correspondence. Like the narrator, who does not truly belong in Dunnet Landing, Jewett does not truly belong in Boston, but both find their adoptive homes and companions more than congenial. The narrator trudging off to the schoolhouse to write is a reflection of Sarah in her Pinny Lawson role: the narrator says, "I walked away with a dull supply of writing-paper and these provisions, feeling like a reluctant child who hopes to be called back at every step" (114). However, Mrs. Todd, like Annie, was seldom the agent of distraction; the narrator was more likely to be taken fishing by William. And as Dunnet Landing represented a larger world for Almira Todd, compared with Green Island where she grew up, so Boston gave Jewett "a large place [to live in] where more things grew" (51). There is even a comparison of Mrs. Todd to a mouse, recalling one of Jewett's nicknames for Fields. Mrs. Todd rose earlier than the narrator, as Annie rose before Sarah; the narrator says of Mrs. Todd, "Long before I was fairly awake I used to hear a rustle and knocking like a great mouse in the walls, and an impatient tread on the steep garret stairs that led to Mrs. Todd's chief place of storage" (76).

Other parallels exist in the nature of the real and the fictional relationships, especially in the mutual protectiveness that exists not only between Mrs. Todd and the narrator but also between Mrs. Todd and Blackett and between Mrs. Todd and Joanna. Perhaps the most suggestive of these relationships appears in one of several stories that Jewett wrote after the initial publication of *Country of the Pointed Firs,* "The Queen's Twin," published in 1899.

In 1896, Annie and Sarah took a tour of the West Indies with their good friends the Aldriches, or Lily and T. B. A., as they called them. During the lengthy tour their boat was becalmed and Annie missed a charity conference she was scheduled to attend. Not only was it frustrating to have their plans disrupted by an event completely out of their control, but also they found T. B. A. harder to live with in close quarters than in brief social contact. Annie kept a trip diary during the cruise, and it consisted largely of anecdotes about Aldrich.

Aldrich kept them entertained with potshots at mutual acquaintances, among them Charles William Eliot, who was out of favor with Annie because of his opposition to co-education at Harvard:

> He is greatly distanced by the temperament of the President of Harvard[:] ["]I always feel a cold wind blowing when I am in the room with him before I find out what the matter is. He is so cold that I expect some day in a warm room that one leg will drip down into his shoe like part of an iceberg and disappear.["] T. B. A. is a keen student of English and he is always making a merry hunt after our mistakes[.] To use the word "people" for persons as everybody does is a sign of great weakness in English to his eye—He has even caught Washington Irving tripping in his plural verb! (18 Feb. 1896)

Annie enjoyed his comments except on the occasions when they interfered with her sanctities:

> He talked while he smoked after dinner, *most* cheerfully under rating [sic] Longfellow, praising Tennyson's poetry, but with a feeling of bitterness toward the man whom he never knew[,] having gazed at his abode through the grill of his closed gate with Boughton his neighbor who said that "he was rude sometimes to persons who went to see him!" Well, well, I thought this is a dearly loved poet, let me hold my love and my patience, and so presently I went away by myself to read and write a letter before going to bed. (18 Feb. 1896)

Then the weather changed and they found themselves stranded upon the ocean; trying to make the best of it, Annie remarked, "But it *is* a curious change for busy minds and hearts such as Sarah's and mine and we have to hold on hard not to be impatient."

Annie noted that the delay "tried S. O. J.'s patience and mind sadly" (22 Feb. 1896). There was nothing to do but sit and talk, and Annie's capacity for "idle" conversation was taxed to its limit. Aldrich took the opportunity to repeat Henry James's opinion of Elinor Howells:

> T. B. A. said in speaking of Howells and our love for him—"Yes," Henry James said to me "I like Howells immensely and should like to see more of him, but somehow I do not altogether like his conjugal appendage"! (2 ? Feb. 1896)

On 26 February they were still aboard ship, and Annie wrote, "This is the Conference at Chardon St. I am lazily swinging in the harbor at Nassau. . . ." Being immobilized was so distasteful to Annie that she wondered whether vacations were quite moral:

> More and more I understand that schemes for enjoyment, simply, in this world are for
> the most part aside from the Divine plan. We are here to labor for others and to seek to
> know the purpose of life and its opportunities; to do such work as we can find to do with
> all our might—. (28 Feb. 1896)

Aldrich shocked Annie by his statement that he would "accept comfort at any time
rather than intelligence," which Annie felt "strikes at the root of all morality."

They breathed a sigh of relief upon reaching Boston a few days after the ship landed
in Palm Beach on 4 March, but a series of illnesses and accidents began at this time
which would alter their lives forever. Sarah's younger sister, Caroline Eastman,
suffering from an illness which proved fatal, died in April of 1897. Sarah's mother
had died in 1893, and her older sister Mary was now in Berwick alone. At about the
same time, her Uncle William (Dr. William G. Perry) fell ill and she was obliged to
remain in Berwick to help nurse him; she wrote to Annie:

> Uncle W. is very comfortable today and had a good night. I can't help sending you
> bulletins, for everything depends upon what kind of a day it is with him whether I must
> stay where he is and help him as best I can to pull through the sad hard hours.

When Uncle William had recovered sufficiently to get along without them, Annie and
Sarah packed for their third trip to Europe together, but this time Sarah's sister Mary
and their nephew Theodore Eastman accompanied them.

Judging from Annie's trip journal, she and Sarah felt considerably hampered by the
additions and occasionally made side trips by themselves. They visited with Georgina
Hogarth, who had been corresponding with Annie regularly ever since they had met
in 1869, and made a pilgrimage to the home of Madame de Sévigné. They spent some
time in Provence visiting the poet Frederic Mistral and his wife, of whom Annie said,
"Unhappily, they have no children. Evidently they are exceedingly happy together
and do not miss what they have never had" (Howe *Mem.* 296).

In mid-June of 1898, when they were still abroad, Annie received a telegram
informing her of the sudden death of her sister Lissie. Since they could not have arrived
home in time to attend her funeral, they continued their journey, but Annie was deeply
shaken by the death of her favorite sister. A small memorial about her life, written by
Richard Burton, said of her:

> Miss Adams stood among the first of those brave spirits who, casting away old prejudices,
> dared to believe that a woman might dedicate her life to a profession. In choosing and in
> following her independent career, she became a stimulus and an example to other women.
> (4–5)

The memorial mentioned that she had shown her work in the "French Salon" and had
particularly excelled in portrait painting. Like Annie, Lissie had a woman friend, Miss
Burnap, with whom she shared both a home in Baltimore and a summer house at Watch
Hill.

In March of 1900, about a year and a half after they had returned from their trip
with Mary and Theodore, Sarah and Annie made a fourth trip to Europe, this time by

themselves. They visited Greece, Turkey, Italy, and France. Upon their return, they found themselves suddenly in the twentieth century; Louisa Dresel rode a bicycle, Sarah sometimes hired a motor car so that she and Annie could go for drives in Berwick (AFL 162; Frost 138). The Charles Street house received indoor plumbing, then an elevator, and Annie and Sarah were able to chat on the telephone between visits.

But other things changed for the worse as well. After the deaths of both mother and sister, Sarah felt obliged to keep her sister Mary company more often and felt guilty if she stayed too long with Annie in Boston, while Annie seldom spent more than a few weeks of the early summer with Sarah in South Berwick. Throughout the winter, she worked regularly with the Associated Charities, filling a number of offices for them, including everything from Director or Vice-President down to visitor or teacher. She rarely acquiesced to Sarah's pleas to share her exile in Maine and, perhaps even more frustrating for Sarah, Annie accepted their separations with equanimity and relative calm. Annie explained Sarah's frequent absences from Boston in a letter to the Aldriches:

> Sarah finds that Mary needs her more and more; that is to say, Mary stays in town a good deal with us and when she returns for long winter stretches alone at S. B.—it is less easy for her to get on of course than when her mother and sister were there for her to help and to keep house for—the result is that Sarah does not find it easy to make long flights. She has been in town quite regularly this winter but she can run back for a night or two whenever she is needed—but you will understand all this without further explanation. (HH 19 March 1902)

In 1897 Annie's *Life and Letters of Harriet Beecher Stowe* appeared to favorable reviews. In 1899 Annie responded to the death of Mary Cowden Clarke with an article called "Two Lovers of Literature" and published another called "Notes on Glass Decoration" about Sarah Wyman Whitman's stained glass windows in the Harvard Chapel. Annie rounded out the year with an essay on George Eliot and a short biography of Nathaniel Hawthorne, while Sarah published *The Queen's Twin*, one of her most popular volumes.

Both women continued to be productive in the first years of the new century, despite colds and rheumatism, but so far both had escaped really serious illness. In 1900 Annie reviewed a biography of Dr. Southwood Smith, the English expert on sanitary reform; wrote a short piece on Mary Mitford, her husband's old friend; and published *Orpheus,* the long poem which Sarah considered her best work. In 1901 Sarah published *The Tory Lover,* her single (and unsuccessful) excursion into historical romance, and Annie contributed an essay on the "New England Classics" to a book club anthology.

Sarah spent the winter of 1901–1902 in Boston, her first long stay since 1897. On the third of September, 1902, Sarah celebrated her fifty-third birthday with her family and friends in South Berwick. While she was taking a ride in her pony carriage with her sister Mary and two other friends, the horse slipped on loose gravel, throwing both Sarah and Rebecca Young, the treasurer of the Berwick bank, over the head of the horse (Frost 130). Miss Young received only bruises, but Jewett suffered injuries to her head and spine from which she never completely recovered.

11.

"Both a Sharer
and a Sustainer"
1902–1910

> She had come to Mrs. Fields as an adoptive daughter,
> both a sharer and a sustainer.
> —Henry James, referring to Sarah Orne Jewett

Many months passed before the extent and seriousness of Sarah's injuries were known. The loss of both physical mobility and mental alertness and the tedious confinement which lay ahead were not yet a reality when Sarah wrote this note to Annie a few days after the accident:

> I did miss you dreadfully—and oh this morning what a tired Pinny! but she will stay in bed later and is not hurt in life or limbs but thought she had come most to an end when she was [on?] waking up—Fuff not to scold her—I know she will not. (n.d.)

At the end of three weeks Sarah had not markedly improved.

Sarah told the Aldriches that she had received injuries to her head and spine and was suffering from loss of balance, intense pain at the back of her neck, and violent headaches. She could not write at all and could do little reading, as she explained to Annie:

> I shall be better by and by, and the stories will begin to write themselves down again but the truth is that most of the time now I am really ill. It frets me even to think about copying and all the rest of it. (Frost 132)

As the months passed, Sarah continued to be unable to concentrate or even stay awake for long periods; according to Willa Cather's introduction to *The Country of the Pointed Firs,* she could not summon enough strength to finish "William's Wedding." All her life she had been a night owl and a late sleeper, but now she retired early and slept late, writing to Annie, "I am getting to be a sleepyhead like you, and so I have come into a land in which it seems always afternoon." The only work Sarah did in these years was writing letters, editing the letters of her and Annie's friend Sarah Wyman Whitman, and a few other odd bits of writing, such as revising a circular for Annie:

Dear Fuffy I wish you would read this very badly written form for the little circular and
see if you do not think it would be more appealing! If you approve and will return it to
me right away I will copy a lot of them and send to you on Friday—I don't feel like doing
any other writing and I would rather do them for you than not—.

Since she could not write, Sarah helped in the garden and reread favorite books. She
wrote to Annie:

Last night I had a perfect delight re-reading Dorothy Wordsworths [Tour] in Scotland.[1]
. . . It is just *our* book the way we enjoy things isn't it, when we are footing it out of doors.

Their separation was particularly difficult when company came to Charles Street
and Sarah, for so many years Annie's co-hostess, could not be at her side. She longed
to be in Boston:

And now the ball is over, and I suppose a tired hostess, and the chairs all going upstairs
again, and the dear room will look like a green garden that no wind ever blows over! I
do so long to hear if it went off to your mind, and if the company liked the singing, and
where it was you hung the lantern! and oh, dear! a thousand questions! (AFL 185;
Matthiessen 124; 1902?)

Jewett's accident irreversibly altered Annie and Sarah's life together. Sarah had felt
obliged to keep her sister Mary company after the death of Caroline; now she needed
Mary to take care of her. Her nostalgic love of South Berwick made it the best place
for her during the long period of crisis and recovery; in an 1895 interview Jewett had
said about her tie to Berwick: "I was born here and I hope to die here leaving the lilac
bushes still green, and all the chairs in their places" (Frost 136; Heaton 29). Her doctor
advised against moving her for some time, and even after she was allowed to travel
Charles Street would have been considered dangerously busy and exciting.

Annie continued her work with the Associated Charities, but Sarah eagerly awaited
Annie's visits to Maine and tried to persuade her to come more often:

I can hardly wait to see you dear Fuff—oh *don't* put off coming again, it seems as if I
couldn't wait at all when I think of it—and as if I should feel so much better when you
get here.

Annie responded, "It does seem strange not to have you night and morning" (n.d.).
Because her doctor had advised Sarah to convalesce in a place where she could
spend a good deal of time outdoors and be unbothered by visitors, she had gone to
Mouse Island in Boothbay Harbor, Maine, an isolated resort where she and Annie had
spent a holiday years earlier. However, four months after the accident, she was denied
even a short trip to Boston for Christmas and was bitterly disappointed:

I don't say much about Christmas dear Fuff but you will know that it goes very hard with
me that I can't think of being with you. After all, as I said to myself this morning, it would
be a great deal harder not to be together, if we didn't care about each other anymore! if

there were any *real* separation I mean, but we are closer than ever in love and friendship and belongingness, aren't we? It is wonderful with all the chances and changes of life that I could always manage to have part of Christmas Day in Charley Street for twenty years without any break—and we mustn't mind *too* much if an unlucky tumble keeps your Pin away this year! (Dec. 1902?)

After nine months Sarah was still not well enough to go to Manchester for Annie's birthday, but she had made sure that someone else would be there to celebrate:

Dearest little heart! For the first time in a great many years I am not going to be with you on your birthday morning and you can think how it grieves me. Only I shall love you and think of you a. the more. . . . I came near to [calling?] and begging you to come over but I thought it would trouble you—I hope to get to you soon or to have you here I can't get on without it much longer. . . . Much love to Jessie or Rose[2] so remember that ~~love~~ lovely birthday when we went to Chamounix [sic]. The first was to Ireland. (5 June [1902])

After the birthday, Rose Lamb wrote Sarah a letter describing the events of the day:

[Rose] said you looked so lovely too—like the blessed damosel and I wanted to hug a white dressed Fuffy right away then—and I daresay rumple her all up—. . . . Goodbye my own dear dear beautiful darling from your own Pin—. (n.d. loose page)

Although they seldom saw each other, they exchanged letters daily and Annie sent Sarah little presents to make up for her absence. Sarah was in pain and must have felt discouraged, but she made an effort to keep up her spirits, with her dog Timmy to help her:

When I was going up to bed last night at half past seven "dark under the table!" I stopped in the hall where the box is and put my fingers in to get two pieces of the oat-cake. And they seemed to be a new shape and Bigger—And they were cookies!!—Oh it made a great party; Mary had to come up the stairs to have some handed to *her* and *Timmy* came galloping from somewhere and when he was told that he couldn't have any, *said* nothing but some minutes afterward I looked behind me as I was undressing, and there sat Timmy waiting and looking with his little keen head as sharp as a bird's! So Timmy got a whole half of a cooky, for his deep appreciation! It made a great evening!! but when I began to eat mine I felt a little homesick, and they had to be just as good as they were to console my heart—I had been reading the Singing Shepherd back in the parlour late in the afternoon and I am always thinking a great deal about you and the dear house—I wish over and over again that I could come (it is so hard to say no when *you* want anything! but I should be sure to be so tired for two or three days after the little journey, and you might think it was worse than it is and worry and then *you* would be all tired out and that would worry me anew—oh no dear, we had better wait a little while longer—. . . . Mary just heard about Timmy and the cookies—and said "of course he waited—his Aunt Annie sent those cookies for *him!*" (dated 1902 by AF)

Annie and Sarah still wrote frequently about their reading and, in Annie's case, their writing. When Edith Wharton's *House of Mirth* appeared in the *Atlantic,* Annie recognized Wharton's talent but found her view of the world too negative:

By the way I have read the Aug. & Sep. of The House of Mirth—surely she has a very powerful hand. How her people live to sight—and in what a horrid world. We scarcely recognize our planet so far—do we? (n.d.)

Annie started an article on Sophia Hawthorne and sent it to Sarah, who evidently did not find it up to snuff. Annie replied:

What a help you are to the dear! Every word you say about the S. H. paper is true, but I wish you had liked it, or rather that it had been worth liking a little just a little better. But I am sure it needs quiet thought and the kind of work I can perhaps do at Manchester and I was in a "driving hurry" to get the material together for that I knew I could not get in the country—that you think I am on the way to something more is a great deal. . . . But what a tired foolish note this is—I fear I was never built to write prose—even letters go hard! (n.d.)

Annie's writing continued to frustrate her, and she came to judge even her poetry harshly, remarking once in a note to Sarah that she wished "they could drown my old verses."

In 1903 Annie was unpleasantly reminded of the old quarrel between the Fieldses and the Hawthornes when Julian Hawthorne published his second book about his father, *Hawthorne and His Circle*. This time, instead of omitting mention of the Fieldses altogether, he declared that James Fields had destroyed nonchalantly the manuscript of *The Scarlet Letter*. Annie decided to send Julian a letter denying his accusation. Originally she intended to have her say about the situation in general, as this draft shows:

My dear Julian:
    There is one passage which I think it would be well for you to illuminate from your last book[,] the one in which you speak of Mr. Fields as inappreciative of the "Scarlet Letter" and therefore of having burned the manuscript. If you will re-read what your father has said upon the subject of being appreciated and helped by his publisher I think you will cross out of your mind as well as off the page any such remark or thought. Your father told me one day after saying that he was glad to have me accept and treasure the ms. of the "House of the Seven Gables" "I wish I had the ms. of the Scarlet Letter to give you also; but I put it up the chimney." You may imagine therefore how this passage in your book struck me: ~~nor have I been able to understand the lack of dignity [illegible] you have shown all through these long years in forgetting the friendship which your father himself took every opportunity to express and make evident.~~ Nothing is of much moment now except for the truth for your own sake therefore you will I am sure cross off the passage speaking of "lack of appreciation" and tell correctly if you choose also of the burning of the manuscript which your father sincerely regretted. (BPL; 1904?)

Julian's curt reply charged Mrs. Fields with having misread the passage and dismissed her account of the disappearance of the manuscript:

I was interested in your note this morning, and sorry that you should have got the impression that my book contained the statement you supposed. What I wrote, and have often said, was that Mr. Fields did not at that time anticipate the value that would attach to Hawthorne's mss. and that therefore he neglected to save the ms. of The Scarlet Letter from the printers. I never of course charged him with "burning it." Had you read the passage in question, you would not have been subjected to the annoyance of imagining such a thing.

On the other hand, I fear you are in error in thinking that the ms. was burned or destroyed by my father. In the conversation you describe, he was probably referring to something else. However, the important thing is that the ms. is gone. (BPL 22 June 1904)

Julian was right in one thing; the passage never mentions "burning" but states that the manuscript was "destroyed by James T. Fields's printers—Fields having at that time no notion of the fame the romance was to achieve, or of the value that would attach to every scrap of Hawthorne's writing" (*Circle* 52). However, no one who knew the Fieldses at all well could credit this notion. They had always held the work of Hawthorne in the highest esteem, and their house was full of memorabilia such as manuscripts and first editions. If James and Annie misjudged the value of a manuscript, they were far more likely to overestimate than underestimate. Annie must have decided against making her general charge of injustice, since the passage does not appear in the actual letter.

By 1903 Sarah was significantly better, although not yet well enough to stay in Boston for any length of time because, as she wrote to Dorothy Ward, the daughter of Mrs. Humphry Ward, "The temptations of Town are much greater than the temptations of dear Berwick" (AFL 201–02; 14 Dec. 1904).

Sarah was still not writing, but she made an effort to keep up with Annie, reading the letters of St. Theresa after Annie published an article about her in 1903. Sarah passed on to Annie a request for an article on Mme Blanc from Robert Underwood Johnson, then editor of the *Century*. Sarah derived vicarious satisfaction—and frustration—from Annie's writing when she could not pursue her own:

> I laughed a little laugh—with a little tear in my mind's eye too—over your note on the back of the envelope when I had read the brief Atlantic paper as I had not done before. My Fuff must have been a little tired!—but I am going to give her a hug and tell her it is beautiful to take things in *large*—only not to tell *the accurate* that *they* are—in details wrong!! Fuffy to gayly say sometimes—"Oh I daresay you are right!" and *still* possess the field! Details are good in *their* place too! (1904?)[3]

In 1904, Annie published a short biography of Charles Dudley Warner for McClure Phillips's Contemporary Men of Letters series, her last book except for Sarah's letters. Annie also made her last trip abroad, to Taormina, Sicily, without Sarah.

Although Sarah probably still hoped to write again, she looked back over her work as on a completed career. Jewett's last piece of sustained writing was an introduction to Sarah Wyman Whitman's letters, published in 1907. Editing these letters caused Sarah to think about the principles underlying such an edition. In a letter to Frances Parkman, she quoted the *Spectator* review of the recently issued *Letters of Queen Victoria*:

I just opened an October "Spectator" that I had not seen, and here in a review of the Queen's Letters some wise person says: "We realize of course that it is exceedingly difficult to print Documents or Letters entire owing to reasons of space. *At the same time it cannot be doubted that a letter is a living thing with an individuality of its own, and if the head and tail are cut off, and two or three pieces taken out of the body, that individuality is lost."* This is my own strong instinct. I have felt Her at my elbow so often in reading these proofs that it has been hard not to follow *our* dislikes or preferences, but I would not for anything be *prepotente*. I think we should think of the author first however in every case. That's our plain duty.

But so few of us know what a stern judge *print* is in itself; what a sifter and weigher of values, how astonishing its calm verdict when a book is *done*. (AFL 204–05)

This passage expresses Sarah's ideas about editing letters, ideas which Annie undoubtedly shared. To Victorians such as Sarah and Annie, the challenge facing an editor was how to reconcile the conflicting goals of maintaining a letter's integrity and protecting its author against charges of impropriety or poor writing. When Jewett edited Whitman's letters, she compromised between the two and was only partly satisfied with the result: "Too much choosing has cost the letters dear; they sometimes do not read like letters at all in these unrelated fragments." Annie would also find the choices difficult when she edited Sarah Jewett's letters.

In the years between 1904 and 1909 Annie stayed busy, again participating in a literary club, composed now of elderly ladies and gentlemen, which met once a week at 148 Charles Street for dinner. In a 1905 notebook Annie recorded the history of the Boston Authors Club, also referred to by Annie as the "small Home Club of 1905" (Diary MHS). Although not from Boston, Edith Wharton attended at least once. Other participants included Helen Bell, Gelett Burgess, the Aldriches, Mr. and Mrs. Bliss Perry, Henry James, Julia Ward Howe, and Robert Collyer. Sarah attended at least once, for Annie wrote: "I was truly pleased with the success and glad that dear S. O. J. could come for they all sincerely wished to see her." Before the last meeting, Annie wrote: "There is only one more dinner and so will end a series which has given me much pleasure" (HL). Although Annie showed little sign of slowing down, changes were inevitable; after one meeting Julia Ward Howe remarked to her nephew Mark that Annie Fields had shrunk (Howe *Mem.* 10). In 1907 William Dean Howells "found Mrs. Fields looking pathetically but prettily old, and very little; Miss Jewett quite stately beside her" (*Sel. Letters* 28:227; 22 Sept. 1907). Howells had gone to Manchester where he had "lunched with Dame Fields, to celebrate Miss Jewett's 180th (as she claimed) birthday" (227n).

In August of 1907 Annie began keeping a regular diary again, her first diary except for trip journals since 1869. The diary, inscribed "A brief record of life and its interests from the first date as below," begins as more of a scrapbook than a diary. Annie filled it with newspaper clippings about her friends—mainly obituaries—and copied quotations of interest into the book. She also slipped pictures of friends, copies of her own poems, letters to the editor, Christmas cards, reviews, and wedding announcements into the book. Two of the notes inserted at the beginning of the diary were from Edith Forbes, Ellen Tucker Emerson's sister, who wrote to thank Annie and Sarah for sending flowers to Ellen's funeral. Ellen died on 14 January 1909, only a few weeks before Sarah's first stroke. Like a great many of the women in the Fields-Jewett circle, Ellen had enjoyed an intimate friendship with another woman: Edith Forbes's note read, "But poor Miss Legate will suffer more than any one else—it seems to break up life for her after twenty years together—." Soon, Mrs. Forbes would be saying the same of Annie.

In 1908 Annie's lifelong strength began to ebb. Sarah mentioned her fears about Annie's health frequently in her letters to mutual friends, writing to Mrs. Humphry Ward and her daughter from Manchester on 8 June:

> [(]You must just take my love and blessing and believe how happy you made our dear A. F. and me.) She is much better now than when you saw her, the air here is always just the right thing, and I love to see her in her little pale gray dress sitting on the piazza looking seaward over the green treetops. She *is* tired, with getting away from Town more than from getting here, but she will soon be rested. (AFL 233)

Annie continued to be the focus of attention throughout 1908. Although Sarah herself was less than well, she was sufficiently recovered to spend the winter of 1908–1909 with Annie. On 27 November Sarah wrote to Willa Cather, who had become a kind of joint protégée of hers and Annie's:

> I was sorry to miss the drive to the station and a last talk about the story and other things; but I was too tired—"spent quite bankrupt!" It takes but little care about affairs, and almost less true pleasure, to make me feel overdone, and I have to be careful—. . . . Emerson was very funny once, Mrs. Fields has told me, when he said to a friend, "You formerly bragged of ill-health, sir!" But indeed I don't brag, I only deplore and often think it is a tiresome sort of mortification. I begin to think this is just what makes old age so trying to so many persons. It seemed a very long little journey, and I could hardly sit up in my place in the car. I have never been very strong, but always capable of "great pulls."
>
>   I expect to be here [in Berwick] until Monday the seventh, unless dear Mrs. Fields should need me. I have just had a most dear and cheerful note from her, and we spoke by telephone last evening. (AFL 245–46)

The previous summer, Sarah had confided in Cather that she feared Annie's life was in danger (Cather; Frost 134).

Willa Cather had become close to both women, and Sarah gave some literary advice to her which illuminates both Jewett's work and her relationship with Annie:

> And now I wish to tell you—the first of this letter being but a preface—with what deep happiness and recognition I have read the "McClure" story,—night before last I found it with surprise and delight. It made me feel very near to the writer's young and loving heart. You have drawn your two figures of the wife and her husband with unerring touches and wonderful tenderness for her. It makes me the more sure that you are far on your road toward a fine and long story of very high class. The lover is as well done as he could be when a woman writes in the man's character,—it must always, I believe, be something

of a masquerade. I think it is safer to write about him as you did about the others, and not try to be he! And you could almost have done it as yourself—a woman could love her in that same protecting way—a woman could even care enough to wish to take her away from such a life, by some means or other. But oh, how close—how tender—how true the feeling is! the sea air blows through the very letters on the page. (AFL 246–47)

Jewett's statement must display either naiveté (Sarah was oblivious of the fact that readers might consider love between women indecent) or the conviction that love between women was so natural that she could not conceive of any negative connotation concerning it.

Although Sarah was preoccupied with fears about Annie's health, it was her own which was in danger. On 31 January 1909, only the second winter which Sarah had spent with Annie since the winter of 1901–1902, Sarah suffered an attack of "apoplexy"—a stroke (cf. CL 173). On 4 February 1909, Annie wrote in her diary:

My dear S. O. J. was stricken down early Sunday morning a small blood vessel giving way in the brain. They think she is recovering today though we have had anxious days and nights. This was four days ago—. . . . It appears a strange moment to start in for a little diary. . . . Jessie Cochrane is here & her sister Mary, two nurses ([The] nurses do not sleep in the house or I could with difficulty manage it) Theodore her medical nephew and the Dr. coming from time to time.

From this point on, the story of Annie's life is predominantly the story of Sarah's illness, her death, and Annie's mourning for her.

Reading Annie's diary for these months is a poignant experience, attesting as it does to her deep love for Sarah and the sorrow she felt when she realized that her death was imminent. Annie would not have wanted an idly curious public to read of her despair as Sarah's death approached or of her grief and longing to join Sarah and their many friends who had passed to "the other side" and all but commanded Mark Howe to destroy the diary and her correspondence with Jewett. Despite his own conservative instincts in the matter of Annie and Sarah's relationship, he kept the greatest part of her papers, including this diary, intact.

Annie would have been proud to know that later generations could read her record of love for Sarah with interest and respect. It is the least self-conscious of all her writing. She didn't worry about the propriety of her words, although she knew that she should have been worried. She didn't care about getting the facts straight or recording for posterity; posterity was far from her mind. The result is a moving portrait of love.

By 10 February Sarah's condition had changed little. Annie recorded the names of her many concerned visitors, including Willa Cather, who made a special trip from New York. On 11 February Sarah was still too ill to be moved. Annie wrote:

We cannot see the way before us. Our dear invalid still lies sleeping and half waking by turns—she is often very amusing & told the nurse last night that she wanted John to buy a five cent mousetrap to catch me with! We are anxious to keep her quiet, so I go very seldom into her room.

Nearly a month later, Annie wrote:

> Every day seems to bring some good reason why I should not write my personal record on these pages—perhaps some record of our friends is still better worth having and this shall not altogether slip, at least—. (10 March 1909)

Annie wrote that Jessie Cochrane had left but that Mary Jewett and the two nurses remained. She inserted a circular describing the work for a new city charter and a Finance Committee into her book. On 8 April Mme Modjeska was added to the list of friends who had died.

Sarah remained in Boston until 21 April, when she was transported to South Berwick by a special railway car. She was carried into the large bedroom at the front of the house where Annie usually stayed (hence "your bed"), probably because it was closer to the head of the stairs and she could look out the window onto the street. On 22 April Annie received a scrawled note from Sarah:

> Dearest Annie, Here I am in your bed and finding it very comfortable only I wish I could see you coming in and hear you[r] dear little "cheep" at the door. . . . I was so glad we could not say a word yesterday as I came away I could not speak for crying a[ll] the way down stairs but the dear rooms did loo[k] so beautiful.

At the top of the note Annie wrote in pencil "She left me in Charles St—April 21st."

Annie received only a few notes more from Sarah, who did not recover and longed for Annie but sensed the hopelessness of the situation:

> Dearest Annie   I do so long to see you—I believe it would do me more good than any thing you always help me to get a good hold on the best of myself but I still feel too weak to plan any journeys. They still have to carry me [illegible] from one room to another and I don't know what to do about me[.] I had so hoped [illegible] to be out of rooms and in the garden [illegible].

It was becoming clearer to both Annie and Sarah that recovery was not imminent. The two women concentrated on communicating their love to each other: "Good night dearest Annie with so many things left unsaid, or rather all said but not written—" "Dear Pinny, I fear this is not a very cosy letter—but we love to be together dear and I will make what I can of these fragments!" At the top of one note, Annie wrote: "Written May 3^D, 1909 3 months & 3 days after she was stricken down A. F." The back reads, "Thursday 20th—My courage and hope ended with this note—AF." And yet again, "Written May 20th when she had been at home a month—June 24th she died—."

Annie's seventy-fifth birthday passed without Sarah; she must have received a few words from her, perhaps this note scribbled on a card: "Dear dear darling Fuffy I love you—." With it is a note in Annie's handwriting, probably to herself: "I have your poor dearest little note! Alas! What a strange thing to have you absent! [signed] Your own / Annie June 6th 1909" On the reverse is written: "My Sarah."

On 21 June Annie began to prepare their friends for Sarah's death; she wrote to Lily Fairchild:[4]

> You probably do not know that our dear Sarah lies at the point of death at South Berwick. She no longer suffers, no longer hears any echoes from this, our world. I went to see her last week and stayed two days. She is quiet and beautiful and does not suffer. She told me the last few things she had in mind and seemed to love to have me there. She soon relapsed into sleep—a sleep from which she will not entirely awaken. (HH)

Sarah died on 24 June and was buried in South Berwick on Sunday 27 June, a fact which Annie did not record until the first of July. She struggled to regain a normal existence, staying with Jessie Cochrane in Manchester, where she received many notes of sympathy from their mutual friends. Lily Fairchild, Willa Cather, Louise Guiney, Rose Lamb, Helen Bell, and Jessie Cochrane were close to her in this time. Annie, now seventy-five, found herself surrounded by friends and well-wishers, but bereft for a second time of the person closest to her.

As a result of Sarah's death, Annie and Mary Jewett were drawn together, and although they were never intimate, they visited and consulted with each other over Sarah's letters and her manuscripts, of which they were joint executors. At the end of July Jessie left for Rome. Robert Collyer and Mary Jewett visited in August. After everyone had left, Annie tried to reconcile herself to Sarah's death:

> I think on My dear Sarah in her new estate, of her release, of the happy presence which she spreads around us, of her dear beautiful helpful generous self who will not come back, no, no, no! We do not ask it, nor wish it indeed. (20 Aug. 1909)

One of Jewett's last and best stories, "The Queen's Twin" (1899), envisioned a love which transcended physical presence and prefigured the course of Annie's and Sarah's lives after 1902. Because Annie and Sarah spent more time apart between 1902 and 1909 than in previous years, their letters came to reflect a communion that depended less heavily on physical presence than it had before. Their notes emphasized the spiritual bond between them; both women acknowledged that, by now, words were unnecessary and inadequate, as when Annie wrote to Sarah, "Goodbye dearest, do not write when you feel tired and we will never say, because we can't[,] how much we miss each other—your A."

At first, "The Queen's Twin" seems an unlikely candidate for an illustration of reciprocity and unspoken communication among its characters. The story is about Abby Martin, an aging woman who now lived alone in a secluded area near Dunnet Landing. Abby Martin's birthday and wedding day were the same as Queen Victoria's, and Abby had augmented the resemblance by naming her children after the royal family. She had a whole roomful of portraits and news stories about the Queen and her family, and she made a voyage to England to catch a glimpse of the Queen.

Her fascination with the Queen would in itself be nothing unusual. The extraordinary part of Jewett's conception is the bond which exists between Abby Martin and Queen Victoria—a bond which does not require either the physical presence or even the knowledge of the person loved. Even though Queen Victoria is oblivious to the existence of Abby Martin, she can still participate in the exchange of thoughts and feelings—an exchange of humors, as it might have been called centuries ago. As Abby Martin explains to Mrs. Todd and the narrator of *Country of the Pointed Firs*:

> I sometimes seem to have her all my own, as if we'd lived right together. I've often walked out into the woods alone and told her what my troubles was, and it always seemed as if she told me 't was all right, an' we must have patience. (144)

Abby Martin benefits from a kind of spiritual companionship which she has initiated herself, without any apparent knowledge on the part of Queen Victoria.

But Abby is not convinced that Queen Victoria is ignorant of their bond, for she says, transforming the Queen into just another old lady like herself:

> When I think how few old friends anybody has left at our age, I suppose it may be just the same with her as it is with me. . . . But I've had a great advantage in seeing her, an' I can always fancy her goin' on, while she don't know nothin' yet about me, *except she may feel my love stayin' her heart sometimes an' not know just where it comes from.* [Emphasis added.] An' I dream about our being together out in some pretty fields, young as we ever was, and holdin' hands as we walk along. (144)

Annie's diary and the letters she wrote to a few, selected friends indicate that she felt herself to be the beneficiary of just such a disembodied love. To Lily Fairchild, who also believed that it was possible to communicate with the spirits of the dead, Annie wrote of herself and Mary Jewett:

> Happily for both of us dear Sarah was often away and we both have had periods when we have missed her dear bodily presence for if we really belong together and care for each other our spirits can go on together without daily communication. However, it is indeed true that having laid aside her painful body she now seems very near to me in many loving ways which are all her own and I feel greatly comforted & companioned by her.

Thus, "The Queen's Twin," one of Jewett's last and finest stories, occupied a pivotal position in her life, for it both reflected and predicted the course of Jewett's important relationship with Annie Fields.

12.

"The Unspeakable Past"
1910–1915

> It is meanwhile the sympathy of old friends from far
> back like yourself, of "those who know," as Dante
> says, that is the reward of my attempt to reach back a
> little to the unspeakable past.
> —Henry James to Annie Fields, 1914

Annie's remaining friends meant more to her now, as did visits from the children of old friends such as May Morris, the daughter of William Morris, who visited Annie during Christmas of 1909, and Ethel Arnold, the daughter of Matthew Arnold, who came in April of 1910. When returning to Boston from Manchester a few months after Sarah's death, Annie wrote:

Today I make ready to go to Boston and our home there without her but my loving servants are doing all they can and her spirit pervades the place. The afternoon is glorious and less cold than of late for it has been icy and my heart was cold but she seems to be with me today again. (20 Oct. 1909)

In December of 1909 Annie was visited by Reginald Somers Cocks, an English friend of the southern writer Grace King and a Tulane professor. Annie still had the ability to surprise with her unorthodox opinions, as King's description of their encounter shows:

He was impressed to awe by the majestic hostess, but terms of sociability did not fail to succeed the first stiff moments of conversation, when, as he related to me, in her beautiful voice, with its precise tones, "she asked me what the people of New Orleans thought of Mr. Washington. I myself had never thought about him, but I answered truthfully that I had never heard a word against him. I was very glad to hear that she responded with warmth in her voice and even went on to eulogise Mr. Washington in the way I had been accustomed to hear in America. And she was still talking about him when I made my adieux. It was not until I was outside that I realized that she was talking about Booker, and not the father of his country, to whom her words of praise were admirably adapted." (King 93)

In February Annie marked the anniversary of the onset of Sarah's last illness. In March she was visited by Herbert Ward, the husband of Elizabeth Stuart Phelps, whose marriage had so amazed Annie and Whittier years before. Mr. Ward brought a story by his wife which described a luncheon at Charles Street attended by Phillips Brooks and Oliver Wendell Holmes.[1] Annie remarked, "If she could use the names of the persons I think it would be widely read but that is of course impossible and the common world has little time to give to guessing—" (2 March 1910).

Annie turned a Christmas visit from Henry James into an occasion to write a capsule sketch of him in her diary:

> Henry James has been here in one of the "let-ups" of his long illness and sadness. He is living with William's family in Cambridge. His affectionate nature, his eager interest in his friends, his life in his affection now not centered solely in his brother's children but quickened by that as it were into a larger life for all who have ever been his, all these things make him inexpressibly soothing yet stimulating as a companion[.] I have seldom enjoyed an hour more than the one spent in the light of his fine sympathy—He asked about Sarah's letters—said he should like to see them—that he wished to write a few words in introduction or what I might call "éclaircissement" of her gift—.
>
> I hear he continues to be fairly well in health & is writing, so I trust he is at work with her papers and her memory first before entering on the larger & more fatiguing work of William's Life which I hear the H. M. & Co. publishers have asked him to do—.

Now that Annie's parents, her sister Elizabeth, James, and Sarah Jewett were gone, she had cause to reflect on those who were left, including her sister Sarah. Annie looked back over her relationship with this sister:

> My sister Sarah was 87 years old yesterday—She is ill and not likely to live through this winter. We have not been very intimate sisters as she is nearly twelve years older than I and I was married shortly after leaving school. Then a few years after she went to Europe for nearly twenty years—She has been very very lame all her life and cut off from many of life's joys for which she has always had a strong appetite. Altogether her going cannot be a definite loss out of my own life; and yet these strange ties of relationship which we so little understand hold their claim upon us.

Contrary to Annie's prediction, Sarah Adams outlived her by a year.

Annie frequently received visits from the young men who had taken the place of Howells, Aldrich, and Scudder in the publishing world. Henry James had called Charles Street "a waterside museum" in *The American Scene,* and Annie was very much a museum piece to the new generation. George Woodberry, Thomas Whittemore, Ferris Greenslet, Bliss Perry, and Mark Howe all visited and wrote to her with some regularity. Whittemore read aloud to her and reported to Annie and five other ladies on the French philosopher, Henri Bergson, of whom Annie did not entirely approve:

> Although I appreciate his clear mindedness and power of statement my mind does not naturally work in these traces—I seem to leave the great fields & sea shores and mountain lands where my thought loves to linger and find myself in some beautiful rooms full of noble furniture arranged for a life of thought and leisure. I then walk with Bergson into

another room where that furniture and these belongings are made and told how they are put together and asked to follow the hand of the designer. It is all very curious and beautiful but I am not interested and long for the flowery upland paths—I may do the subject great wrong, but this is the aspect it wears to me—. (30 Aug. 1911)

Woodberry was another of the younger friends with whom Annie discussed both past and contemporary literature. After reading Edwin Arlington Robinson and Louise Imogen Guiney, she gave Woodberry her impressions:

I have seen a small volume of his work which seems to me very true, natural and modern withal—also just, and not last poetic, but I put this first quality last because the whole measure was too slight to know if the real "fire and fury of the brain" were really after all in possession. I have not heard of much new writing of the imagination, and the stories seem to me so lacking in that quality[;] and all writing is for all readers[,] of course[,] who seem to be story readers—Behold a dark view! Nor quite a true one! (15 Sept. 1910)

Of Edgar Allan Poe, she wrote to Woodberry:

I am reading your Life of Poe with much interest because, although he was before my time, all his treatment of Longfellow and his association with Willis were known to my husband and hence to me. . . . The common world even & readers of poetry have been a good deal befogged respecting Poe's poetry—should they value it or should they not? and if they happened to be charmed by it—why? No especial new thought was there. The alliance with music of which you speak is very true—but what a sad apparition he was! It makes me remember Lanier who should have counted Poe as his best example in his book on poetry & music but I do not recall his name in L's pages. The Poe book is most successfully put together—. (19 Sept. 1909)

Annie's letters to Woodberry reveal a woman who was sometimes lonely but interested in the modern world and surprisingly unsentimental about the past. When Annie began work on a memorial immediately after Sarah's death, George Woodberry was one of several people with whom Annie discussed her work:

I have made a brief introduction to my own letters with which the little volume will end because it appeared to be needed to round the whole and [I] will not say as Emerson did after he had carefully elimanated [sic] from Thoreau's verse all of which did not to him seem quite inevitable, and sent the mss. to his sister at her request; I fear "she will spoil my Greek statue"! as indeed she did by replacing everything in her power and more. No, I have endeavored to cut profitably for her Sarah's keen taste and judgement, without cutting out the dear human element which was a distinguishing quality of her character. (12 June 1910)

In March of 1911 Annie gave Sarah's letters to the printers, commenting that Henry James was ill and "still unfit to write" (7 March 1911). Alice Meynell was then invited to write an introduction but she deferred to Annie in the matter, suggesting that anything she wrote should be only "something to accompany or follow a preface from your own hand" (HL, n.d. [1910?]).

When the edition of Sarah's letters appeared in October of 1911, Annie's unsigned preface stood alone. She wrote in her diary:

> This summer has again passed Sarah's Letters have just appeared and now I go again to town without her—Her love does not let me go and I wonder sometimes when I may join again those I love—There are many still here who are very very dear and I can still thank God and pray for strength to wait until *His* will says this too is finished.

The book which Annie created was the standard volume of Sarah's letters for many years. A fully documented edition of letters in the Colby College Library has come out, but the letters in Annie's book (which are in the Houghton Library) have never been reprinted. Annie attempted to put the letters in chronological order, but most were undated and her dating is unreliable. Annie's task was immensely complicated by the letters' intimacy and "childish diction." Following the principles that Sarah used for her edition of Sarah Whitman's letters, she found it difficult to retain the integrity of the letters and satisfy her sense of propriety.

Annie's original manuscript, however, was truer to Sarah's letters than was the published edition, which had been expurgated by a committee of two, Mary Jewett and Mark Howe, Sarah's literary executor. Apparently Mary Jewett first balked at printing the nicknames, although it was Howe who persuaded Annie to eliminate them:

> I must say that I agree with Miss Mary Jewett regarding the nicknames—especially where an assumed childish diction is coupled with them. An occasional "Pinny," I should think might be left, but four-fifths of them—I think—should go for the mere sake of the impression we want the book to make on readers who have no personal association with Miss Jewett and cannot hear just how some of the playful bits would sound, spoken by her. You can hear them all and of course it is hard to give them up. In the end, however, I doubt—with Miss Mary Jewett—whether you will like to have all sorts of people *reading them wrong.* (12 April 1911)

Did Annie understand from this how people were likely to misread the nicknames? A bit of typescript that was almost certainly intended to be included in the *Letters* suggests that Annie and Sarah were aware of the nicknames' ambiguous nature.[2] The lines do not appear in either the Fields or the later Cary edition of Jewett's letters, and the original is not at the Houghton Library with the rest of the letters edited by Annie:

> Monday night, 1889
> Dearest,—
>   I was startled at the thought, *What,* if we should come to biographers, would they think of the name of Fuffatee! But there it goes again, and I remember for consolation that nearly all I know of the spouse of the first Norman duke is her nickname of Popaelia means puppet or little dolly, or something as fine and ducal! (HL)

Not only were the nicknames deleted, but also whole sections of letters, perhaps even entire letters, were destroyed, probably by either Annie or Howe. Expurgating the letters must have caused anguish, but as Sarah had pointed out to Mrs. Parkman, "So few of us know what a stern judge *print* is in itself; what a sifter and weigher of values, how astonishing its calm verdict when a book is done" (n.d.).

As this statement suggests, the fear that their relationship might be regarded as sensational was not Annie's only motivation for destroying letters. Her awareness that someday scholars would be reading her papers shows up at the beginning of her first diary, begun in 1863. Annie's concern about rejected poems, the formal style of some of the "private" writing in her diaries and letters, her ambivalence about entrusting private thoughts to the blue notebooks—all indicate that Annie was concerned with the quality of her "literary remains." Annie knew that her notes and voluminous collection of books and papers would be valued, and throughout her life she was culling and selecting.

Letters were destroyed systematically by Annie and Sarah as they wrote them, not only after Jewett's death; among the letters at the Houghton is a note from Annie to Sarah which reads, "Dearest! I feel so mean in exchange for your dear notes to send you mere nothings. Destroy notes of course enclosed unless I mark them to be saved!" If the intention of all concerned was to keep the intimate nature of the Fields-Jewett relationship from the public, the effort was a failure. The letters which remain present a vivid picture of their great love for each other.

In 1912 Annie read the life of Mark Twain and his *Joan of Arc* and waited to die: "I hope to wait as cheerfully as he did for the trumpet call and as usefully, but I am ready" (25 Jan. 1913). Henry James wrote to Annie about *Notes of a Son and Brother* as a fellow survivior:

> I really like to think of those who know what I am talking about—& and such readers are now of the fewest. We both have had friends all the way along, however, & I mustn't speak as if we were too bleakly stranded today. The only thing is, none the less, that almost nobody understands what we mean, do they?—we can say that to each other (& to Mrs. Bell & to Alice Howe) even if we can't say it to *them*—I think of you very faithfully & gratefully & tenderly, & am yours affectionately always *Henry James.* (25 July 1914)

Annie refused to remain in the past that nobody understood and retained her interest in the present. Near the end of her life she wrote about the war being waged in Europe:

> The whole thing has been so sudden that the fire may be quenched as quickly though somebody yesterday said "this was so general it may last for 30 years"[.] To my uninstructed vision this seems a very mistaken surmise because modern appliances could kill off the whole human race by that time—. (30 July 1914)

Annie died on 5 January 1915 after a brief illness. Her memorial service was held in the library of the Charles Street house at sunset, where her coffin lay overlooking the Charles River. Isabella Stewart Gardner laid a purple pall which she had bought for her husband's funeral over Annie's coffin.[3] The body was cremated and her ashes were buried in Mt. Auburn Cemetery near those of her parents, sister Elizabeth, and husband.

Her death signalled the newspapers to reminisce about the golden age of literature of which Annie was nearly the last representative; in the *Boston Transcript,* eight separate articles commented on Mrs. Fields's death. As one of the more perceptive articles, quoting from the New York *Sun,* explained:

> It was not that she had made especially notable contributions to literature during her long life, although in former days keen analysis, poise and high order of intelligence gave distinction to a manuscript signed "Annie Fields." But with her passing probably comes to an end that group of extraordinary men and women residing in and around Boston whose genius, talent, true cultivation, produced an array of books worth reading and worth preserving.

The article went on to say that as the wife of James T. Fields,

> Mrs. Fields at once saw the part she was destined to play in the drama of life then progressing; and right well did she play it.... She made the most of herself while making the most of her husband; together they went forward side by side, to the last comrades and true lovers—and much, very much, of the success of Mr. and Mrs. James T. Fields was due to the second name in that ideal partnership.

An article by E. H. Clement called "The Personal and Social Side of Mrs. Fields" began:

> It is not too much to say that Mrs. James T. Fields tacitly succeeded to the title of first woman citizen of Boston on Mrs. Julia Ward Howe's death. Her long life, active and useful to the end, bridged the most brilliant half century of Boston's three hundred years—"all of which she saw and a part of which she was," to a very distinguished degree. Poet, scholar, litterateur, and intimate of the greatest among literary folk, at home and in England, she was also in later life a studious publicist and practical social organizer—the Associated Charities being, it is safe to say, more Mrs. Fields's monument than that of any other single individual.

An article on the Fields library noted:

> It was perhaps not less the charm of Annie Fields' personality than the potency of the name of a great American publisher and the fact that both Mr. and Mrs. Fields were authors, that not only unlocked for them the door of every author's home in England and America, but set forth for them the finest fare of literary friendship.

Other obituaries included one placed on the records of the Associated Charities of Boston, which noted that

> Unlike many older people she was living in the world of today—its sufferings and its ideals—although more than to most people the world of the past was open to her and full of significance.

Annie's will was complicated and her benefactors suffered from the numerous unofficial addenda she made on little slips of paper. A bequest to Louise Imogen

Guiney was never given because Annie had overestimated the value of her estate; a gift to a home for children could not be carried out because it had been absorbed by another home with a different name.

Annie had rewritten her will on 3 September 1909, shortly after Sarah's death, revoking a previous will which had probably left much of her estate to Sarah. Deciding how to dispose of her property was evidently stressful. In the new will, Annie left manuscript books and poems to Harvard and the Dartmouth Library and paintings to the Boston Museum of Fine Arts. She left money and mementoes to her three nephews and her niece; Louisa Beal's stepchildren; her sisters; two cousins; her namesake, Annie Fields Alden (the daughter of Henry Mills Alden of *Harper's*); a friend, Eva von Blumberg;[4] and annuities for her servants. The house and land at Manchester she gave to her nephew Zabdiel Boylston Adams, and she asked that all other real estate be sold.

In addition to generous sums of money which were to be given outright to Jessie Cochrane, Annie Fields Alden, and Louise Imogen Guiney, Annie asked that the income from the real estate be put into a trust fund for them. To the Associated Charities of Boston Annie left $40,000 as a pension fund for retired employees, specifying that Zilpha Smith and Frances A. Smith, two of her first charitable visitors, should receive pensions upon their retirement. She made gifts to Dartmouth College, the Portsmouth high schools, and the Old People's Memorial Fund, with the residue of the estate going to Zabdiel Boylston Adams.

Annie wanted the Charles Street house to be demolished; it now stood in the midst of a commercial district and she could not bear for it to go the way of stately houses in unfashionable districts. The Charles Street garden remains, according to Annie's wish, but the small, grassy plot wedged between two apartment buildings and divorced from the river by an expressway bears little resemblance to the showplace it once was.

Annie's instructions to Mark DeWolfe Howe, her literary executor, were by no means clear. In February of 1910, she told him:

> I cannot tell you what a comfort it is to me to be able to leave all my letters and scribblings in your hands knowing that you will use nothing publicly which is not worth while. Pray destroy everything which is of no public value and *that I think* will mean *everything*. You will find numbers of autographs, I mean brief notes which you could let Libbie, the auctioneer or some such person sell for your advantage (to get a little present for Fanny!).

In April of 1911 she told him that letters which had never been used in print "might best be burned. Later in the evening she said that her chief concern for papers, books, etc. not specially designated, is that they should go to persons who will care for them." An unwitnessed codicil of September of 1911 added that "In case it should seem worth while to write any small Memorial, (which I consider more than doubtful and should much prefer should not be done unless for some reason not ~~closely~~ altogether connected with myself)" DeWolfe should "consult George E. Woodberry." As a result of Mrs. Fields's various requests, Howe wrote *Memories of a Hostess,* a book derived from Annie's diaries but not a biography of her. Many of her letters were preserved intact while some were mutilated and others destroyed.[5] Annie's literary legacy is a large one; thousands of documents—letters written to or by her, notebooks, diaries, manuscripts, and scrapbooks—remain.

A book on the history of Houghton Mifflin says that Annie expected Howe to write a biography of her and had expected Houghton Mifflin to publish any book based on her manuscripts. Annie may have hoped a biography would be written, but preferred, with characteristic modesty, to say otherwise. She would have liked *Memories of a Hostess,* and we must be grateful to Howe for preserving what he did instead of taking Annie at her word. By the time Howe's book was ready for publication, however, he was part of a new publishing venture, the Atlantic Monthly Press, and gave the book to them. Thus Houghton Mifflin, the direct descendant of her husband's firm, did not publish the book based on the Ticknor & Fields years.

The house in Manchester still stands, but it went out of the family in the 1930s. It has been modernized but remains in essence as it was in Annie's lifetime. Its current owner points out Annie's room and those in which Sarah Jewett and Willa Cather customarily stayed.

Just as Annie had written about the writers and literary figures she had known, so her younger friends wrote about her. She was mentioned in several articles and books while she was alive, including Elizabeth Stuart Phelps Ward's *Chapters from a Life,* William Dean Howells' *Literary Friends and Acquaintance,* and an article by Louise Imogen Guiney in *The Critic.* The interdiction on writing about living friends was not as strong in the early part of the twentieth century as it had been twenty years before.

Some interesting pieces were prompted by Annie's death, including an article by Frances Morse, "Mrs. Fields's Bequest" to Associated Charities, and Henry James's "Mr. and Mrs James T. Fields." Harriet Prescott Spofford's *A Little Book of Friends,* which opens with a description of Annie Fields, was published in 1916, a year after Annie's death. Later memoirs appeared in Grace King's *Memories of a Southern Woman of Letters,* Robert Underwood Johnson's *Remembered Yesterdays,* Laura Richards's *Stepping Westward,* Mark Howe's *A Venture in Remembrance,* and Willa Cather's *Not Under Forty.* Reminiscences appear in Elizabeth Shepley Sergeant's memoir of Willa Cather and Helen Howe's memoir of her father's generation, *The Gentle Americans.* Frances Morse, writing for the Associated Charities, noted the two distinct sides of Annie's life:

> To many men and women Mrs. Fields, throughout her life, was associated with every effort to better conditions for those who start at a disadvantage; to another large group, including friends in England and in France, she was a woman of letters who herself had written delightfully and memorably. Thus, she seemed to live two full and active lives, each drawing from deep sources of human interest, and each illuminating the other. (290)

Morse repeated a comment about Annie attributed to "one of the Associated Charities staff who had known her the longest":

> She was a woman of power, not only an idealist; she brought others up to her ideal, and carried them along with her in her and their work. She threw in generously all her gifts of pen and speech to carry into action the causes she believed in. (290)

The writer Grace King described her first visit with Mrs. Fields, who she said was called "Annie Adams" by her friends, at Manchester-by-the-Sea:

> She was more than I expected. Her great beauty had never been mentioned as one of her charms—the regular face, fine eyes, and undulating black hair combed into a knot behind. . . . I cannot remember what she said or what I replied, but it was a "famous interview."

Robert Underwood Johnson, who had travelled across the Atlantic with Annie and Sarah in 1892, recalled:

> I found Mrs. Fields full of reminiscences of the authors she had known in Boston or in England. Thackeray and Dickens, Emerson, Longfellow and Holmes were among the high-lights of her talk, which was always kindly, even where she had to make criticisms.

Johnson also remembered an English visitor who had described Annie as "the lady who had sugar of different sizes," which he thought "would have amused Mrs. Fields herself, for her sense of humor was very keen" (394).

The most perceptive of all essays about Mrs. Fields is Willa Cather's "148 Charles Street." Cather said of Annie Fields, who outlived most of her generation and recorded its story for future generations, that "She had the very genius of survival" (67). But posterity made Cather a liar for many years. Changing literary evaluations have turned Annie Fields into a kind of classic statue—beautiful and symmetrical, but distant and remote.

Distance is partly why Annie Fields was forgotten so quickly after her death. When the newspapers eulogized her with a plethora of articles, they eulogized a whole era—an era that nearly everyone was glad to bury. The Victorians were so completely repudiated by their literary descendants they might not have existed. Writers of the Modern Age looked back to the Romantics; they could not bear to share the world with Tennyson and Longfellow. Annie's world was an instantly extinct civilization, an era of dinosaurs or prehistoric scratches on caves which tourists look at with little interest and less sympathy. James's coinage "the waterside museum" evokes perfectly the attitude of the modern literary world toward someone so ancient.

Annie Fields could not have lived her life today; literary hostesses, Boston marriages, and Annie's classical verse are decidedly obsolete. The work of a great hostess, like that of a great mother or wife, is soon forgotten by history. The work of a writer in minor genres such as the memoir, the journal, or letters disappears quickly from memory and is seldom remembered once its immediacy has passed. All these accomplishments are more likely to be those of women, for women, even comparatively wealthy women like Annie Fields, are constantly interruptible. Yet the value to literature of a literary observer such as Annie is indisputable; in an apparently unpublished review of *Authors and Friends,* Sarah Orne Jewett wrote:

> Sometimes we hear it said that we should never have known Dr. Johnson, that he would have been forgotten long ago if it had not been for his biographer, and there are those who believe that in spite of the many services which the writer of Authors and Friends has rendered to her city and her time as a philanthropist and public servant in far-reaching

ways, in spite [of] the reticence of the sketches, the living quality of the descriptions, the renewal of those personal atmospheres which seemed to have passed away forever[,] must be very touching to many hearts. . . . It is very natural that with such personal allusion, such revivifying of old days as one finds in Authors and Friends, the men and women of Boston, especially all those who were in any wise neighbors or companions should find the book enchanting. . . . It was fortunate that such a book should be made by such an author and friend as ~~Mrs Fields the writer~~ in whom these great men and women were quick to recognize an unmistakeable kinship.

It is ironic that most forgotten women writers have been accused of writing about the ephemeral and women's affairs, but Annie Fields, who wrote about the mostly male literary establishment, the classics, and war, has been the most forgotten writer of them all. She would have been remembered longer if she had produced the tight stories of a Mary Wilkins Freeman, a Kate Chopin, or a Sarah Orne Jewett.

Revitalized interest in the life of Annie Fields has resulted partly from an interest in "Boston marriages," an intrusion into private life which would have appalled Annie. But then again, Annie once told Willa Cather that "She was not . . . 'to escape anything, not even free verse or the Cubists!'" and Cather remarked that "She was not in the least dashed by either." So perhaps Annie would have taken the interest in her love for Jewett in stride.

There are many other reasons to be interested in Annie Fields, reasons which she would have understood completely. The role she played in the Boston publishing world is unique, and her documentary record makes it possible to study a long period of American literature and American life. Her ideas about charity organization and the role she played in transforming the face of social work make hers one of the most interesting contributions to that field in her time. She also exerted a major influence on a woman writer who, together with Stowe, Chopin, and Wharton, has emerged as one of the important American woman fiction writers, and she fostered the careers of numerous others.

Annie Fields's point of view is characteristically nineteenth century. Even if they told us nothing else of interest, her diaries would tell us a great deal about how her era thought and felt. Her point of view is also characteristically feminine. She was not a prototypical feminist or antifeminist but the much more common mixture. The complexity of her views and the movement of her diary between literary and personal worlds makes the diary more, not less, valuable and interesting to scholars and readers, especially those interested in women's lives.

Although there are gaps in the record, more is known about Annie's education and family background than is known about most women of her time and more remains to be discovered in manuscripts and other records. Her liberal views about abolition, religion, and feminism blatantly contradict the view of her that has prevailed. Annie Fields should play a more important role in the next generation of nineteenth-century literary histories. The record should show that Annie Adams Fields, not just Mrs. James T. Fields, must be taken into account in writing the literary history of her age.

Notes

1. Early Life and Marriage, 1834–1859

1. The descriptions of Boston in 1834 and 1854 follow Koren, State Street Trust Company, and Gilman.

2. See Rossiter in Works Cited section of Bibliography, below. The Massachusetts Historical Society identifies Mrs. Fields as the "Boston Lady."

3. Taken from Henry Wadsworth Longfellow's poem "A Psalm of Life." The second word of the second line quoted by AF should be "may." Emphasis added by Mrs. Fields.

4. Annie Adams Fields. Diaries, MS, Fields Coll.,Massachusetts Historical Society, Boston. This collection contains fifty-three numbered blue-book diaries belonging to Annie Fields and one bound diary belonging to James T. Fields in which Annie wrote. The numbers were presumably added by Mark DeWolfe Howe, Annie's literary executor. All quotations from or references to Annie's journals or diaries are from this collection unless otherwise noted.

5. The following discussion of Alice James is based on the biography by Jean Strouse.

6. Scrapbooks, Fields Coll., Huntington Library. Subsequent references to miscellaneous items in this collection will be identified by the abbreviation HL.

7. Tilton is in error in her biography of Oliver Wendell Holmes when she identifies this woman as Annie Fields. The incident, recorded by Holmes in a diary, occurred in 1850 when Eliza was Fields's wife.

8. Louise Imogen Guiney to Annie Adams Fields, 26 Aug. [1904–1909]. Fields Coll., Huntington Library.

9. For various descriptions of 148 Charles Street, see Tryon 213–15; Matthiessen 70; Cather 53–62; and Guiney, 367–69.

10. Annie Fields to Laura Winthrop Johnson, MS, Fields Coll., Huntington Library. Subsequent references to this collection of letters will be identified in the text by the abbreviation LWJ and a date or approximate date when available.

11. James T. Fields to Annie Adams Fields, n.d., Fields Coll., Huntington Library.

2. "The Sleeping Partner," 1859–1870

1. For a description of this colony from a literary point of view, see Mellow's biography of Nathaniel Hawthorne.

2. Carroll Smith-Rosenberg's article "The Female World of Love and Ritual" provides an illuminating discussion of nineteenth-century marriage.

3. A.L.S. James T. Fields to Annie Adams Fields. Fifty-eight letters are in the Fields Coll. of the Huntington Library. Subsequent references to this collection will be abbreviated as JTF/AF in the text.

4. *Récit d'une Soeur* (1866) by Mrs. Augustus Craven (née Pauline de La Ferronays) was an enormously popular family memoir by a former member of the French aristocracy. Published in English as *A Sister's Story,* the book describes the deaths of the author's mother, father, two sisters, brother, and his wife, which occurred within a few years of each other. The romance Annie refers to was that of Mrs. Craven's brother and his wife.

5. This passage is an extreme example of the allusiveness common to members of the Fields literary circle. "Redde" means "to read aloud" in Middle English.

"Byron and common sense" refers to the Scottish Common Sense philosophers and more specifically to Byron's poem "English Bards and Scottish Reviewers: A Satire" (1809), which alludes to Comus (the god) and Virtue.

Milton's *A Masque presented at Ludlow Castle* (1634), better known as *Comus,* depicts a chaste and virginal Lady who becomes separated from her two brothers and successfully resists the seductive wiles of Comus, the son of Bacchus and Circe and a god of sensual pleasure. Annie is probably referring to lines 166–84.

6. *Cymbeline* IV.ii.257. *The Riverside Shakespeare,* ed. G. Blakemore Evans (Boston: Houghton Mifflin, 1974), 1548.

According to the OED, "in the nineteenth century it became somewhat common to invent nonce-words" with the ending "mania." According to A. R. Humphreys, the editor of the Oxford *White-Jacket,* Melville uses the term "mania-a-potu" in *White-Jacket* as an alternative name for delirium tremens.

7. For this brief comparison of Annie to a contemporary executive wife I am indebted to Margaret Helfrich's study of executive wives.

8. Louise Tharp, in her book about the Peabodys, and Ellen Ballou, in her history of Houghton Mifflin, both characterize the Fieldses as egotistical and self-serving. However, neither writes from an unprejudiced point of view, since Tharp is defending Sophia Hawthorne, and Ballou is defending Scudder in their quarrels with James and Annie. See Tharp 270–73 and Ballou 62, 435–37.

9. Rotundo suggests that Annie regarded herself as an unofficial historian of her husband's firm.

10. "The Ruined Maid's Lament" has been removed from the Burns canon. It appeared in various nineteenth-century editions by James Hogg (the "Ettrick Shepherd") and William Motherwell and was also included in some of Allan Cunningham's editions. The poem begins, "Oh meikle do I rue, fause love, / Oh sairly do I rue, / That e'er I heard your flattering tongue, / That e'er your face I knew."

3. Literary Ambitions, 1860–1870

1. Julia Dorr was a daughter of Rufus Choate and a member of Boston's literary society.

2. This is a reference to *The New England Tragedies,* which contains "John Endicott" and "Giles Corey of the Salem Farms." The book did not appear until October of 1868 and was reviewed by Howells in the *Atlantic* 23 (Jan. 1869), 133–34. Annie's entry shows what close contact she and Fields had with Longfellow, for on 18 February he wrote to George Washington Greene that he had written one tragedy and was halfway through the other (Hilen 5:213).

3. The poems were published in May, July, and December of 1862, and January, March, and September of 1863.

4. Ernest, Alice, Edith, and Annie Allegra were the names of four of Longfellow's five children (Arvin 132). Fanny, mentioned below, shared her name with Longfellow's second wife, Fanny Appleton, who died in 1861. Erminia is the name of a heroine in Tasso's epic, *Jerusalem Delivered.* "Asphodel" is the name of the traditional flower of immortality which grows in the Elysian Fields *(Odyssey* XI.538; *Comus,* 109n838.)

5. The author of this epigram may be Ponce Denis Ecouchard Lebrun (1729–1807), a French poet known for his epigrams and his violent temper.

4. Family and Friends, Housekeeping and "True Womanhood"

1. Saxton's biography *Louisa May* convincingly describes Alcott's feelings toward Annie and James. Saxton's description of the Fieldses' motives and attitudes may be less reliable. See especially 215, 257, 271, 288–89, 294, 298, 323–24, and 333.

2. Frederick Robertson (1816–1853) was an Anglican clergyman whose five volumes of sermons emphasizing the principles of spiritual life were widely known and extremely popular. Ticknor & Fields began publishing Robertson's sermons in 1857 and volumes appeared continuously throughout Fields's tenure.

3. Anne Whitney (1821–1915) first exhibited her work in Boston and New York in 1864. In

1873 she received a commission for a full-length statue of Samuel Adams. In 1875 she won first place in an anonymous competition to sculpt a statue of Charles Sumner, but she was denied the commission when the judges discovered she was a woman. She completed the statue in 1902, and it now overlooks Harvard Square.

4. Probably a reference to Mrs. Richard Henry Dana, Jr. (Sarah Watson). The Danas were summer neighbors of the Fieldses in Manchester.

5. Kate Dewey was probably a daughter of Orville Dewey (1794–1882), a Unitarian clergyman and relative of Ralph Waldo Emerson.

6. See Welter, "The Cult of True Womanhood."

7. Mrs. Emma Dorothy Eliza Nevitte Southworth (1819–1899) was a popular novelist. Mrs. Davis (not Rebecca Harding) may have been Mary Fenn Davis (1824–1886), a member of the New York women's club Sorosis (see below), or perhaps Pauline Kellogg Wright Davis (1813–1876), an amateur painter and a suffragist.

8. During this convention, held at the Horticultural Hall in November of 1868, the New England Woman's Suffrage Association was formed, and Julia Ward Howe elected president. Six months later the more radical National Woman Suffrage Association was formed, and in November of 1869 the New England Woman's Suffrage Association changed its name to the American Women Suffrage Association. This more conservative organization included men and focused on suffrage to the exclusion of other social issues. Annie and James aligned themselves with the latter group, which also included Julia Ward Howe, James Freeman Clarke, T. W. Higginson, Mary A. Livermore, and Lucy Stone as members and leaders. See Flexner 154–58.

9. The New England Woman's Club was founded in 1868. For more about the women's club movement and its relationship to the suffrage movement and to women writers, see Blair, *The Clubwoman as Feminist.*

5. The Dickens Years, 1867–1870

1. My account of Dickens relies primarily on the biography by Edgar Johnson and on Arthur Adrian's book about Dickens's sister, Georgina Hogarth, who became a lifelong correspondent of Annie's after they met in 1869. In fact, Annie's diaries and her letters from Georgina, now at the Huntington Library, were one of Adrian's major sources.

2. The evidence was collected in a slim volume by Ada B. Nisbet called *Dickens and Ellen Ternan.*

3. John Bigelow (1817–1911) co-edited the New York *Evening Post* with William Cullen Bryant and was later U.S. consul general at Paris (1861–1865) and U.S. minister to France (1865–1866). He mentioned his knowledge of the Dickens-Ternan affair in the first volume of his autobiography, *Retrospections of an Active Life* (1910).

4. See Tryon, Austin, and Johnson for accounts of this widely described event.

5. Paul Du Chaillu (1831–1903) was an African explorer born in France. His book *A Journey to Ashango-Land* (New York: Appleton, 1867) was reviewed somewhat negatively in the *Atlantic,* July 1867, 122–23. He published *Stories of the Gorilla Country* in 1868.

6. John Gorham Palfrey (1796–1881) was a Unitarian clergyman who edited the *North American Review* from 1835 to 1843, served in the House of Representatives between 1847–1849, and wrote the four-volume *History of England* (1858–75).

7. "Delicate, gentle, fairy-like beings begotten by fallen spirits who direct with a wand the pure in mind on the way to heaven" (Benet 3:840).

8. See the articles by Randall Stewart for a complete discussion of this quarrel and analysis of the financial matters.

9. The following passage from one of Whittier's letters to Lucy Larcom has mistakenly created the impression that Dodge succeeded in enlisting Whittier to her side:

Gail Hamilton advised me not to think of going [to the Fieldses']. The lack of domestic peace & harmony there—Mrs. F's brusque, rough way, & Mr. F's exacting and tyrannical behavior—would, she said, make my visits anything but agreeable. (WL 4:118; 7 Feb. 1866)

However, as Pickard points out in his edition of Whittier's letters, Whittier was simply repeating a passage in a letter that Dodge had written to him that was clearly intended to be ironic. Both letters were written in 1866 when Dodge and the Fieldses were still on good terms.

10. See Julian Hawthorne's *Nathaniel Hawthorne and His Wife* (1884) and *Hawthorne and His Circle* (1903).

11. Boston: Fields, Osgood, & Co., 1869. Dedication: "To Annie Fields, this little volume, descriptive of scenes with which she is familiar, is gratefully offered."

12. This passage is a loose imitation of several exchanges between Eugenius and Yorick. According to James A. Work, the Latin meaning of "Eugenius" is "well-born, noble, and generous," and the character was based on Sterne's friend John Hall-Stevenson. The imitation may have been suggested to Dickens by the word "fields" in Sterne's passage, which he then picked up as a pun on Fields's name. The name "Eliza" undoubtedly derives from the name of Sterne's great love, Mrs. Elizabeth Draper, to whom he wrote the *Journal to Eliza*. Thus understood, the passage constitutes a tremendous compliment to both Annie and James. See the Work edition 28n1.

13. Dr. Gabor Naphegyi (1824–1884) was the author of *The History of Hungary, and Sketches of Kossuth* (1849), *Among the Arabs* (1868), and *The Album of Language: Illustrated by the Lord's Prayer in One Hundred Languages* (1869).

14. Mrs. Frederick Lehmann (Jane Chambers) and Mrs. Rudolf Lehmann (Amelia Chambers) were sisters as well as sisters-in-law, since both were daughters of Robert Chambers, the Scottish publisher. Rudolf Lehmann, a well-known painter, painted four portraits of Robert Browning, who was a close friend.

15. Edward Flower (1805–1883) served several terms as Mayor of Stratford, where he and his wife Celina Greaves entertained Americans at their home, The Hill, built in 1865.

6. Charity Work: "A Dangerous Eagerness"

1. Probably a reference to Joseph Butler (1692–1752), Bishop of Durham, whose *Fifteen Sermons* were widely read and praised.

2. "New Uncommercial Samples" (5 Dec. 1868), 12–17.

3. My discussion of the conditions prevalent in Boston at this time is based on Handlin, *Boston's Immigrants*.

4. Handlin 15, 89, 93–94, 109–22.

5. My discussion of Annie's projects and activities is based on her diaries, her letters to Laura Winthrop Johnson, and Huggins, *Protestants against Poverty*. Huggins has examined the records of the Associated Charities, now in the offices of the Boston Family Service Association, which I have not seen.

6. See Dickens's story "The Holly Tree."

7. Letters in the collection of the Huntington Library.

8. Fanny Quincy Howe, the wife of Annie's friend and literary executor, Mark A. DeWolfe Howe, corresponded for over ten years with a prostitute named Maimie Pinzer. Both Mr. and Mrs. Howe were protégés of Mrs. Fields, and it is likely that Annie Fields knew a great deal more about the lives of Boston prostitutes than she recorded in her diaries. See Rosen, ed., *The Maimie Papers*.

9. Mrs. Caswell, a missionary to the American Indians, was greatly admired by Annie. See Huggins 171–73.

Mary A. Livermore (1820–1905), had volunteered for the Northwest Sanitary Commission during the Civil War and later worked for temperance, suffrage, and other causes in Boston.

Stowe's story is called "The Minister's Housekeeper" and it appeared in *Oldtown Fireside Stories.*

10. A.L.S. Octavia Hill to Annie Adams Fields, 26 Oct. 1875, Houghton Library.

11. See "Problems of Poor Relief" (Feb. 1878) and other articles in the Bibliography written between 1872 and 1889.

12. See Huggins's account (174–76) and Annie's account in her diaries beginning 31 July 1874.

13. This is the same structure adopted by James for his series called "My Friend's Library," in which Annie is "my friend."

14. See JTF to AF HL 16 Nov. 1874, and letters from Abby Morton Diaz to Annie Fields in HL (n.d.). There is an article on Mrs. Diaz in *Notable American Women* 1:471–73.

7. Home and Family, 1870–1881

1. See J. T. Fields, "Some Memories of Charles Dickens" (1870). On 15 June 1871 Annie mentioned "writing out my memories . . . for J. to use" in one of his "Whispering Gallery" articles. Howe notes in *Memories of a Hostess* that a number of the passages about Dickens quoted from Annie's diary appeared in slightly altered form in *Yesterdays with Authors.*

2. For a complete discussion of Manchester and its place in the summer life of Bostonians, see Garland's *Boston's North Shore,* especially chapter 7, "Of Autocrats and Actors," 254–71.

3. This information comes from Mrs. Neal, the current owner of the Fieldses' Manchester house, who kindly showed me the house in 1980.

4. James C. Austin states in his book on Fields that Annie "made it [Manchester] her permanent home" after Fields's death (426) and that Jewett lived there with her (320).

5. For more information about these lectures, see AF/*JTF* 187–89.

6. President Charles Eliot Norton bitterly opposed the admission of women to Harvard. See Howells, D.

7. Thomas Couture (1815–1879) was a popular French genre painter and the teacher of Manet.

8. Beecher was accused of committing adultery with Mrs. Tilton by Victoria Woodhull in 1872 and tried in 1875. The civil case ended in a hung jury. Annie commented frequently about the progress of the case in her diary and in her letters to LWJ in 1874. See Wilson 336–41.

9. Perhaps a sister-in-law of Annie's co-worker at the Associated Charities, Mrs. James A. Lodge.

10. Quoted in Garraty 157 from Gosse's essay "The Custom of Biography."

8. A New Kind of Partnership, 1881–1886

1. Quoted from Donovan, "The Unpublished Love Poems of Sarah Orne Jewett," 1.

2. Mark A. DeWolfe Howe implies in *Memories of a Hostess* (283–84) that James T. Fields selected Jewett as the ideal companion for Annie after his death. I have never seen any allusion to this "selection" in the primary materials. Although I do not think Fields would have disapproved of the friendship that arose between Annie and Sarah, neither do I think the friendship developed because he planned it.

3. Neither Jewett nor Fields wrote complete dates on letters, often writing only a day of the week or nothing at all. When Fields compiled her edition of Jewett's letters between 1909 and 1911, she penciled dates on many of the letters, but these dates are unreliable. I give Fields's date, if there is one, or my own guess, if there is enough evidence upon which to base one.

4. "The Child in Sarah Orne Jewett," in *Appreciation of Sarah Orne Jewett,* ed. Richard Cary (Waterville, Me.: Colby College Press, 1973), 223–28.

5. For Henry James's attitude toward his sister's relationship with Katherine Loring, see Strouse.

6. Faderman discusses the Jewett-Fields relationship in the chapter "Boston Marriage" in *Surpassing the Love of Men,* 197–203. Donovan discusses the nature of the relationship in her article "The Unpublished Love Poems of Sarah Orne Jewett," 26–31. Both writers qualify their use of the word "lesbian." These are the best discussions of the relationship to date. See also Donovan's excellent study *Sarah Orne Jewett* (1980), 12–18.

7. The argument I make here parallels that in the essay "A Closer Look at the Fields-Jewett Relationship," in Nagel, Gwen L., *Critical Essays on Sarah Orne Jewett* (Boston: G. K. Hall, 1984).

8. "Little books" is a reference to Annie's having published several of the small-format volumes favored by publishing companies at the time. She also undoubtedly had a houseful of such books.

9. See Richard Cary's explication of the nicknames in his 1967 edition of the letters, 96–97n3. Some of the other women who had nicknames were Mrs. James Lodge (Marygold), Celia Thaxter (Sandpiper), and Louise Imogen Guiney (Linnet).

10. Frost says that Annie Fields gave Jewett the nickname, but I have not seen the letter he refers to. See Frost 69.

11. No one seems to know what the "T" of "T. L." stands for—perhaps "Tom" because of Jewett's story "Tom's Husband."

12. See Pool, n4 above; also Cary, *Sarah Orne Jewett,* 19–20.

13. For discussions of *A Country Doctor,* see Donovan, *Sarah Orne Jewett,* 64–69; and Morgan, "The Atypical Woman."

14. *The Mate of the Daylight and Friends Ashore* (Boston: Houghton Mifflin, 1884), 210–33. See discussion in Donovan, *Sarah Orne Jewett,* 52–53.

9. The Developing Writer, 1883–1895

1. Jewett is referring to *The Story of the Normans* (1887).

2. "Chrysalides" was published in the *Atlantic Monthly* in 1883 and in *The Singing Shepherd.*

3. Richfield Springs, New York, was one of many "springs" and "baths" to which Annie and Sarah went for their health, primarily in the hope of easing Sarah's rheumatism.

4. I did not find this poem in Annie's poetry notebooks and manuscripts at the Huntington Library—it may have been destroyed.

5. See Bentzon, *La Condition de la femme aux Etats-Unis* (1894). Grace King provided a short biography of Madame Blanc in *Memories of a Southern Woman of Letters.*

6. "Revisiting a Green Nook" appeared in *Scribner's* in 1890 and in *The Singing Shepherd.*

11. "Both a Sharer and a Sustainer," 1902–1910

1. The edition Jewett read is probably *Recollections of a Tour Made in Scotland, a.d. 1803,* published in 1874 by G. P. Putnam's Sons.

2. Jessie Cochrane was a pianist from Louisville, Kentucky, whom Annie and Sarah befriended. Rose Lamb (1843–1927) was a one of Annie's co-workers at the Associated Charities. She had studied watercolor with William Morris Hunt and was a close friend of Celia Thaxter's (CL 97n).

3. This letter may be about an error Annie made in an 1899 article on the Cowden-Clarkes, which gave Mary Cowden-Clarke's year of death as 1897 instead of 1898. The *Century* issued an errata statement in the 1899 index.

4. Although Lily Fairchild played an important role in Annie's last years, I have been unable to place her. Cary mentions an Elizabeth Fairchild who would have been about the same age as Jewett and was friendly with her as early as the 1870s, but "Lily" would be an unusual nickname for Elizabeth. The Boston Public Library, which holds the letters, gives the correspondent's name as Mrs. Charles N. Fairchild. A man named Charles Fairchild was a junior partner in the

paper manufacturing firm of S. D. Warren & Co. and knew Howells and other members of Annie's circle well (Ballou 196–227). Lily may have been his wife.

12. "The Unspeakable Past," 1910–1915

1. Carol Farley Kessler alludes to this story in her book on Elizabeth Stuart Phelps. Evidently Phelps was only planning the story when her husband mentioned it to Annie, because Kessler writes that "When she died Phelps was at work on a short story sequence in which she planned to treat 'American urban life as shown in men's clubs of a certain type.'" Phelps's husband, Herbert Ward, printed an outline of his wife's unfinished story after her death.

2. In the collection of the Huntington Library.

3. Information from Mrs. Bole. Frances Adams Wallace, Annie's great-niece, wrote in her copy of Morris Carter's book *Isabella Stewart Gardner and Fenway Court* that she helped Mrs. Gardner take the pall from her aunt's coffin and fold it. The pall is mentioned in Carter's book, 254.

4. I have not been able to identify Eva von Blumberg.

5. Her diaries are in the Massachusetts Historical Society; other letters and notebooks are in the Huntington Library. Many additional papers, including the letters exchanged between Annie and Sarah, are in the collection of the Houghton Library at Harvard.

Bibliography

Works Cited

Included in this list are works cited in parentheses throughout the text or works referred to in the text that are not generally well known. Works referred to in the text that are standard sources have usually been omitted.

Adams, Andrew N[apoleon]. *A Genealogical History of Henry Adams of Braintree, Massachusetts, and His Descendants; also John Adams of Cambridge, Massachusetts, 1632–1897*. Rutland, Vt.: Tuttle, 1898.

Adrian, Arthur A. *Georgina Hogarth and the Dickens Circle*. London: Oxford Univ. Press, 1957.

Ahlstrom, Sydney E. *A Religious History of the American People*. 2 vols. Garden City, N.Y.: Image-Doubleday, 1975.

Amory, Cleveland. *The Proper Bostonians*. New York: E. P. Dutton, 1947.

"Artistic: Miss Edmonia Lewis at Florence." *The Commonwealth*, 21 Oct. 1865, n.p.

Arvin, Newton. *Longfellow: His Life and Work*. Boston: Atlantic Monthly–Little, Brown, 1962.

Austin, James C. *Fields of the Atlantic Monthly: Letters to an Editor, 1861–1870*. San Marino, Calif.: The Huntington Library, 1953.

Ballou, Ellen B. *The Building of the House: Houghton Mifflin's Formative Years*. Boston: Houghton Mifflin, 1970.

Barnard, Henry, ed. *Educational Biography: Memoirs of Teachers, Educators, and Promoters and Benefactors of Education, Literature, and Science*. Reprinted from the *American Journal of Education*. Part I. Teachers and Educators. New York: F. C. Brownell, 1859.

Bentzon, Th. [Blanc, Therese de Solms]. "La Condition de la femme aux Etats-Unis. Part 2: Boston. Section V: Mrs. J.-T. Fields—Salons et Intérieurs." *Revue des Deux Mondes*, 1 Sept. 1894, 109–15.

Blair, Karen J. *The Clubwoman as Feminist: True Womanhood Redefined, 1868–1914*. New York: Holmes & Meier, 1980.

Bole, Nancy [Annie Fields's great-niece]. Personal interview.

Brooks, Van Wyck. *The Flowering of New England, 1815–1865*. [New York:] E. P. Dutton, 1936.

Burns, Robert. *The Works of Robert Burns: With Life by Allan Cunningham*. New [2nd] ed. London: Henry G. Bohn, 1854. One of the very few editions which contain "The Ruined Maid's Lament."

Burton, Richard. *Elizabeth Adams: A Life Sketch*. [Baltimore:] Privately printed, Sept. 1898.

Carter, Morris. *Isabella Stewart Gardner and Fenway Court*. Boston: Houghton Mifflin, 1925.

Cary, Richard, *Sarah Orne Jewett*. Twayne's United States Authors Series [TUSAS] 19. New York: Twayne Pubs., 1962.

———. ed. *Sarah Orne Jewett Letters*. Enl. and rev. ed. Waterville, Me.: Colby College Press, 1967.

Cather, Willa. *Not Under Forty*. New York: Alfred A. Knopf, 1936.

Clarke, Edward Hammond. *Sex in Education; or a Fair Chance for the Girls*. Boston: J. R. Osgood, 1873.

Clement, E. H. "The Personal and Social Side of Mrs. Fields; the Many Notable Figures in Literary History Who Were Attracted to Her Personality." *Boston Evening Transcript*, 6 Jan. 1915, p. 18, col. 2–4.

Collins, Philip, ed. "Public Readings." Intro. to *Charles Dickens: The Public Readings*. Oxford: Clarendon, 1975.

Collyer, Robert. Rev. of *James T. Fields,* by Annie Adams Fields. *The Dial,* Jan. 1882, 203–06.

Craven, Mme Augustus [née Pauline de La Ferronays]. *Récit d'une Soeur: Souveniers de Famille.* 2 vols. Paris: Didier, 1866.

Dickens, Charles. "Aboard Ship." In "New Uncommercial Samples," *All the Year Round,* 5 Dec. 1868, 12–17.

_____ . "The Holly-Tree Inn." *Household Words,* 15 Dec. 1855, 36 pp.

_____ . *The Nonesuch Dickens.* Vol. 3: *The Letters of Charles Dickens, 1858–1870.* Ed. Walter Dexter. Bloomsbury: The Nonesuch Press, 1938.

_____ . "A Small Star in the East." In "New Uncommercial Samples," *All the Year Round.* 19 Dec. 1868, 61–66.

[Dodge, Mary Abigail.] *A Battle of the Books.* Ed. and pub.Gail Hamilton [pseud.]. Cambridge: Hurd and Houghton, 1870.

_____ . *Gail Hamilton's Life in Letters.* Ed. H. Augusta Dodge. Biographical sketch by Harriet Prescott Spofford. 2 vols. Boston: Lee and Shepard, 1901.

Donovan, Josephine. *New England Local Color Literature: A Women's Tradition.* New York: Frederick Ungar, 1983.

_____ . *Sarah Orne Jewett.* New York: Frederick Ungar, 1980.

_____ . "The Unpublished Love Poems of Sarah Orne Jewett." *Frontiers: A Journal of Women Studies,* Fall 1979, 26–31.

Duberman, Martin. *James Russell Lowell.* Boston: Houghton Mifflin, 1966.

Emerson, Edward Waldo. *Early Years of the Saturday Club, 1855–1870.* Boston: Houghton Mifflin, 1918.

Emerson, George B. *Reminiscences of an Old Teacher.* Boston: Alfred Mudge & Sons, Printers, 1878.

_____ . *The Schoolmaster.* Part 2 of *The School and the Schoolmaster.* Boston: Wm. B. Fowle & N. Capen, 1843.

Faderman, Lilian. *Surpassing the Love of Men: Romantic Friendship and Love between Women from the Renaissance to the Present.* New York: William Morrow, 1981.

Fields, James T. "My Friend's Library." *Atlantic Monthly,* Oct. 1861, 440–447.

[Fields, J. T.] "Some Memories of Charles Dickens." *Atlantic Monthly,* Aug. 1870, 235–45.

Fields, James T. *Underbrush.* Boston: J. R. Osgood, 1877.

_____ . *Yesterdays with Authors.* Boston: J. R. Osgood, 1872.

Flexner, Eleanor. *Century of Struggle: The Woman's Rights Movement in the United States.* Rev. ed. Cambridge: The Belknap Press of Harvard Univ. Press, 1975.

Friedrich, Otto. *Clover, a Love Story.* New York: Simon and Schuster, 1979.

Frost, John Eldridge. *Sarah Orne Jewett.* Kittery Point, Me: Gundalow Club, 1960.

Garland, Joseph E. *Boston's North Shore: Being an Account of Life among the Noteworthy, Fashionable, Wealthy, Eccentric and Ordinary, 1823–1890.* Boston: Little, Brown, 1978.

Garraty, John A. *The Nature of Biography.* New York: Knopf, 1957.

Gilman, Arthur. *The Story of Boston: A Study of Independence.* Great Cities of the Republic. New York: G. P. Putnam's Sons, 1889.

Guiney, Louise Imogen. "Authors at Home: Mrs. James T. Fields in Boston." *The Critic,* 4 June 1898, 367–69.

Hale, Nancy. Intro. to *The Peterkin Papers,* by Lucretia P. Hale. Boston: Houghton Mifflin, 1960.

Handlin, Oscar. *Boston's Immigrants: A Study in Acculturation.* Rev. and enl. ed. Cambridge: The Belknap Press of Harvard Univ. Press, 1959.

Hawthorne, Julian. *Hawthorne and His Circle.* New York: Harper, 1903.

_____ . *Hawthorne and His Wife.* Boston: Ticknor, 1884.

Heaton, Eliza Putnam. "The Home of Miss Jewett." *Boston Sunday Herald,* 18 Aug. 1895, 29.

Helfrich, Margaret L. *The Social Role of the Executive's Wife.* Bureau of Business Research Monograph No. 123. Columbus: The Ohio State Univ. Bureau of Business Research, [1965].

Holmes, Oliver Wendell. *A Mortal Antipathy.* Vol. 7 of *The Standard Library Edition of the Works of Oliver Wendell Holmes.* Boston: Houghton Mifflin, 1892.

Howard, Brett. *Boston: A Social History.* New York: Hawthorn Books, 1976.

Howe, Helen. *The Gentle Americans, 1864–1960: Biography of a Breed.* New York: Harper and Row, 1965.

[Howe, Julia Ward.] "How to Regard the Great Organ." *The Commonwealth,* 13 Nov. 1863, [1].

Howe, Julia Ward. "Lyrics of the Street." *Atlantic Monthly.* "The Telegrams," May 1862, 555–56; "The Wedding," July 1862, 98–99; "The Charitable Visitor," Dec. 1862, 720; "The Fine Lady," Jan. 1863, 119; "The Darkened House," March 1863, 372; "Play," Sept. 1863, 380.

Howe, M. A. DeWolfe. *Memories of a Hostess: A Chronicle of Eminent Friendships. Drawn chiefly from the diaries of Mrs. James T. Fields.* Boston: The Atlantic Monthly Press, 1922.

_____. *A Venture in Remembrance.* Boston: Little Brown, 1841.

Howells, Dorothy Elia. *A Century to Celebrate: Radcliffe College, 1879–1979.* Cambridge, Mass.: Radcliffe College, 1978.

Howells, W. D. *Selected Letters of W. D. Howells.* George Arms, Richard H. Ballinger, and Christoph Lohmann, gen. eds. 6 vols. Boston: Twayne—G. K. Hall, 1979–1983.

_____. *Literary Friends and Acquaintance: A Personal Retrospect of American Authorship.* Vol. 32 of *A Selected Edition of W. D. Howells.* Ed. David F. Hiatt. Edwin H. Cady, gen. ed. Bloomington: Indiana Univ. Press, 1968.

Huggins, Nathan Irvin. *Protestants against Poverty: Boston's Charities, 1870–1900.* Foreword by Oscar Handlin. Contributions in American History, No. 9. Westport, Conn.: Greenwood, 1971.

James, Henry. *The American Scene.* New York: Harper, 1907.

_____. "Mr. and Mrs. James T. Fields." *Atlantic Monthly,* July 1915, 21–31.

Jewett, Sarah Orne. *The Country of the Pointed Firs and Other Stories.* Selected and arranged by Willa Cather. New York: Doubleday, 1956.

_____. Intro. to *The Letters of Sarah Wyman Whitman.* Cambridge, Mass.: The Riverside Press, 1907.

Johnson, Edgar. *Charles Dickens: His Tragedy and Triumph.* 2 vols. New York: Simon and Schuster, 1952. Rev. and abr. ed. New York: Penguin, 1979.

Johnson, Robert Underwood. *Remembered Yesterdays.* Boston: Little, Brown, 1923.

Kessler, Carol Farley. *Elizabeth Stuart Phelps.* Boston: Twayne, 1982.

King, Grace. *Memories of a Southern Woman of Letters.* New York: Macmillan, 1932.

Koren, John. *Boston, 1822–1922: The Story of Government and Principal Activities during One Hundred Years.* Boston: City of Boston Printing Dept., 1923.

Lathrop, Rose Hawthorne (Mother Alphonsa). *Memories of Hawthorne.* Boston: Houghton Mifflin, 1897.

Longfellow, Henry Wadsworth. *The Letters of Henry Wadsworth Longfellow.* Ed. Andrew Hilen. 5 vols. Cambridge: The Belknap Press of Harvard Univ. Press, 1967–1982.

Matthiessen, Francis Otto. *Sarah Orne Jewett.* Boston: Houghton Mifflin, 1929.

Mellow, James R. *Nathaniel Hawthorne in His Times.* Boston: Houghton Mifflin, 1980.

Morgan, Ellen. "The Atypical Woman: Nan Prince in the Literary Transition to Feminism." *Kate Chopin Newsletter,* Summer 1976, 33–37.

Morse, Frances R. "Mrs. Fields' Bequest." *Survey* 35 (1915), 290.

Nagel, Gwen L. and James. *Sarah Orne Jewett: A Reference Guide.* Boston: G. K. Hall, 1978.

Neal, Mrs. [current owner of Thunderbolt Hill]. Personal interview.

Nisbet, Ada B. *Dickens and Ellen Ternan.* Berkeley: Univ. of California Press, 1952.

Notable American Women: A Biographical Dictionary, 1607–1950. Edward T. James ed. Janet Wilson James, assoc. ed. 3 vols. Cambridge: The Belknap Press of Harvard Univ. Press, 1971.

Oldham, Ellen M., ed. "Mrs. Hawthorne to Mrs. Fields." *Boston Public Library Quarterly,* July 1957, 143–54. Ed. from a ms. by A. F.

"One Word More." *The Commonwealth,* 4 Dec. 1863, n.p.

Pfister, Harold Francis. *Facing the Light: Historic American Portrait Daguerreotypes.* City of Washington: Smithsonian Institution Press for The National Portrait Gallery, 1978.

Pool, Eugene Hillhouse. "The Child in Sarah Orne Jewett." In *Appreciation of Sarah Orne Jewett: 29 Interpretive Essays.* Ed. Richard Cary. Waterville, Me.: Colby College Press, 1973, 223–28.

Roman, Judith A. "A Closer Look at the Fields-Jewett Relationship." In *Critical Essays on Sarah Orne Jewett.* Ed. Gwen L. Nagel. Boston: G. K. Hall, 1986.

Rosen, Ruth, and Sue Davidson, eds. *The Maimie Papers.* Intro. Ruth Rosen. Old Westbury, N.Y.: Feminist Press, 1977. Letters written 1910–1922 from Maimie Pinzer to Fanny Quincy Howe.

Rossiter, William L., ed. "Recollections of Old Boston: From a Conversation with a Boston Lady of the Period." In *Days and Ways in Old Boston.* Boston: R. H. Stearns, 1915, 39–44. An interview attributed to Annie Fields by the Massachusetts Historical Society.

Rotundo, Barbara Ruth. "Mrs. James T. Fields, Hostess and Biographer." Ph.D. diss., Syracuse Univ., 1968.

Rusk, Ralph L. *The Life of Ralph Waldo Emerson.* New York: Columbia Univ. Press, 1949.

Saxton, Martha. *Louisa May: A Modern Biography of Louisa May Alcott.* Boston: Houghton Mifflin, 1977.

Sergeant, Elizabeth Shepley. *Willa Cather: A Memoir.* Philadelphia: Lippincott, [1953].

Sklar, Kathryn Kish. *Catharine Beecher: A Study in American Domesticity.* New York: W. W. Norton, 1973.

Smith-Rosenberg, Carroll. "The Female World of Love and Ritual: Relations between Women in Nineteenth-Century America." *Signs,* Autumn 1975, 1–29.

Spofford, Harriet Prescott. *A Little Book of Friends.* Boston: Little, Brown, 1916.

State Street Trust Company. *Boston: One Hundred Years a City, 1822–1922.* Boston: Walton Advertising and Printing Co., 1922.

Stewart, Randall. "Pestiferous Gail Hamilton, James T. Fields, and the Hawthornes." *New England Quarterly,* Sept. 1944, 418–23.

———. "The Hawthornes at the Wayside, 1860–1864: Selections from Mrs. Hawthorne's Letters to Mr. and Mrs. Fields." *More Books: The Bulletin of the Boston Public Library,* Sept. 1944, 263–79.

———. "Hawthorne's Last Illness and Death: Selections from Mrs. Hawthorne's Letters to Mr. and Mrs. Fields." *More Books: The Bulletin of the Boston Public Library,* Oct. 1944, 303–13.

———. "Editing Hawthorne's Notebooks: Selections from Mrs. Hawthorne's Letters to Mr. and Mrs. Fields, 1864–1868." *More Books: The Bulletin of the Boston Public Library,* Sept. 1945, 299–315.

———. "Mrs. Hawthorne's Financial Difficulties: Selections from Her Letters to James T. Fields, 1865–1868." *More Books: The Bulletin of the Boston Public Library,* Feb. 1946, 43–52.

———. "Mrs. Hawthorne's Quarrel with James T. Fields: Selections from Letters to Fields by Mrs. Hawthorne and Elizabeth Peabody." *More Books: The Bulletin of the Boston Public Library,* Sept. 1946, 154–63.

Stowe, Harriet Beecher. "The True Story of Lady Byron's Life." *Atlantic Monthly,* Sept. 1869, 295–313.

Strouse, Jean. *Alice James: A Biography.* Boston: Houghton Mifflin, 1980.

Tharp, Louise Hall. *The Peabody Sisters of Salem.* Boston: Little, Brown, 1950.

———. *Three Saints and a Sinner: Julia Ward Howe, Louisa, Annie and Sam Ward.* Boston: Little, Brown, 1956.

Thaxter, Celia. "A Memorable Murder." *Atlantic Monthly,* May 1875, 602–15.

Tilton, Eleanor M. *Amiable Autocrat: A Biography of Dr. Oliver Wendell Holmes*. New York: Henry Schuman, 1947.

Tryon, William S. *Parnassus Corner: A Life of James T. Fields, Publisher to the Victorians*. Boston: Houghton Mifflin, 1963.

Ward, Elizabeth Stuart Phelps. *Chapters from a Life*. Boston: Houghton Mifflin, 1896.

Welter, Barbara. "The Cult of True Womanhood: 1820–1860." *American Quarterly*, Summer 1966, 151–74.

Whipple, Edwin Percy. "Recollections of James T. Fields." *Atlantic Monthly*, Aug. 1881, 253–59.

Whiting, Lilian. *Boston Days*. Boston: Little, Brown, 1902.

———. *Louise Chandler Moulton: Poet and Friend*. Boston: Little, Brown, 1910.

Whittier, John Greenleaf. *The Letters of John Greenleaf Whittier*. Ed. John B. Pickard. 4 vols. Cambridge: The Belknap Press of Harvard Univ. Press, 1975.

Wickham, Gertrude Van R. "Dogs of Noted Americans," Part 3: "Sara [sic] Orne Jewett's Dog." *St. Nicholas*, May 1889, 544–45.

Woody, Thomas. *A History of Women's Education in the United States*. 2 vols. New York: The Science Press, 1929.

Contemporary Periodical Reviews, Articles, and Obituaries

Included here are additional contemporary sources used in preparing this book. Works by named or noted authors cited in the text have been included above.

Rev. of *Authors and Friends*. *The Wave*, 28 Nov. 1896, 10.

Rev. of *Authors and Friends*. *Nation*, 4 March 1897, 168–69.

Rev. of *Authors and Friends*. In "Our Library Table." *The Athenaeum*, 27 March 1897, 14.

Boston Daily Evening Transcript, Wed., 15 Nov. 1854. Marriages. "At King's Chapel, this morning, Nov. 15th, by Rev. Dr. Gannett, Mr. James T. Fields to Miss Annie W., daughter of Dr. Z. B. Adams."

Clapp, John Bouve. "Mrs. Fields in Anecdote." *Boston Evening Transcript*, 6 Jan. 1915, p. 18, col. 4.

Dall, Caroline Healey. "Harriet Beecher Stowe's Life and Letters." *Poet-Lore*, Oct. 1898, 579–85.

"The Death of James T. Fields." *Boston Daily Evening Transcript*, 25 April 1881, p. 4, col. 2.

"Death of Dr. Z. B. Adams, of This City." *Boston Medical & Surgical Journal* 51 (1855–56), 545–46.

"Dr. Z. B. Adams." *Boston Medical & Surgical Journal* 52 (1855), 24.

"Famous People at Home." "[No.] 9: Mrs. James T. Fields." *Time and the Hour*, 17 April 1897, 6–7.

Fiske, J. "Reminiscences of James T. Fields." *Atlantic Monthly*, Jan. 1882, 134–35.

[Francis, Susan M.] "Atlantic's Pleasant Days in Tremont Street." *Atlantic Monthly*, Nov. 1907, 716–20.

"From Henry James's 'The American Scene': Mrs. Fields's Drawing Room." *Boston Evening Transcript*, 6 Jan. 1915, p. 18, col. 2–3.

"From Mrs. Fields's 'Authors and Friends.'" *Boston Evening Transcript*, 6 Jan. 1915, p. 18, col. 4–5.

"From Mrs. Fields's 'The Singing Shepherd': 'To One Whose Sight Was Failing.'" *Boston Evening Transcript*, 6 Jan. 1915, p. 18, col. 2–3.

G[ilder], J[eannette] L. "A Book and Its Story: Mrs. Fields and Her Famous Friends." *Critic*, 20 Feb. 1897, 123–24.

"The Good Physician." Obit. of Dr. Zabdiel Boylston Adams. *Boston Daily Evening Transcript*, 26 Jan. 1855.

Guerry, William A. "Harriet Beecher Stowe." *Sewanee Review*, July 1898, 335–44.

Howe, M. A. DeWolfe. "Days with Mrs. James T. Fields and Her Friends." *The Bookman*, Dec. 1896, 308–13.

Rev. of *James T. Fields: Biographical Notes and Personal Sketches, with Unpublished Fragments and Tributes from Men and Women of Letters*, by Annie Adams Fields. *The Athenaeum*, 8 April 1881, 439–40.

"The Late James T. Fields." *Boston Daily Evening Transcript*, 26 April 1881, p. 1, col. 3–4.

"The Late Z. B. Adams, M.D." *Boston Daily Evening Transcript*, 29 Jan. 1855.

"A Lesson and a Memory; The Late Mrs. James T. Fields Left Both to the Wives of Struggling Literary Men—A New York Appreciation." *Boston Evening Transcript*, 13 Jan. 1915, 7.

"Life and Letters of Mrs. Stowe." *The Dial*, 16 Dec. 1897, 384–86.

Rev. of *Life and Letters of Harriet Beecher Stowe. The Critic*, 18 Dec. 1897, 376–77.

Rev. of *Life and Letters of Harriet Beecher Stowe. The Athenaeum*, 1 Jan 1898, 15- 17.

Rev. of *Life and Letters of Harriet Beecher Stowe. The Nation*, 24 Feb. 1898, 152–53.

"The Literati of New England." Rev. of *Authors and Friends. The Dial*, 16 Jan. 1897, 59–60.

"Mr. Fields Was Downtown on Saturday." *Boston Daily Evening Transcript*, 25 April 1881, p. 4, col. 3.

"Mr. James T. Fields." *Boston Daily Evening Transcript*, 25 April 1881, p. 4, col. 4–5.

"Mrs. Fields's Reminisences of Whittier." *The Critic*, 28 Jan. 1893, 47–48.

"Mrs. Fields's 'Shelf of Old Books.'" *The Dial*, 1 March 1895, 154.

"Mrs. James T. Fields." Associated Charities of Boston. Typescript. The Houghton Library, Harvard University.

"Mrs. James T. Fields." *Boston Evening Transcript*, 6 Jan. 1915, p. 16, col. 3.

"Mrs. James T. Fields." *Outlook* 109 (20 Jan. 1915), 115–16.

"Mrs. J. T. Fields Dies at Her Home: Widow of Former Boston Publisher Had Lived at 148 Charles Street for Sixty Years." *Boston Evening Transcript*, 5 Jan. 1915, last ed., p. 1, col. 7.

Sanborn, Frank B. "Frank Sanborn's Appreciation of Mrs. Fields; the Generous Tribute of One Member of the Famous New England Group to Another Member." *Boston Evening Transcript*, 6 Jan. 1915, p. 18, col. 1.

Sargent George H. "The Late Mrs. Fields's Library—Autographed Relics of Her Late Visitors; a Collection Uncommonly Rich in Books Associated with the Many Distinguished Personages Who Were Friends of the Fields' [sic]." *Boston Evening Transcript*, 13 Jan. 1915, p. 19.

Rev. of *A Shelf of Old Books. The Athenaeum*, 2 March 1895, 275–76.

Rev. of *A Shelf of Old Books. The Critic*, 23 March 1895, 218.

Rev. of *A Shelf of Old Books. Overland Monthly*, March 1895, 329–30.

Rev. of *The Singing Shepherd*, by Annie Adams Fields. *Overland Monthly*, Jan. 1896, 123.

Rev. of *The Singing Shepherd, and Other Poems. The Dial*, 16 Feb. 1896, 111–12.

"Some Glimpses of Our 'Immortals.'" Rev. of *Authors and Friends. The Literary Digest*, 13 Feb. 1897, 460–61.

Rev. of *Under the Olive*, by Annie Adams Fields. *American*, 27 Nov. 1880, 107–08.

Wilson, Forrest. *Crusader in Crinoline: The Life of Harriet Beecher Stowe*. Philadelphia: Lippincott, 1941.

"Women's Work in Philanthropy: Opening Charity Conference of New York Women." *Lend a Hand* 1 (1886), 101–03.

"Zabdiel Boylston Adams." *Med. Communicat.* 9 (1860), 48–49. Published in Boston by the Massachusetts Medical Society.

Primary Sources

Books

[Fields, Annie Adams.] *Ode at the inauguration of the great organ in Boston, Nov. 2, 1863.* Recited by Miss Charlotte Cushman. Cambridge: Priv. printed, 1863.
_____ . *Asphodel.* Boston: Ticknor & Fields, 1866.
_____ . *The Children of Lebanon.* Boston: Priv. printed, 1872.
F[ields], A[nnie]. *The Return of Persephone: A dramatic sketch.* Cambridge: Priv. printed, 1877. Dedication tipped in: "To the memory of my mother."
_____ . *James T. Fields: Biographical Notes and Personal Sketches.* Boston: Houghton Mifflin, 1881.
_____ . *Under the Olive.* Boston: Houghton Mifflin, 1881; 2nd ed., 1881.
Fields, Mrs. James T. *How to Help the Poor.* Boston: Houghton, Mifflin and Co., 1883. Repr. 1884, 1885; 1885 copy states "23rd thousand."
_____ . *Whittier: Notes of His Life and Friendships.* Harper's Black and White Series. New York: Harper and Bros., 1893.
_____ . *A Shelf of Old Books.* New York: Charles Scribner's Sons, 1894; 1895.
_____ . *A Shelf of Old Books.* London: Osgood & McIlvaine, 1894.
F[ields], A[nnie] and R[ose] L[amb], eds. *Letters of Celia Thaxter.* Intro. by A. F. Boston: Houghton Mifflin, 1895. Also printed in *Authors and Friends.*
Fields, Annie. *The Singing Shepherd.* Boston: Houghton Mifflin, 1895.
_____ . *Authors and Friends.* Boston: Houghton Mifflin, 1896; 4th ed., 1897; 6th ed., 1897.
_____ . *Authors and Friends.* London: T. F. Unwin, 1896.
_____ . ed. *Life and Letters of Harriet Beecher Stowe.* Boston: Houghton Mifflin, 1897; 1899.
_____ . *Life and Letters of Harriet Beecher Stowe.* London: Sampson Low, 1897; S. Low & Marston, 1898.
_____ . *Nathaniel Hawthorne.* The Beacon Biographies of Eminent Americans. Ed. M. A. DeWolfe Howe. Boston: Small, Maynard, 1899.
_____ . *Nathaniel Hawthorne.* London: K Paul, Trench, Trubner, [c. 1899].
Fields, Mrs. *Orpheus: A Masque.* Boston: Houghton, Mifflin, 1900.
Fields, Mrs. James T. *Charles Dudley Warner.* Contemporary Men of Letters Series. Ed. William Aspenwall Bradley. New York: McClure Phillips, 1904.
Fields, Annie, ed. *Letters of Sarah Orne Jewett.* Boston: Houghton Mifflin, 1911.
_____ . ed. *Letters of Sarah Orne Jewett.* London: Constable, 1911.

Articles

[Fields, Annie Adams.] "The Holly-Tree Coffee Rooms." *The Christian Union,* 21 Feb. 1872, 175.
[_____.] "A Beautiful Charity." *Harper's,* July 1877, 200–05.
F[ields], A[nnie]. "Problems of Poor Relief." *Sunday Afternoon,* 2 Feb. 1878, 136–43.
[Fields, Annie Adams.] "A Glimpse at Some of Our Charities. Part I." *Harper's,* Feb. 1878, 441–50.
[_____.] "A Glimpse at Some of Our Charities. Part II. The Employment, Education, and Protection of Women." *Harper's,* March 1878, 596–608.
[_____.] "Three Typical Workingmen." *Atlantic Monthly,* Dec. 1878, 717–27.
[_____.] "Saint Cecilia." *Harper's,* Nov. 1880, 809–19.
Fields, Mrs. James T. "Upon the Constitution and Duties of a District Conference." *Proceedings of the Eighth Annual [National] Conference of Charities and Correction, Held at Boston, July 25–30, 1881.* Ed. F. B. Sanborn. Boston: A. Williams & Co., 1881.
_____ . *Extracts from a Paper upon District Conferences.* No. 3. Leaflet, Charity Organization Society of the City of New York, May 1882, 4 pp.

A[nnie]. F[ields]. "Mr. Emerson in the Lecture Room." *Atlantic Monthly,* June 1883, 818–32.

Fields, Annie. "Monster Asylums." Letter. *The Nation,* 25 Dec. 1884, 544.

———— . "Acquaintance with Charles Reade." *Century,* Nov. 1884, 67–79.

———— . "Glimpses of Emerson." *Harper's,* Feb. 1884, 457–67.

———— . "Work for Paupers and Convicts." Letter. *The Nation,* 2 Sept. 1886, 194.

Fields, Mrs. Annie. "Lend a Hand, for 'Pain Is Not the Fruit of Pain.'" *Lend a Hand,* Jan. 1886, 7–8.

Fields, Annie. "The Contributors and the Children: The Poet Who Told the Truth." *Wide Awake,* Dec. 1886, 87–88.

———— . "Glimpses of Longfellow in Social Life." *Century,* April 1886, 884–93.

———— . "The Contributors and the Children: [Noble-Born]." *Wide Awake,* April 1887, p. 342.

Fields, Mrs. A. T. [sic]. "Three Real Cases." *Lend a Hand,* Aug. 1888, 455–56.

Fields, Mrs. James T. "A Shelf of Old Books: Leigh Hunt." *Scribner's,* March 1888, 285–305.

Fields, Annie. "The Contributors and the Children: About Clothes." *Wide Awake,* Jan. 1888, 85–87.

Fields, Mrs. James T. "A Helping Hand." *Wide Awake,* Aug. 1888, 143–49.

Fields, Mrs. Annie. "The Aged Poor," *Chautauquan* 9 (1889), 517–19.

Fields, Mrs. James T. "A Second Shelf of Old Books: Edinburgh." *Scribner's,* April 1889, 453–76.

Fields, Mrs. "Special Work of Associated Charities." *Lend a Hand,* April 1889, 285–88.

Fields, Mrs. James T. "Guerin's 'Centaur.'" *Scribner's,* Aug. 1892, 224–32.

Fields, Annie. "Tennyson." *Harper's,* Jan. 1893, 309–12.

———— . "Whittier: Notes of His Life and of His Friendship." *Harper's,* Feb. 1893, 338–59.

Fields, Mrs. James T. "Third Shelf of Old Books." *Scribner's,* Sept. 1894, 338–59.

Fields, Annie. "Celia Thaxter." *Atlantic Monthly,* Feb. 1895, 254–66.

———— . "Oliver Wendell Holmes: Personal Recollections and Unpublished Letters." *Century,* Feb. 1895, 505–15.

———— . "Days with Mrs. Stowe." *Atlantic Monthly,* Aug. 1896, 145–56.

———— . "Reminiscences of Harriet Beecher Stowe." Excerpt from *Life and Letters.* In "Reading from New Books," *The Living Age,* 8 Jan. 1898, 145–47.

Fields, Mrs. James T. "The Inner Life of John Greenleaf Whittier." *Chautauquan* 30 (1899), 194–98.

———— . "Two Lovers of Literature: Charles and Mary Cowden Clarke." *Century,* May 1899, 122–31.

Fields, Annie. "Notes on Glass Decoration." *Atlantic Monthly,* June 1899, 807–11.

———— . "George Eliot." *Century,* July 1899, 442–46.

Fields, Mrs. James T. "Mary Russell Mitford." *Critic,* Dec. 1900, 512.

———— . "Dr. Southwood Smith: Pioneer of English Sanitary Reform." *Charities Review,* March 1900, 28–34.

———— . "Which Are the New England Classics? A Ten-Minute Talk." In *Six New England Classics: Talks and Lectures.* Course V. Booklovers Reading Club. Ed. Fred Lewis Pattee. Philadelphia: The Booklovers Library, 1901, 65–71.

Fields, Mrs. "Notable Women: Mme. Blanc ('Th. Bentzon')." *Century,* May 1903, 134–39.

Fields, Annie. "Saint Theresa." *Atlantic Monthly,* March 1903, 353–63.

Fields, Mrs. "'A Letter from Mrs. Fields' to the Arbella Club, 'A Friendly Circle of Girls.'" Oct. 1912. Privately printed by the Boston Athenaeum.

Poems

[Fields, Annie Adams.] "The Wild Endive." *Atlantic Monthly,* Nov. 1861, 625.

[————.] "Compensation." *Atlantic Monthly,* April 1862, 511.

[————.] "Waiting." *Atlantic Monthly,* Dec. 1862, 764.

West, A. [pseud.]. "My Ship." *Atlantic Monthly,* April 1863, 420.

———— . "Give." *Atlantic Monthly,* May 1863, 643.

_____ . "My Palace." *Atlantic Monthly*, Oct. 1863, 417–19.

_____ . "Andante: Beethoven's Sixth Symphony." *Atlantic Monthly*, Nov. 1863, 583.

[————.] "Sweet-Brier." *Atlantic Monthly*, Aug. 1864, 229–30.

[————.] "The Future Summer." *Atlantic Monthly*, Oct. 1864, 503–04.

[————.] "Riches." *Atlantic Monthly*, Nov. 1864, 530.

West, A. [pseud.]. "The Song Sparrow." *Atlantic Monthly*, Nov. 1866, 599.

_____ . "Elizabeth's Chamber." *Atlantic Monthly*, Feb. 1867, 173.

_____ . "Labor." *Atlantic Monthly*, March 1867, 345.

_____ . "The Household Lamp." *Atlantic Monthly*, March 1868, 362.

_____ . "The Bee and the Rose." *Atlantic Monthly*, Feb. 1869, 187.

_____ . "Threnody [June 9, 1870]." *Atlantic Monthly*, Sept. 1870, 308.

_____ . "My Retreat." *Atlantic Monthly*, Oct. 1870, 440.

_____ . "The Return." *Atlantic Monthly*, Nov. 1870, 521.

A. W. "Children." *Atlantic Monthly*, April 1871, 467.

_____ . "Foreshadows." *Atlantic Monthly*, Sept. 1871, 319.

[Fields, Annie Adams.] "Little Guinever." *Boston Transcript*, 16 May 1872, and *Atlantic Monthly*, June 1872, 730.

A. F. "The Ruined Cottage (New Hampshire Hills)." *Harper's*, June 1875, 51.

_____ . "Where?" *Harper's*, July 1875, 189.

_____ . "The First Breath of Autumn." *Harper's*, Oct. 1875, 744.

_____ . "The Latter Days." *Harper's*, Dec. 1875, 118.

_____ . "April." *Harper's*, April 1876, 769.

_____ . "Song [To dream, and then to sleep]." *Harper's*, Nov. 1876, 876.

_____ . "Lillian's Dying." *Harper's*, Dec. 1876, 64.

_____ . "Good-Morrow." *Harper's*, Aug. 1877, 394.

_____ . "A Return." *Harper's*, Feb. 1878, 353.

_____ . "The Necklace." *Harper's*, Feb. 1879, 234.

A. W. "Defiance." *Atlantic Monthly*, Feb. 1879, 192–93.

Fields, Annie. "Pastor Dankwardt: Pomerania, 1807." *Harper's*, Jan. 1882, 271–72.

_____ . "Changing Skies." *Harper's*, Oct. 1882, 728.

_____ . "Humility." *Harper's*, Jan. 1883, 233.

_____ . "The Folding." *Harper's*, June 1883, 19.

A. F. "Chrysalides." *Atlantic Monthly*, Sept. 1883, 375.

_____ . "The Initiate." *Atlantic Monthly*, Dec. 1883, 745–46.

_____ . "Deisidaimonia: (Holy Fear)." *Atlantic Monthly*, March 1884, 350.

_____ . "Summer Companions." *Harper's*, Sept. 1885, 584.

Fields, Annie. "Ros Solis." *Harper's*, July 1886, 257.

_____ . "An Invitation." *Harper's*, Aug. 1886, 397.

_____ . "Victoria." *Harper's*, Jan. 1887, 251.

[Fields, Annie Adams]. "Prelude." In *A Week Away from Time*. [Ed. Mrs. James Lodge.] Boston: Roberts Brothers, 1887.

Fields, Annie. "A Bride of a Year." *Scribner's*, Sept. 1887, 320.

Fields, Mrs. "The Winging Hour." *Century*, Dec. 1887, 212.

Fields, Annie. "Ephemeron." *Scribner's*, Feb. 1888, 160.

_____ . "The Poet's House." *Scribner's*, Nov. 1888, 593.

_____ . "The King's Seat." *Century*, June 1888, 265.

_____ . "The Way." *Harper's*, Feb. 1889, 373.

_____ . "Song ['Behold another singer,' Criton said.]" *Harper's*, April 1889, 814.

_____ . "Not Strand but Sea." *Scribner's*, May 1889, 635.

_____ . "'I am the Beginning and the End.'" *Scribner's*, Nov. 1889, 614.

_____ . "The Pathless Way." *Atlantic Monthly*, June 1890, 748.

_____ . "Flammantia moenia mundi." *Atlantic Monthly*, Aug. 1890, 235.

_____ . "Bird of Autumn: To ————." *Atlantic Monthly*, Nov. 1890, 606.

_____ . "On Waking from a Dreamless Sleep." *Harper's*, Nov. 1890, 923.

_____ . "Revisiting a Green Nook." *Scribner's,* Oct. 1890, 472.

_____ . "Far Haven." *Harper's,* Dec. 1890, 148.

_____ . "Silence and Solitude." *Harper's,* April 1891, 795.

_____ . "Corban: A Song." *Scribner's,* July 1891, 61.

_____ . "Song and Sorrow." *Scribner's,* Aug. 1891, 170.

_____ . "Winter Lilacs." *Scribner's,* Dec. 1891, 711.

_____ . "The Singing Shepherd." *Harper's,* Dec. 1891, 117.

_____ . "Ode to Spring." *Century,* March 1892, 779.

_____ . "Comatas." *Century,* June 1892, 179.

_____ . "Death, Who Art Thou?" *Harper's,* Oct. 1893, 705.

_____ . "A Birthday in Autumn." *Scribner's,* Sept. 1893, 353.

_____ . "'A Thousand Years in Thy Sight.'" *Harper's,* Jan. 1894, 205.

_____ . "There Is No Other Life but the Eternal." *Scribner's,* Feb. 1894, 170.

_____ . "Coronal." *Harper's,* Dec. 1894, 50.

_____ . "Benevolence." *Scribner's,* June 1895, 751.

_____ . "Regnum Spiritus." *Scribner's,* Aug. 1896, 188.

_____ . "Round the Far Rocks." *Atlantic Monthly.* Jan. 1898, 70.

_____ . "The Morning Star." *Harper's,* July 1898, 194.

_____ . "To the Children." *Home Progress,* July 1913, 33.

_____ . "Midsummer Noon." *Home Progress,* June 1914, 475.

Unpublished Manuscripts

Adams, Elizabeth. To Annie Fields, undated. Six letters. Priv. coll. of Mrs. Benjamin P. Bole.

Davis, Rebecca Harding. Letters. Alderman Library, Univ. of Virginia, Charlottesville, Va.

Fields, Annie Adams. Diaries, MS. Fields Coll. Massachusetts Historical Society, Boston.

F[ields], A[nnie]. "June Among the New Hampshire Hills." Proofs. The Huntington Library, San Marino, Calif.

Fields, Annie Adams. Fields Addenda, Box 1. Three notebooks of poetry, MS. 1. 1857–64. 47 poems. 2. 1864–74. 139 poems. 3. 1870–80. 80 poems. The Huntington Library.

_____ . Fields Addenda, Box 2, Env. 1. "Canticles of Married Love." MS. The Huntington Library.

_____ . Fields Addenda, Box 2, Env. 2–9. Eleven poetry notebooks and unbound poems, MS. 1871–99. The Huntington Library.

_____ . Fields Addenda, Box 3, Env. 7. "A Gentleman of Fire," 8 pp. MS. The Huntington Library. Short story?

_____ . Fields Addenda, Box 3, Env. 9. "Illustrations from Life," 31 pp. MS. The Huntington Library.

_____ . Fields Addenda, Box 3, Env. 11. "Life of St. Catherine," 27 pp. MS. The Huntington Library.

_____ . Fields Addenda, Box 3, Env. 14. Memoir of Robert Collyer, 7 pp. MS. The Huntington Library.

_____ . Fields Addenda, Box 3, Env. 15. "Memoirs of a Physician," 25 pp. MS. Also corrected typescript, 11 pp. The Huntington Library. Book review.

_____ . Fields Addenda, Box 4, Env. 4. "The Walk," 5 pp. MS. The Huntington Library. A religious talk.

_____ . Fields Addenda, Box 4, Env. 5. Speech on the life of Christ, 31 pp. MS. The Huntington Library.

_____ . Fields Addenda, Box 4, Env. 6. Speech in tribute to Julia Ward Howe, 6 pp. MS. The Huntington Library.

_____ . Fields Addenda, Box 4, Env. 7. Speech on patriotism to be delivered on Washington's Birthday, 24 pp. MS. The Huntington Library.

_____ . Fields Addenda, Box 5, Env. 1–6. Notebook containing drafts of 18 speeches on charity work and miscellaneous notes. MS. The Huntington Library.

_____ . Fields Addenda, Box 12, Env. 5. A.L.S. 130 letters, 3 fragments, and 1 poem Annie Fields to Laura Winthrop Johnson, 1864–1884. The Huntington Library.

Fields, James Thomas. Fields Addenda, Box 12, Env. 7. A.L.S. 58 letters to Annie Adams Fields, c. 1854–1875. The Huntington Library.

Index

JUDITH A. ROMAN is Assistant Professor of English at Indiana University East, where she teaches writing and literature.